IMAGES
of America

NEWBURY

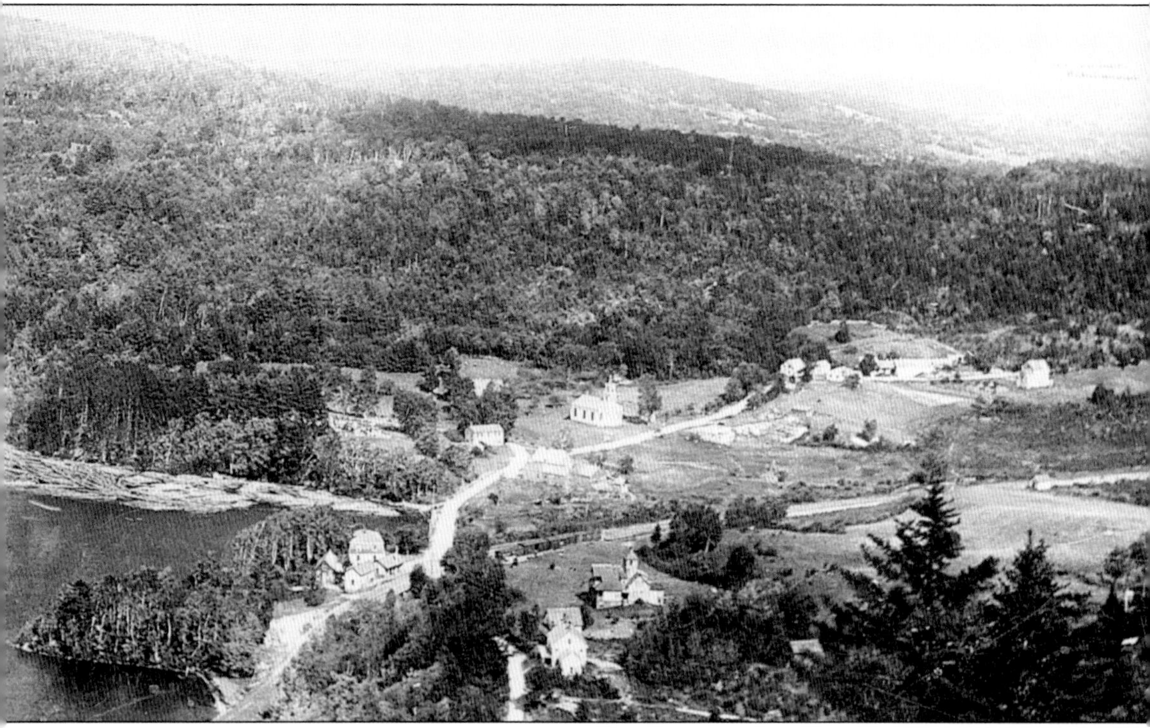

This *c.* 1910 view of Newbury center from the Eagle's Nest is dominated by the Center Meeting House. To its left is the Cilley Tavern and across the road is an empty lot where Matson's Hotel stood (burned in 1909). Across the street from the tavern is Edwin Lear's house and store. Between the harbor and the road (front left) is the railroad station (restored in 1995), freight house (no longer standing), and Durgin's boardinghouse (torn down about 1991). In the right foreground is a house and elaborate barn belonging to Dr. John Coggswell (later demolished). Up the road from the meetinghouse are houses belonging to V. C. Brockway and his son, Charles, both Newbury railroad station agents. Logs along the shore have been sent to the harbor from lumbering operations around the lake, awaiting transport by train. (Town of Newbury.)

On the cover: Friends and family throng Lake Station landing in Newbury as the steamboats *Kearsarge* (left) and *Armenia White* arrive packed with summer residents and vacationers. A private launch complete with fringed canopy has managed to secure a dockside spot as it waits for the passengers to disembark. (Newbury Historical Society.)

IMAGES
of America

NEWBURY

Shelly Candidus
with the Newbury Historical Society

ARCADIA
PUBLISHING

ISBN 978-0-7385-6489-0

Published by Arcadia Publishing
Charleston SC, Chicago IL, Portsmouth NH, San Francisco CA

Printed in the United States of America

Library of Congress Control Number: 2008937678

For all general information contact Arcadia Publishing at:
Telephone 843-853-2070
Fax 843-853-0044
E-mail sales@arcadiapublishing.com
For customer service and orders:
Toll-Free 1-888-313-2665

Visit us on the Internet at www.arcadiapublishing.com

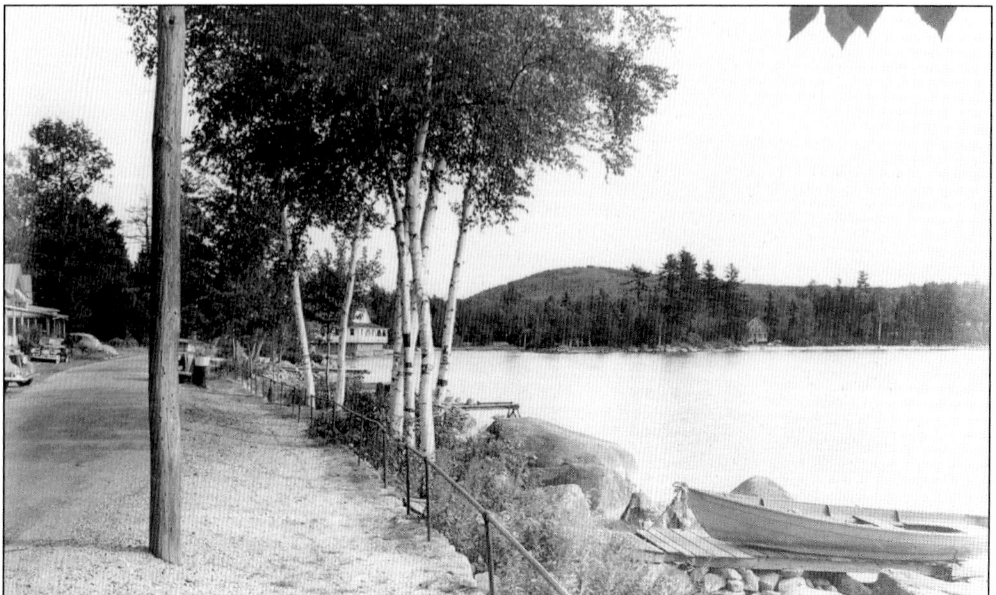

This view of Lake Sunapee with Mount Sunapee in the background was taken from Lake Avenue in Blodgett's Landing. Cressy Point, once the summer home of noted entertainer Will Cressy, is nestled in the pines just to the right of center in the background. (Sally Kassman.)

Contents

ACKNOWLEDGMENTS

This book could not have been compiled without the resources and cooperation of the Newbury Historical Society. Archivist William Weiler scoured the society's archives and traveled far afield to provide pictures and documentation. He also scanned the photographs that are reproduced on these pages. Thanks to president Robert Morris and all the members of the Newbury Historical Society who offered encouragement and support.

Special appreciation goes to those individuals who spent many hours identifying, discussing, and selecting the finest and most appropriate images for inclusion in this book: William Weiler, Gay and Martin Sheary, Judy and Wayne LaPorte, Dennis Pavlicek, and Donna Long provided informed input, which expedited the selection process.

The following people have generously shared pictures from their own collections: Joe and Beverly Digilio, Elizabeth Folsom, Sally Harris, John Hutchinson, Wayne and Judy LaPorte, and many individual contributors. Thanks to Richard Perkins for access to his family's collection of old documents and pictures provided by the Newbury Public Library.

John Greenwood has devoted countless hours to chronicling a pictorial history of Blodgett's Landing on his Web site. Through his efforts, we have accessed pictures from the collection of Sally Kassman, niece of professional photographer William V. D. Kitchen, to illustrate the story of this unique settlement. John Greenwood's Web site also features pictures taken by resident photographer J. B. Warren from the 1880s through 1910, provided by Joe and Beverly Digilio.

Ron Garceau, publisher of *SooNipi Magazine*, has made available images from his extensive collection of historical photographs and postcards of the Lake Sunapee area.

We are indebted to the organizations that shared their resources, time, and expertise, among them the Town of Newbury, Newbury Public Library, New Hampshire State Archives, and Bradford Historical Society.

Finally, we acknowledge with deep gratitude the dedicated work of the late Ernest Sherman, who paved the way in his *History of Newbury New Hampshire, the Beginnings—1740–1800*. In his foreword he writes, "We sincerely hope that a new beginning can be made to gather a group of earnest workers to finish the story, collect the pictures and properly honor the many dedicated citizens who built our town."

We hope this effort does him honor.

INTRODUCTION

In the beginning, after the upheavals of nature and the retreat of the ice, there was the lake, the mountain, and deep forests. The Penacook Indians, with villages in the Merrimack River valley, cultivated small plots of pumpkin, corn, squash, and beans. Hunting was crucial to their survival, and they moved throughout the area with the seasons to pursue game and fish. They found an abundance of both when they made camp in the forested mountain area rising above the lake they called Soonipi—"wild goose waters."

The arrival of the white man brought new opportunities to trade pelts for wampum and foreign goods, but it also brought disease and death to the Native Americans. Smallpox, diphtheria, and influenza cut the Penacook population from 2,500 in 1630 to 1,200 in 1674. Nevertheless, under the leadership of Chief Passaconaway and his son, the Native Americans remained on friendly terms with the white traders throughout the beginning of King Philip's War in 1675. The next year, however, the English, retaliating against hostilities from other native tribes, seized 200 Penacooks. As the fighting continued, the Penacooks eventually fled, some westward and most, with their leader, to join the Abenaki tribe at the Canadian border.

King Philip's War, while lasting only one year, was devastating to both the native population and the English settlers. Seven of every eight Native Americans perished, as did 30 of every 65 settlers. After this war, forays and raids continued well into the 18th century, culminating with the French and Indian War (1754–1763). The climate was hardly conducive to attracting homesteaders, but the land-rich proprietors in Portsmouth persisted in their efforts to establish settlements. In 1751, the proprietors appointed Joseph Blanchard agent to bring settlers into the Lake Sunapee area. Blanchard knew the area well, having surveyed it following the Mason Curve line. He proposed a charter in 1754 for a township he called Hereford. It stipulated that 500-acre lots were to be held for the grantors, and 100-acre lots were designated for homesteaders, a minister, a school, and a meetinghouse. Each settler was bound to clear and enclose for tillage three acres annually for three years, and during that time to have built a dwelling on his land.

The years of turmoil rolled on, and in 1768, the grantees of the Hereford charter told the proprietors that they could not comply with the terms of the charter due to the ongoing hostilities and lack of roads to access the area. Later that year, petitioners from Merrimack asked for a grant of the land "near a pond called Sunapy which Tract of Land Lyes Environed in with Mountains on every side." The proprietors required a survey of the proposed town, thus imposing further delays. In the meantime, Zephaniah Clark, an early settler in present-day Newport, took possession of 100 acres at the base of Mount Sunapee, building a large public house there and becoming the town's first settler.

In June 1771, both James Minot and Capt. John Fisher petitioned the proprietors for the forfeited town of Hereford. Fisher, whose wife was the sister of Gov. John Wentworth, promised to settle the claims of prior petitioners and to fulfill all the conditions of the grant. The proprietors accepted Fisher's petition, pending a survey of the land contained within the proscribed boundaries. Fisher was able to meet the conditions of the grant because of two fortunate circumstances. First, work had been in progress for several years to establish a carriage road to connect Charlestown to Boscawen. This Province Road passed along the southern tip of Lake Sunapee, went eastward toward Sutton, and then westward to Mount Sunapee and present-day Goshen. The second piece of good fortune was the presence of Zephaniah Clark, already familiar with the area. Fisher hired him to complete the required survey, which was accepted by the proprietors. Finally, on February 5, 1772, the charter was granted to Capt. John Fisher for a town to be called Fishersfield. The town was incorporated under that name in 1778 and became Newbury in 1837, when settlers from Newbury, Massachusetts, influenced the name change.

Fisher and his associate, John Peirce, wasted no time in recruiting settlers for the town. Early records kept by Peirce show that 11 families were given 100 acres each for settlement in 1775. These included, in addition to Zephaniah Clark, Ephraim Bradbury, Joseph Chandler, Charles Emerson, William Emery and son, Peter and Oliver Emerson, Samuel Gunnison, and twin brothers Paul and Ebenezer Towle. The motivations for moving into the wilderness for each of these families may have differed, but all must have shared the pioneering spirit: a love of independence, a dedication to hard work, and a dream of a better life.

For the new arrivals, a better life remained a dream, perhaps sustained by the beauty of Mount Sunapee and its adjacent range, the pure waters of the lake, and the bounty of the woodlands. Day-to-day reality was simply hard work. The dense forest had to be cleared to provide for houses—simple log structures of one or two rooms—and to create fields for crops. When the field was cleared, granite rocks—often boulders—had to be moved and became cellar holes and stone walls. To make matters worse, these early settlers arrived as the Revolutionary War burst forth in the colonies, and many Fishersfield men joined their fellow countrymen in the fight for independence. An account by Samuel Gunnison Sr. in neighboring Saville (now Sunapee) reports that in the spring of 1782,

> Some of the families have one cow each, some two, others none at all. We could not find above four families that has bread corn enough to last to the . . . harvest . . . roads are in bad situation and having no mills we are oblidged to go to the next town for everything we may want . . . the poverty in the town is deplorable, many of the families have no money and if the taxes are inforced on them must sell their stock and their families suffer.

While some families relocated because of hardship, others persevered and were joined by more eager to settle in this beautiful wilderness. By 1780, the war had been won, independence had been declared, and attention could be given to town government and to establishing the social elements vital to community life. According to the first census in 1790, there were 331 residents in Fishersfield, and the promise of a better life was beginning to be a reality.

The story of Newbury, evolving from its beginnings through its bicentennial in 1978, is the story of its enduring natural beauty, which sustained the early settlers and over the years brought visitors from many corners of the world to enjoy the mountain, the lake, and the revitalized forests.

One

SETTING BOUNDARIES

The history of New England's territorial boundaries dates back to the early 1600s, when King James I granted a charter for a corporation known as the Council of Plymouth. In 1622, this corporation conferred to Capt. John Mason a patent for an extensive, vaguely defined territory called the Province of Maine and, in 1629, additional patents that included land to be called New Hampshire. This area was defined by measuring from the Merrimack River north along the seacoast to the Passcattaway River and thence west threescore miles. London geographers mistakenly believed that the Merrimack flowed easterly throughout its course and thus the boundary of the territory of New Hampshire was set in a distinctive southeasterly curving line. Newbury and many neighboring towns incorporate the Mason Curve as a boundary.

Succeeding generations of Masons became embroiled in litigation over land titles and town boundaries until 1746, when John Tufton Mason, sole heir, conveyed his province to 12 proprietors in Portsmouth. The location of the Mason Curve was a subject of controversy between the Mason Proprietors and the State of New Hampshire for many years, since the curve set boundary lines between state grants outside of the curve and townships granted by the proprietors on its inside. In 1788, the proprietors and the state reached an agreement clarifying the proprietors' right to much of the disputed land, and the Mason Curve was adopted as absolute.

The Fishersfield charter granted to Capt. John Fisher by the Mason Proprietors in 1772 divided the town into 500-acre lots for the proprietors, 100-acre lots for settlers, and lots for the minister, a house of worship, a school, and a training field. Rod widths were set for roads. The major road connecting Fishersfield with neighboring towns was Province Road, built on the imprint of old Native American footpaths and trapper trails. Establishing Province Road was slow, back-breaking work for men already challenged to clear their own fields, but slowly the old trails were groomed to accommodate teams and coaches. Province Road became the first carriage road across the state between the Connecticut and Merrimack Rivers. It was vital for moving Revolutionary War troops and supplies and providing a route for people, goods, and mail to travel between towns and into outlying districts. Many segments of this road are in use in present-day Newbury.

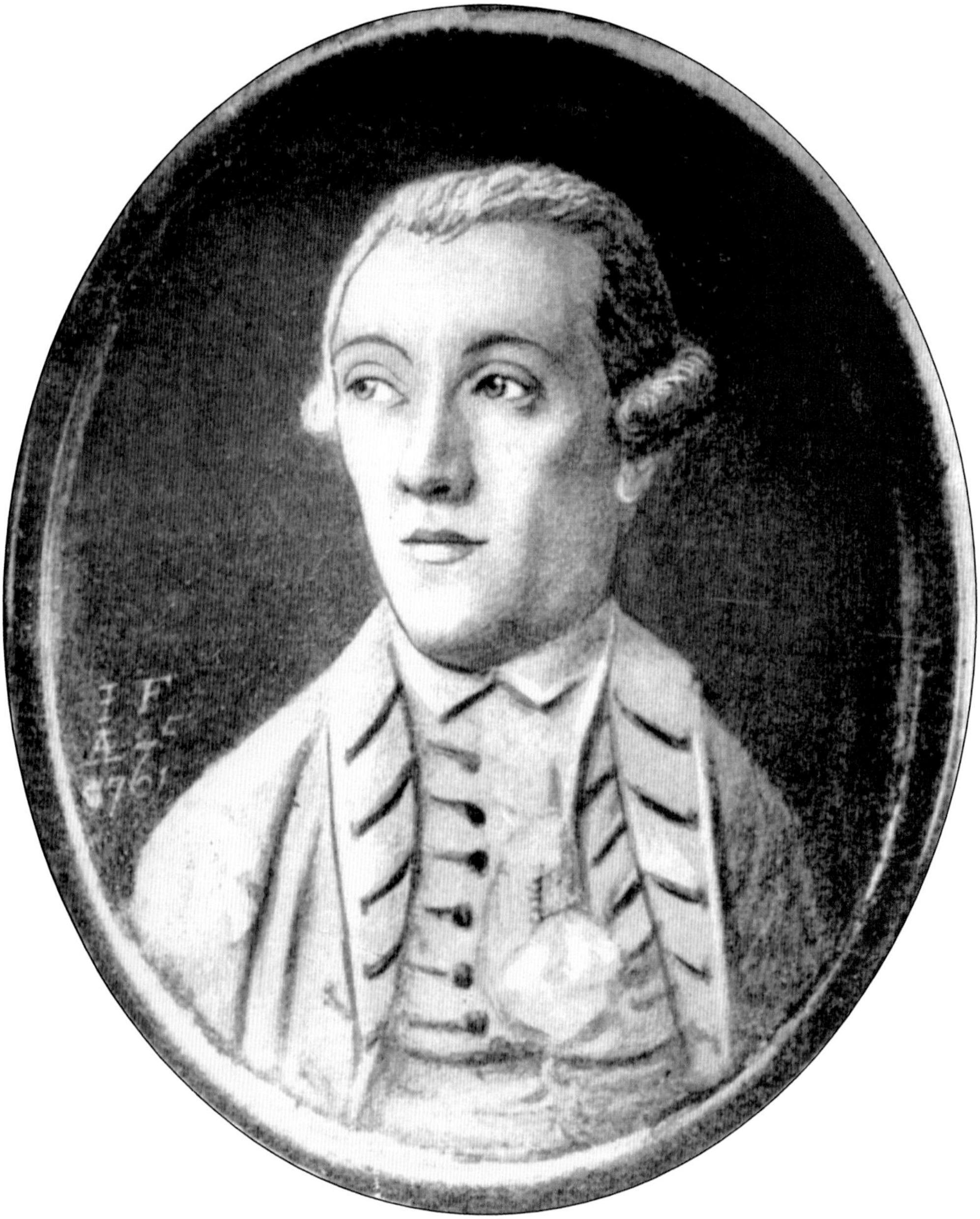

Capt. John Fisher was born in 1736. In 1763, he married Anna Wentworth, sister of Gov. John Wentworth, who was also a Mason Proprietor. He is reported to have been a director of the Bank of England at that time. He then came to New England and bought property in the Portsmouth area where he was a naval officer. He became collector of customs at Boston in 1773, at the same time attending to charters he held and was pursuing for territories in New England. He gained the charter for Fishersfield (now Newbury) in 1772 but left the details of its fulfillment to his agent, John Peirce. After the Revolutionary War broke out, he set aside his interests in New England and departed for England in 1775 to become undersecretary of state under Prime Minister William Pitt, the younger. Fisher died there on June 1, 1805. (New Hampshire Historical Society.)

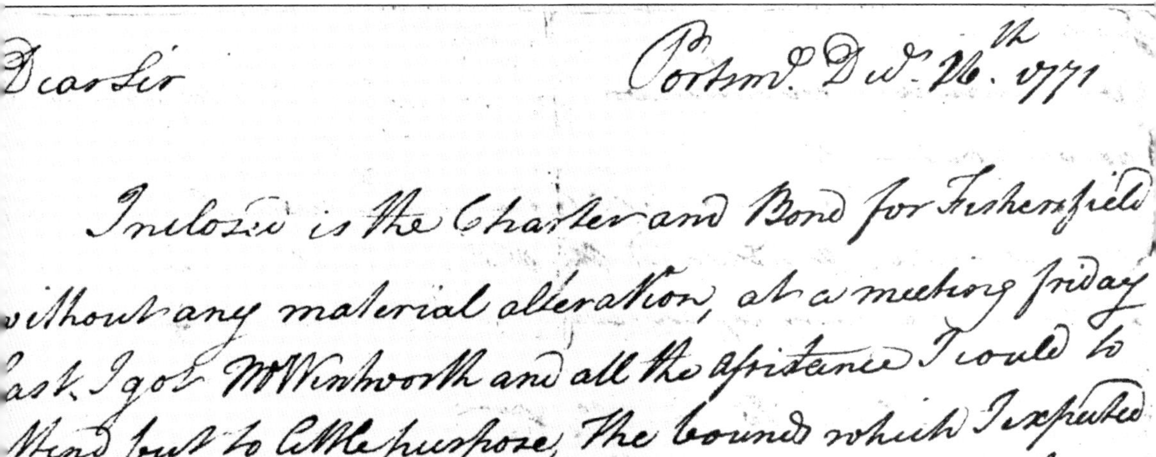
Dear Sir Portsmo. Decr. 16th. 1771

Inclosed is the Charter and Bond for Fishersfield without any material alteration, at a meeting friday last, I got Mr Wentworth and all the assistance I could to attend but to little purpose, the bounds which I expected they would have alterd without any difficulty they were the most obstinate against, I say they intend to measure all the Towns up from the Province line & in that case they shall have 10 or 15m Acres left between No. 8 and Fishersfield which they'l divide, the Article of reentry they would not alter, and that as the Charter now stands their is no article which does not lay in the power of you to fullfill — The meeting House is to be built in

This is part of a letter from John Peirce (agent) to Capt. John Fisher reporting on his negotiations with the Mason Proprietors for the Fishersfield grant. It reads, "Inclosed is the Charter and Bond for Fishersfield without any material alteration, at a meeting Friday last, I got Mr. Wentworth and all the assistance I could to attend but to little purpose. The bounds which I expected they would have alterd without any difficulty they were the most obstinate against. I say they intend to measure all the Towns up from the Province line & in that case they shall have 10 or 25 [thousand] Acres left between No. 8 and Fishersfield which they'l divide. The Article of reentry they would not alter, and that as the Charter now stands their is no article which does not lay in the power of you to fulfill." Peirce adds, "Several others were merely against it, said that they had offerd you great terms before," and he urges Fisher to sign the bond in its present form, since "we can never expect a more favourable meeting." (New Hampshire State Archives.)

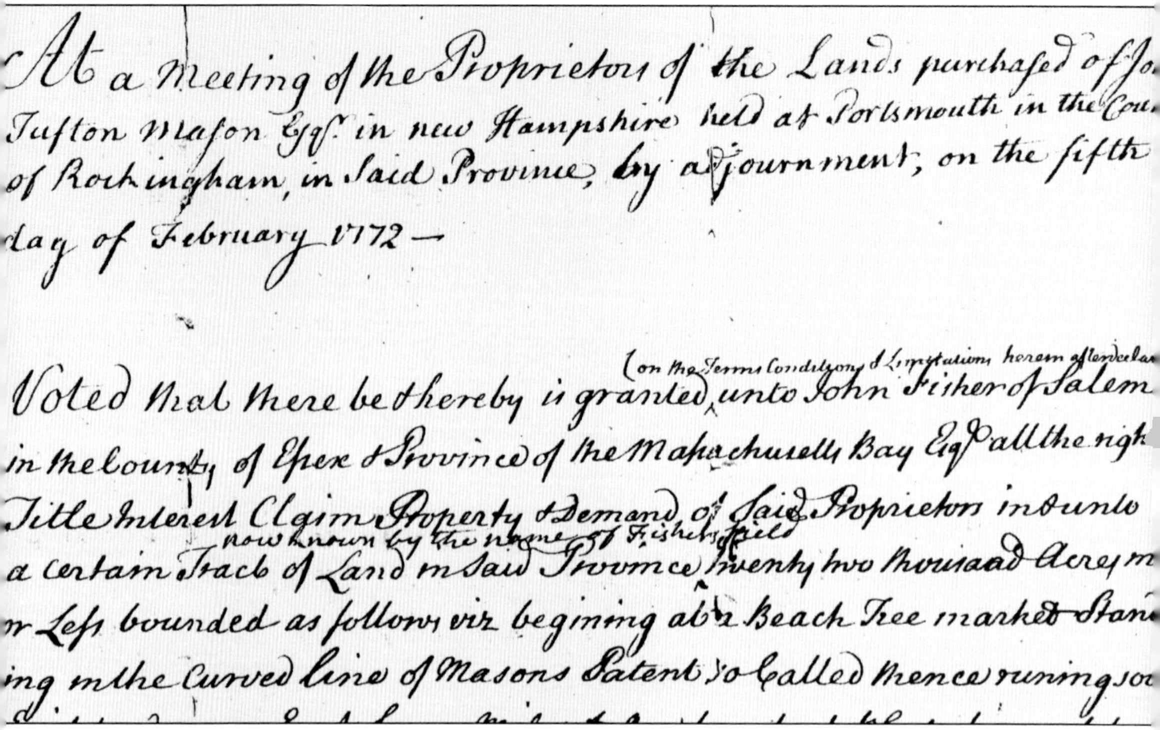
At a Meeting of the Proprietors of the Lands purchased of Jo
Tufton Mason Esqr in new Hampshire held at Portsmouth in the Cou
of Rockingham, in Said Province, by adjournment, on the fifth
day of February 1772 —

Voted that there be & hereby is granted (on the Terms Conditions & Limitations herein after declar) unto John Fisher of Salem
in the County of Essex & Province of the Massachusetts Bay Esqr all the righ
Title Interest Claim Property & Demand of Said Proprietors in & unto
a certain Tract of Land in Said Province (now known by the name of Fishersfield) twenty two thousand Acres m
or Less bounded as follows viz begining at a Beach Tree marked Stan
ing in the Curved line of Masons Patent so Called thence runing so

The Fishersfield charter was granted to Capt. John Fisher on February 5, 1772. It reads, "At a meeting of the Proprietors of the Lands purchased of John Tufton Mason Esqr in New Hampshire held at Portsmouth in the County of Rockingham in Said Province by adjournment, on the fifth day of February 1772—Voted that there be & hereby is granted . . . unto John Fisher of Salem in the County of Essex and Province of the Massachusetts Bay Esqr all the right Title Interest Claim Property & Demand of Said Proprietors in & unto a certain Tract of Land in Said Province now known by the name of Fishersfield twenty two thousand Acres more or Less bounded as follows viz beginning at a Beach Tree marked Standing in the Curved line of Masons Patent so called." The grant describes lot sizes for proprietors and settlers, lands for specific uses, and widths for town roads. Provisions include the grantors' right to "reserve all white Pine Trees fit for his Majestys use growing on the Premises." (New Hampshire State Archives.)

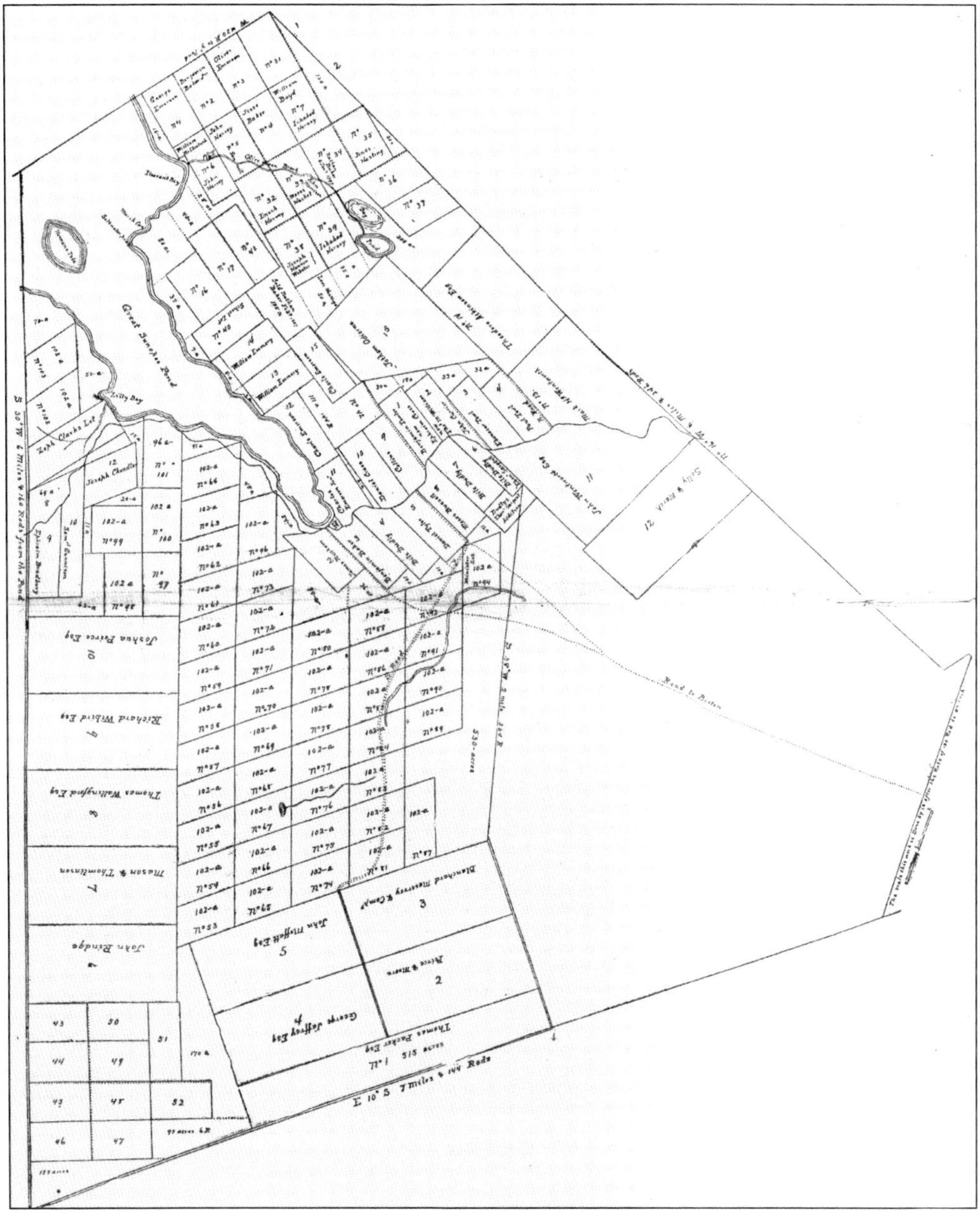

Innkeeper and surveyor Zephaniah Clark, Fishersfield's first settler, made this map in 1775. The 500-acre lots reserved for the Mason Proprietors are easily distinguished from the 100-acre settlers' lots. Gov. John Wentworth drew lot No. 11 on the Sutton line bounded by Province Road, while his father drew adjacent lot No. 13. Zephaniah Clark's land lies on the west side of Lake Sunapee at the present-day traffic circle. He and his neighbors, Samuel Gunnison and Joseph Chandler, were active in early town government. Charles Emerson owned the land at the southern end of the lake where the Cilley Tavern was soon built. His home was the site of the first town meeting on January 17, 1779. (Town of Newbury.)

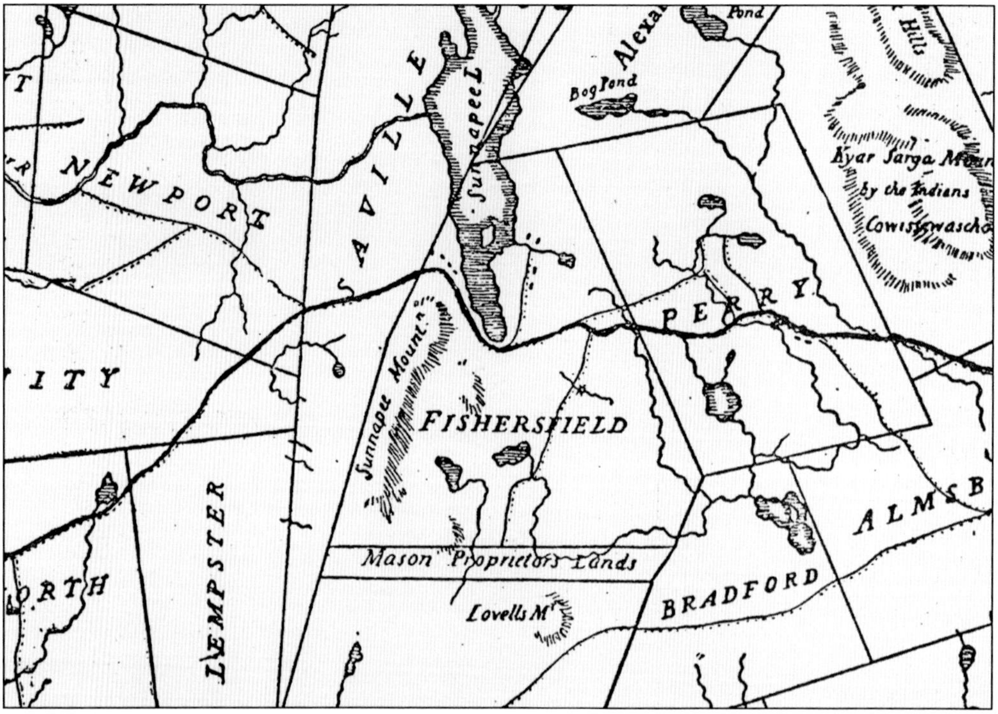

A detail from Samuel Holland's map of 1773 shows Province Road as a darker line running east from Charlestown to Boscawen, where unfinished portions are indicated by a dotted line. The Mason Curve forms the western border of Fishersfield and bisects Great Island in Lake Sunapee between Fishersfield and Saville (now Sunapee). The "Proprietors Lands" mentioned in John Peirce's letter to Capt. John Fisher are shown in a band on the southern town border. (William Weiler.)

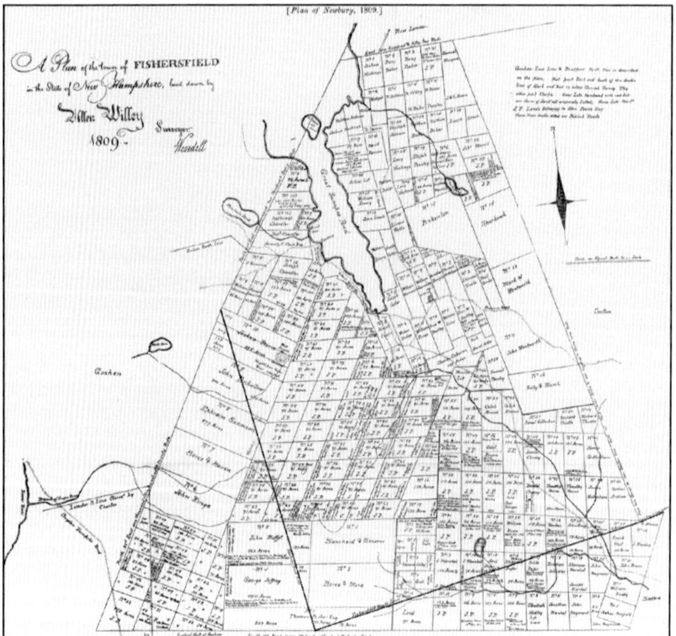

Allen Willey's map of 1809 shows many property changes from Zephaniah Clark's 1775 map. More lots have been assigned ownership and dozens of lots are designated "JP" for John Peirce. When Fisher returned to England in 1775, he deeded half the town to Peirce and gave him power of attorney for the rest. This map shows parts of Fishersfield annexed to Goshen, Lempster, and Bradford. (Town of Newbury.)

Two

BREAKING GROUND

The same natural beauty and resources that draw present-day visitors to Newbury for recreation were there for the first settlers in 1775, but for them these resources provided the stuff of life. The forest supplied logs for the first houses, consisting of one or two dark and drafty rooms, which seldom outlived their first occupants.

Cabins were followed by framed houses, 20 feet square, and double houses, 40 by 20 feet, which were a sign of prosperity. Even so, they were built for utility, with simple lines and small windows, a great open fireplace for heat and cooking, and a large flue that drew the heat up the chimney and created icy indoor drafts. Furniture was crafted from the abundant fine woods at hand. Doorways were often hung with animal skins to keep out the elements. Early wooden doors were leaned against the doorway and moved by hand to enter or leave, since hinges were unavailable. Game provided food and hides, which were used for outdoor wear and shoes. Women wove flax and wool for additional garments.

From sunrise to sunset, all family members labored to establish homesteads. Clearing the land was a duty under the terms of the charter, and it was imperative for survival. As the forest slowly gave way to open fields, there lay exposed great outcroppings of granite. Stones that could be moved by men and oxen were fashioned into walls and cellar holes. Crops could then be planted and harvested to sustain man and beast. In addition to daily labor, there were wild animals to vanquish, roads to be built, and wars to be fought for the common good. Gravestones in Newbury's cemeteries bear testimony to the toll that hardship and illness took on the early settlers.

Socializing was limited during this period when families had little time or easy access to enjoy their neighbors. A meetinghouse, burial ground, and town pound were built on Bly Hill, but this was not a convenient location for far-flung early families. South Newbury village, established in the early 1800s, provided a church, school, town hall, Grange, tavern, blacksmith shop, weigh station, post office, and store to create a lively and accommodating community. Many of the town's oldest buildings are still in use in this historic area.

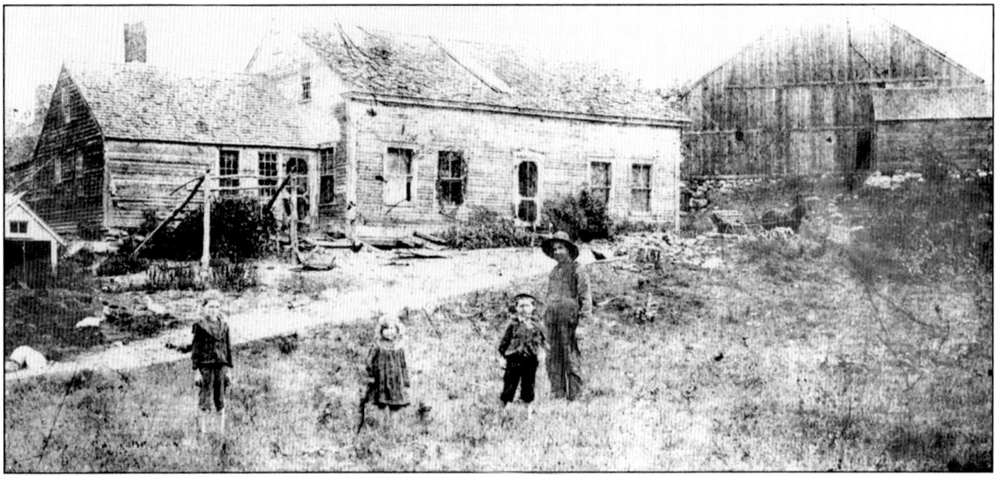

This early homestead, the Bly farm, is located in South Newbury on present-day Sutton Road. Additions seen to the house and a good-size barn indicate a thriving farm. It continues to thrive today as the Schroeder farm and has won a Farm of Distinction Award. The original barn was sold, carefully taken down, and rebuilt on a site in Connecticut. (Sonny Harris.)

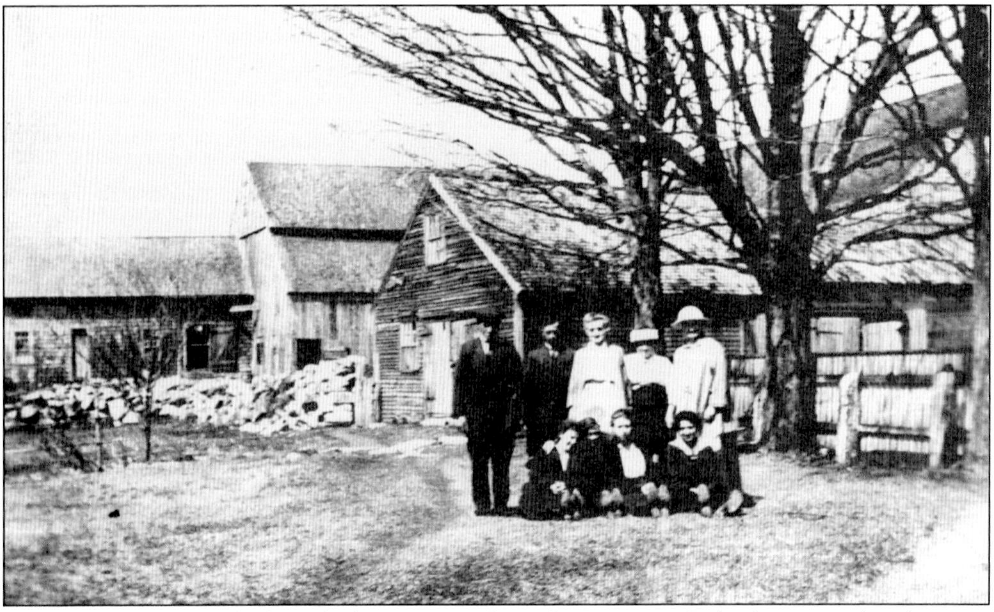

The Digilio farm dates back to the late 1700s and was the Benjamin Baker homestead. Its location on Baker Hill provides sweeping views of Lake Sunapee and Mount Sunapee. The Digilio family bought the farm in 1910 and lives there today. In recent years, some of the land was sold to local businessmen who built a golf course on the open, scenic site. (Joe and Beverly Digilio.)

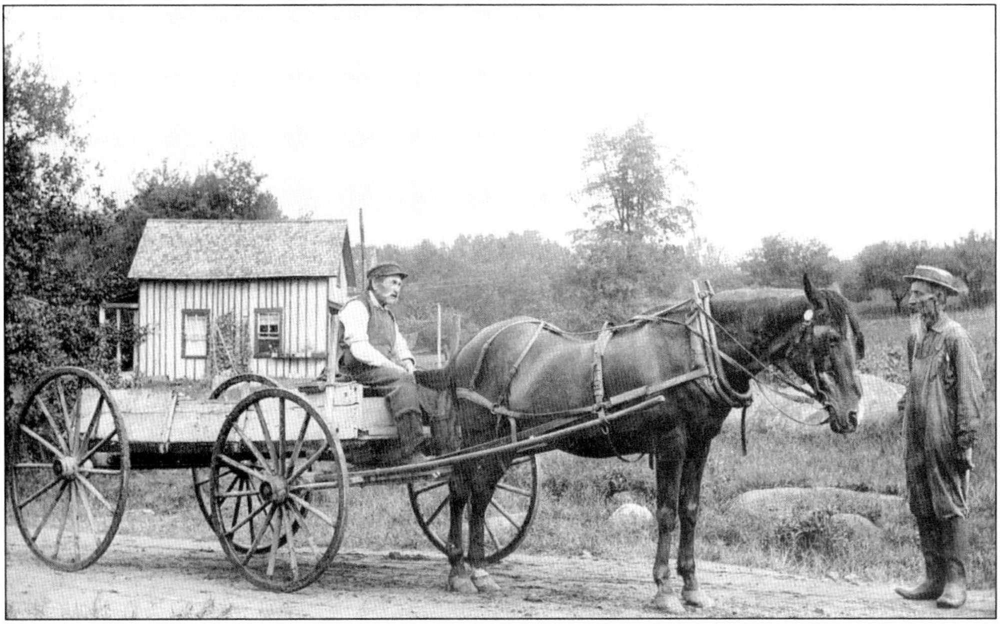

A farmer, out for chores or an errand, stops to greet an acquaintance on the road. The location appears to be Bowles Road, with J. B. Warren's photographic studio in the background. (Tracy Messer.)

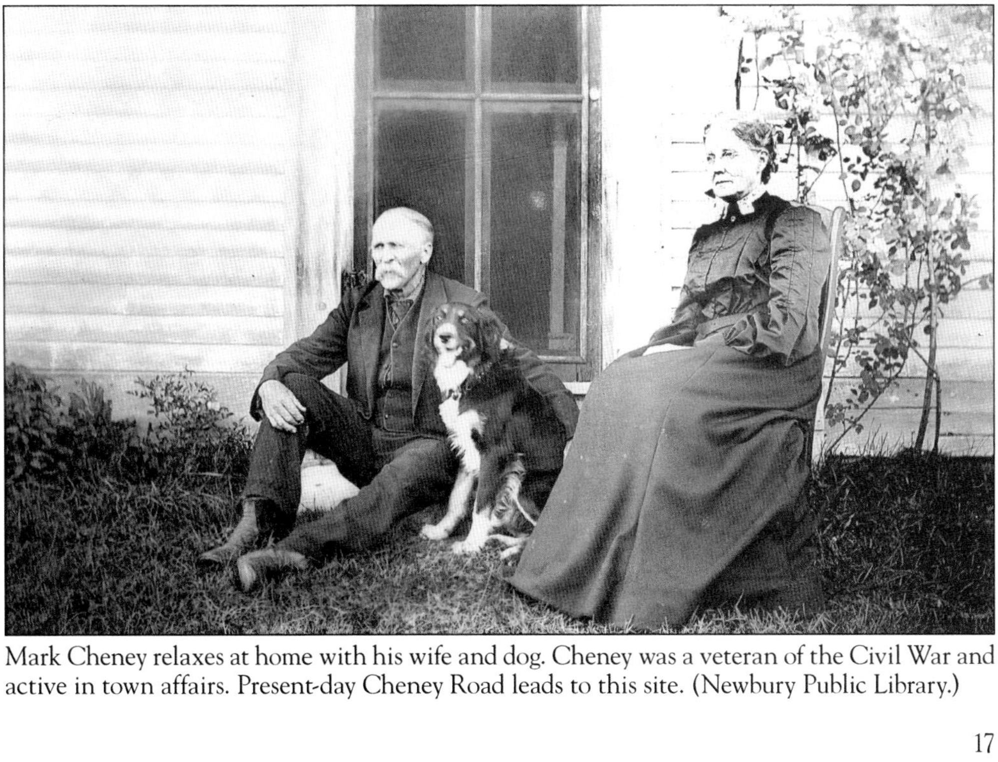

Mark Cheney relaxes at home with his wife and dog. Cheney was a veteran of the Civil War and active in town affairs. Present-day Cheney Road leads to this site. (Newbury Public Library.)

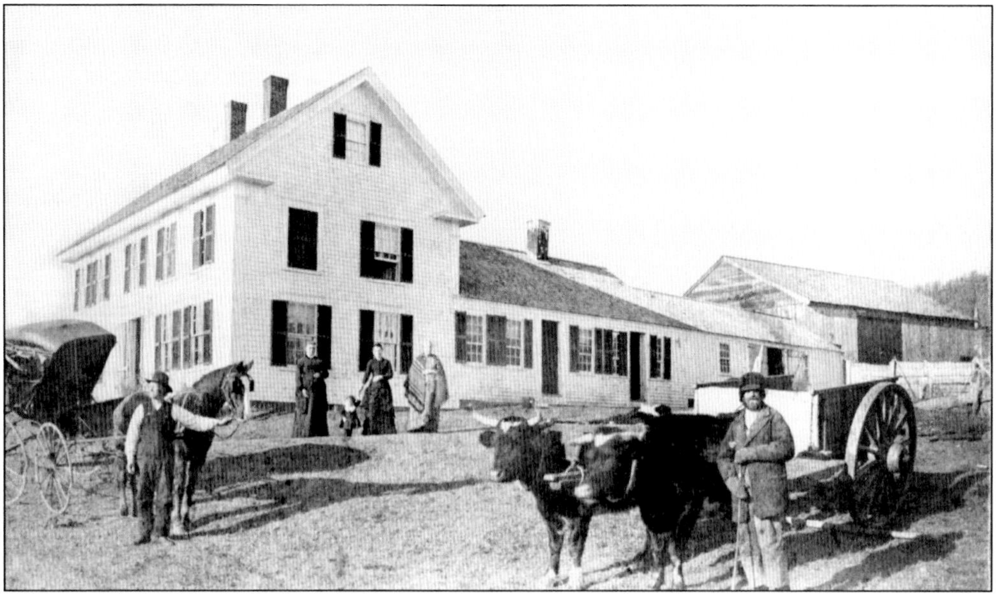

This carefully composed picture of the Osman Bailey house shows several extensions and an open barn. The one-story center section with chimney was the original Proctor house, with the large three-story portion added by Bailey as his family grew and prospered. William Ayer (right, with oxen) married Bailey's daughter. (Nancy Isaacson.)

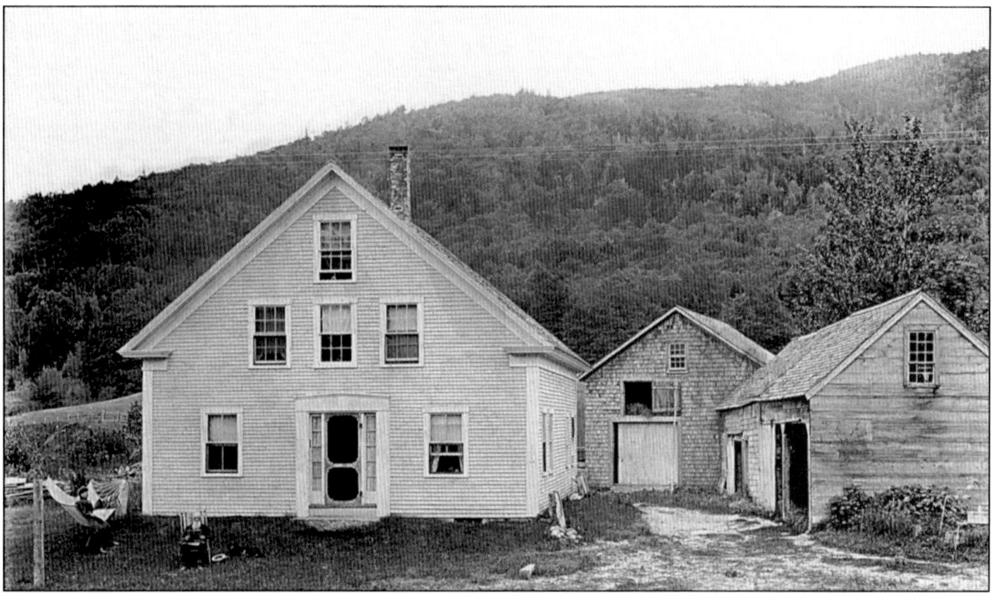

Nathaniel Lear and his wife enjoy a moment of relaxation with their dog, Don. The Lear farm was situated at Newbury harbor across from the Cilley Tavern. It was later the Edwin Lear store. The outbuildings are gone, but the house remains standing today, located at the Newbury harbor gas station site. (John Hutchinson.)

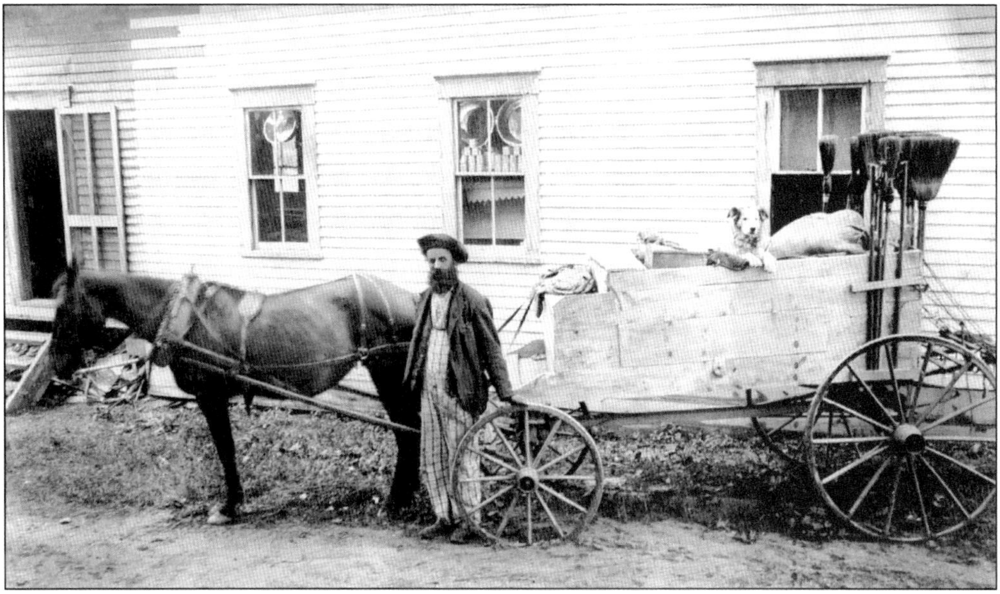

Peddlers were welcomed by early settlers, who were eager to acquire household items. Here Jim Craig makes his rounds. Town records house a scrap of paper attributed to selectman Sprague Morse that reads, "Agreeably to the provisions of an act approved April 1, 1893, I hereby License James Craig a soldier in the late war of rebellion to peddle tin ware throughout the state of New Hampshire for one year." (Newbury Historical Society.)

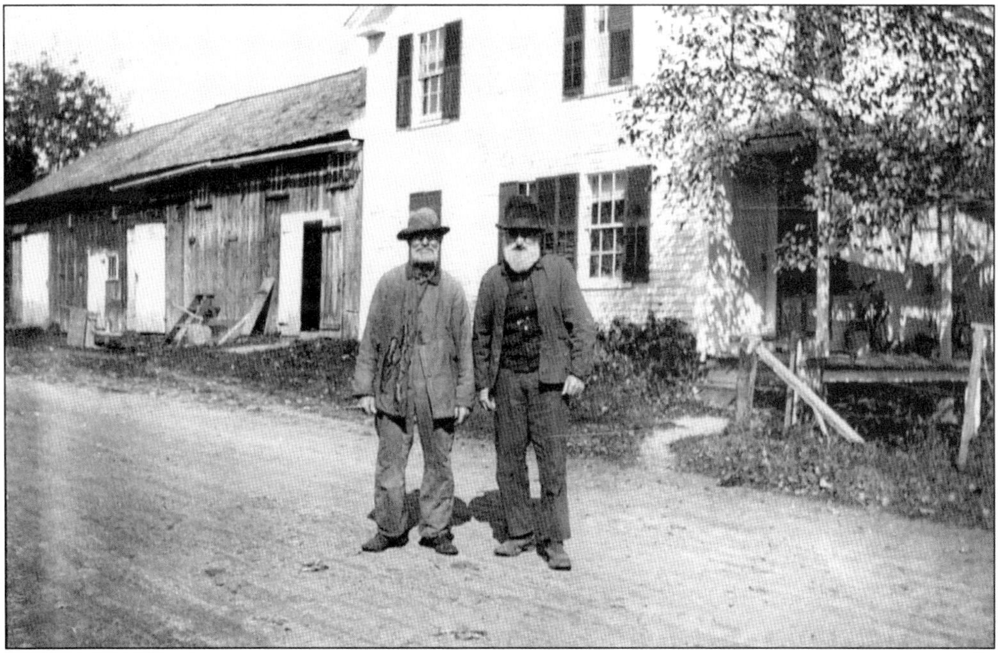

Two unidentified men stand in front of Edwin A. Blodgett's house in South Newbury in 1903. This building was next door to Blodgett's village store and once housed the post office. It has passed through many hands and undergone alterations over the years, losing the ell and front porch. The Romaine family has lived here since the early 1960s. (Sally Harris.)

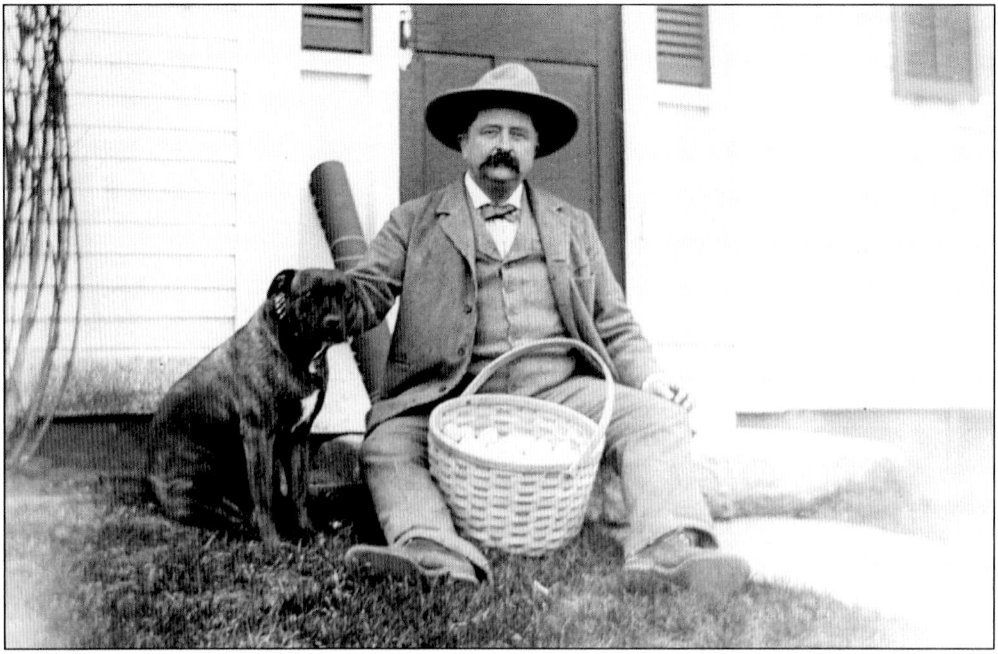

Mark Shultis bought the former Muzzey farm in 1900 and established a highly successful poultry business with several thousand chickens. The arrival of the railroad made the distribution of his fresh produce to major nearby cities possible. Fire destroyed the operation around 1906. Here he and a helper put some of their eggs in a basket. (Sally Harris.)

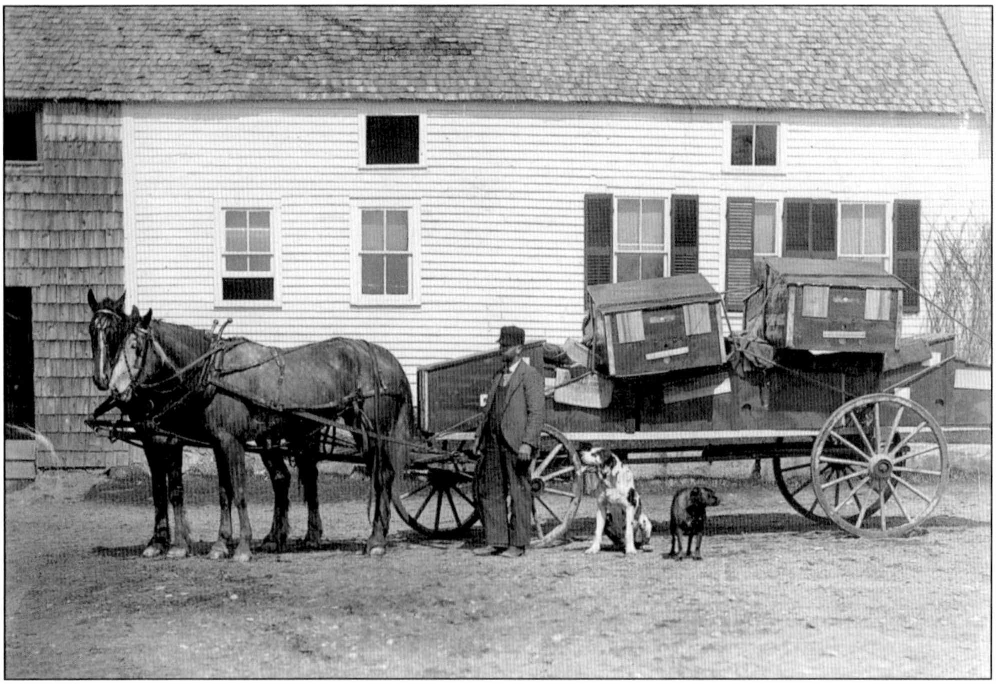

Incubators used to hatch young chicks arrive at the Shultis farm. It is possible that woodstoves or heat lamps used in conjunction with the incubators may have led to the disastrous fire that destroyed the poultry plant. (Sally Harris.)

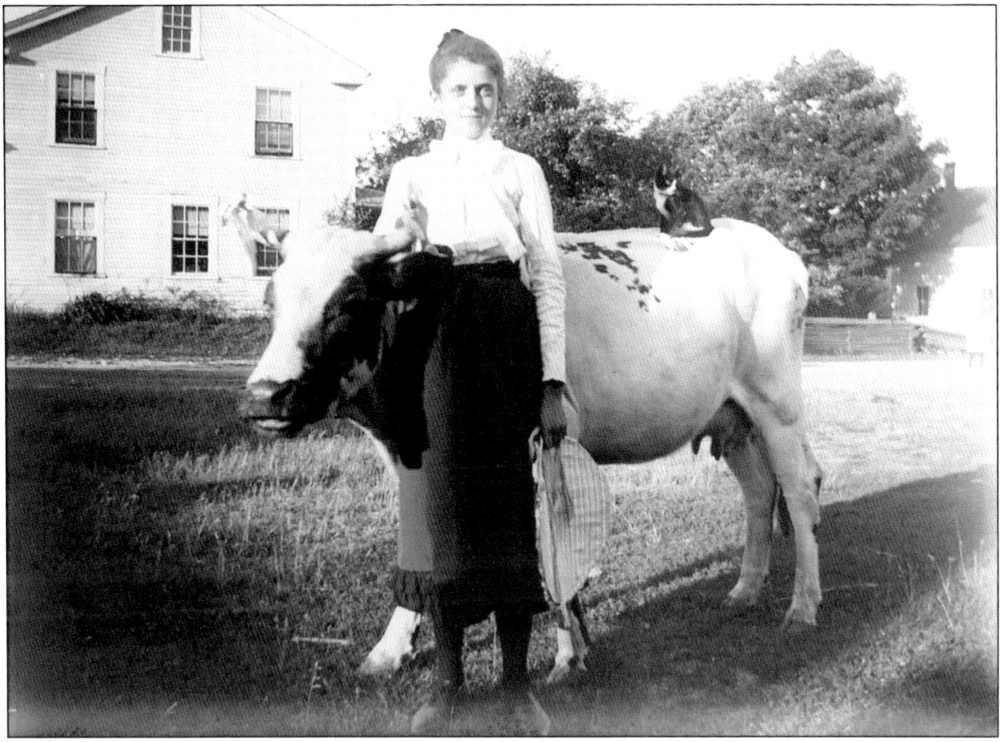

This young lady's name has been lost, but it is evident that she had an affinity for animals. The cow and its feline passenger seem very happy in each other's company. The location is South Newbury, with the Edwin A. Blodgett house in the background. (Brenda Digilio.)

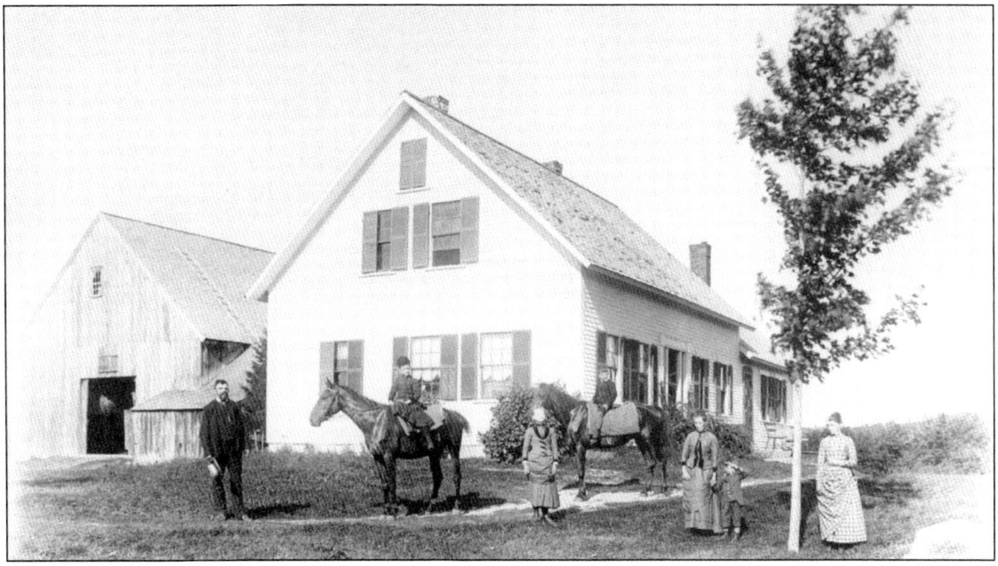

The Charles Henry Gillingham farm, located off Poor Farm Road on the Newbury-Sutton town line, appears neat and prosperous. It is adorned by bushes, outdoor seating, and a young maple tree planted by the family. Pictured here in 1886 are, from left to right, Charles Henry, Mary Avis, Annie, Moody, Elinda (Maud), Ralph B., and Maud Clara Gillingham. (Newbury Historical Society.)

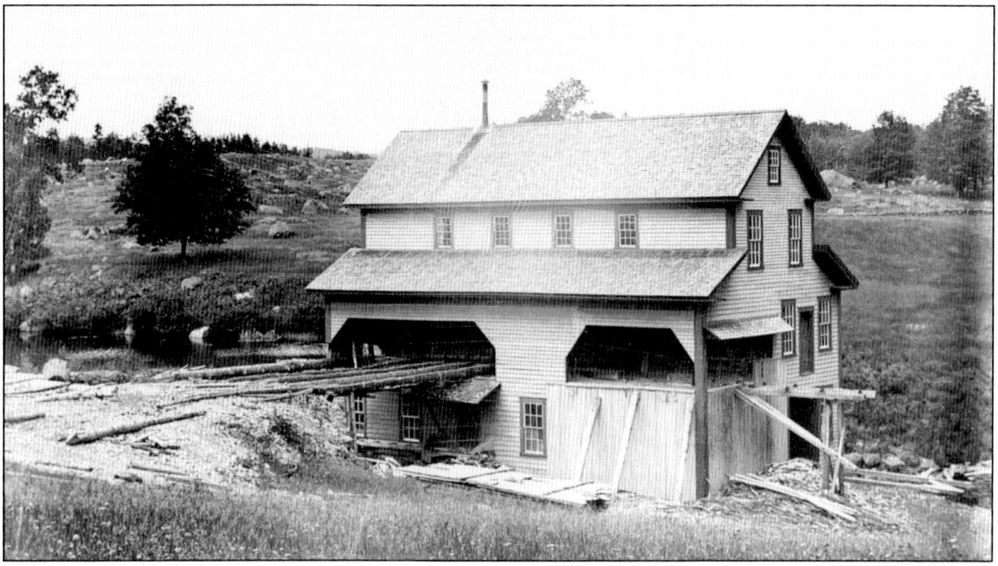

Located in South Newbury on Andrew Brook, Fowler's Mill processed the abundant area lumber into items that were finished in a South Newbury shop. A variety of wooden products were manufactured here, including clothespins and wooden benches. Those benches were used in the original town hall and dozens are used today in the old town buildings in South Newbury and in the current town offices in Newbury center. Below, the children gather on the lawn of the expansive Fowler house, used over the years as a guesthouse and inn. (Above, Brenda Digilio; below, Alex Azodi.)

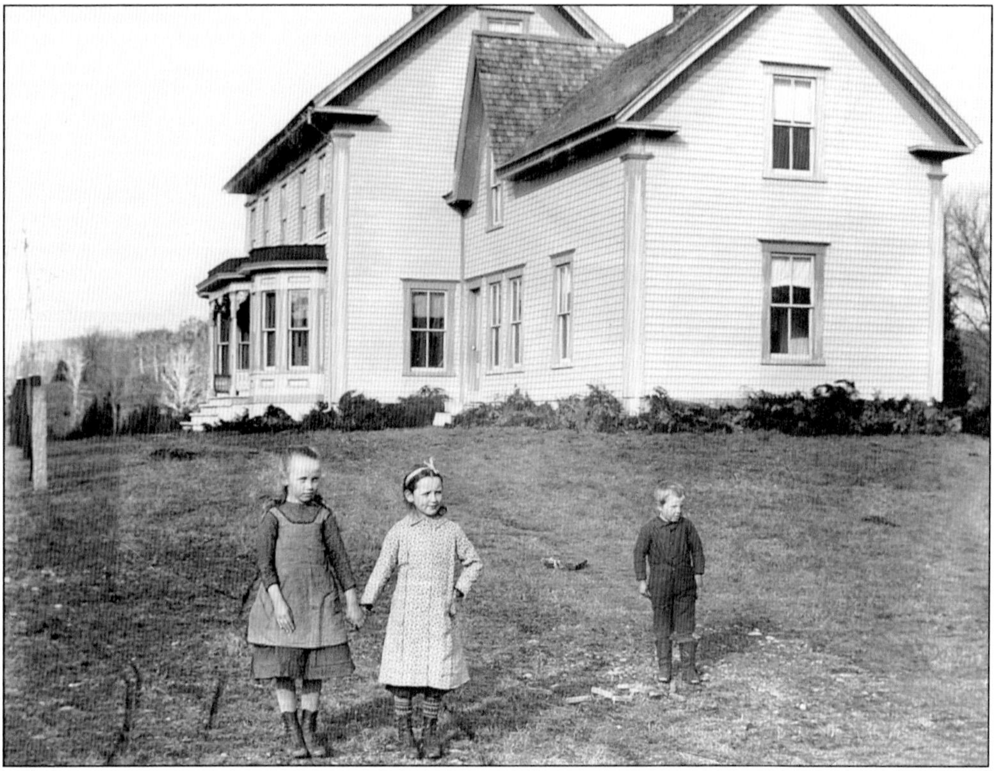

A watering trough located along Village Road in South Newbury offered refreshment to thirsty horses and oxen as they traveled by. (Sally Harris.)

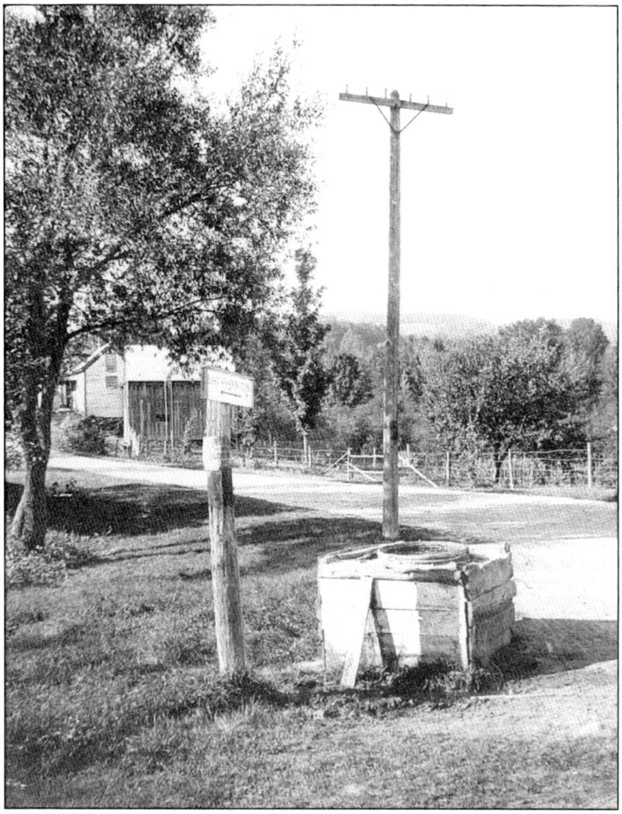

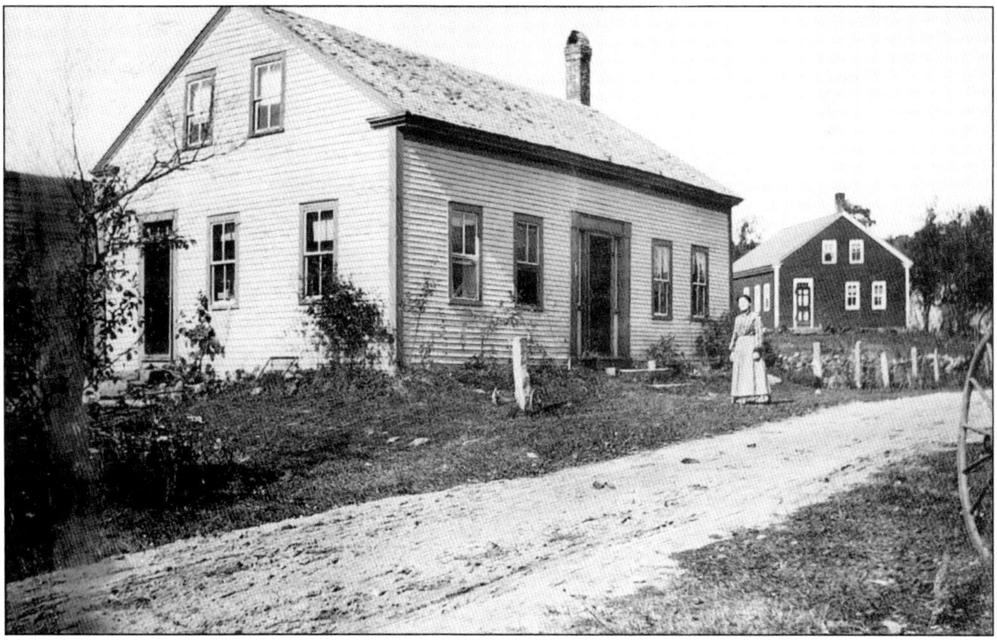

Mark Shultis took this picture in 1902 when he was negotiating to buy this house from Charles H. Cross, son of Nelson Cross. The woman may be Mrs. Charles H. Cross or simply a passerby. The house is at the intersection of Village and South Roads. (Sally Harris.)

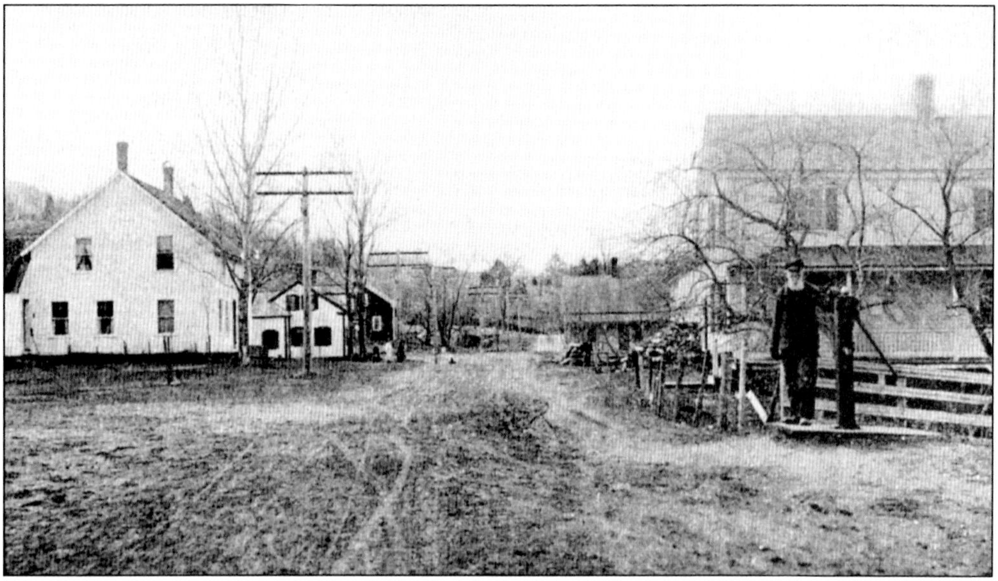

These early South Newbury houses were located at the intersection of Village Road and South Road. The area was home to Rev. Timothy Morse, who bought his tract of land near Lake Todd in 1775 and established a large family that, according to local historian Ernest Sherman's *History of Newbury*, "would multiply until it would tie into most of the old families." In the photograph above, a man stands at the public water pump in front of the Edwin A. Blodgett house. Across the road is the King Gillingham house. South Road curves left between the small white and dark houses. The photograph below is the same scene, some years later, with the roads well defined. (Above, Town of Newbury; below, Sally Harris.)

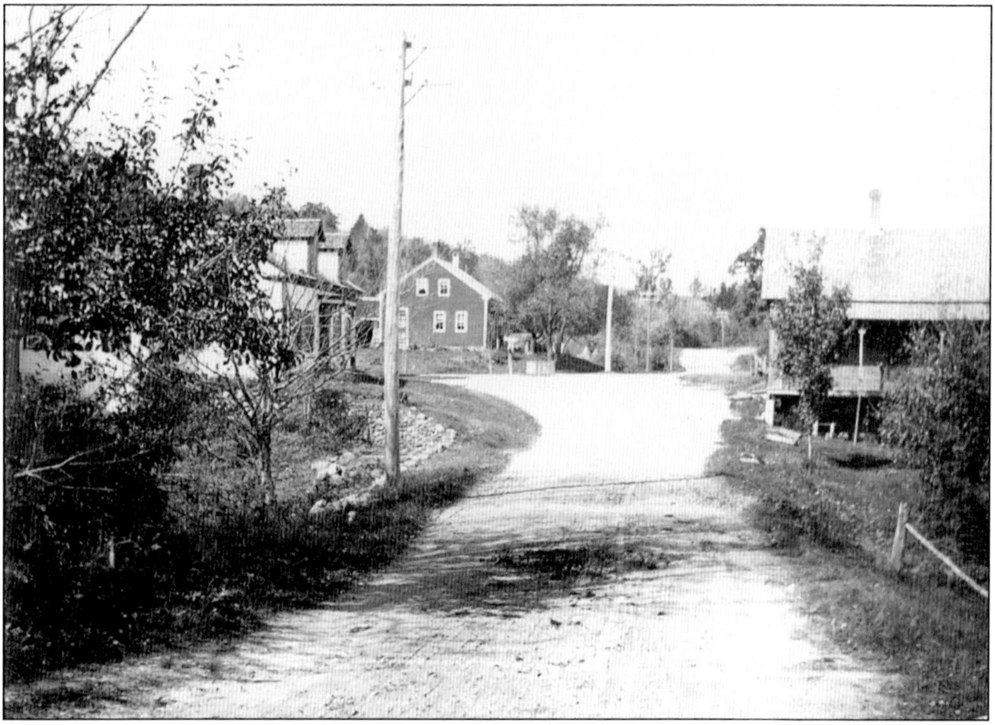

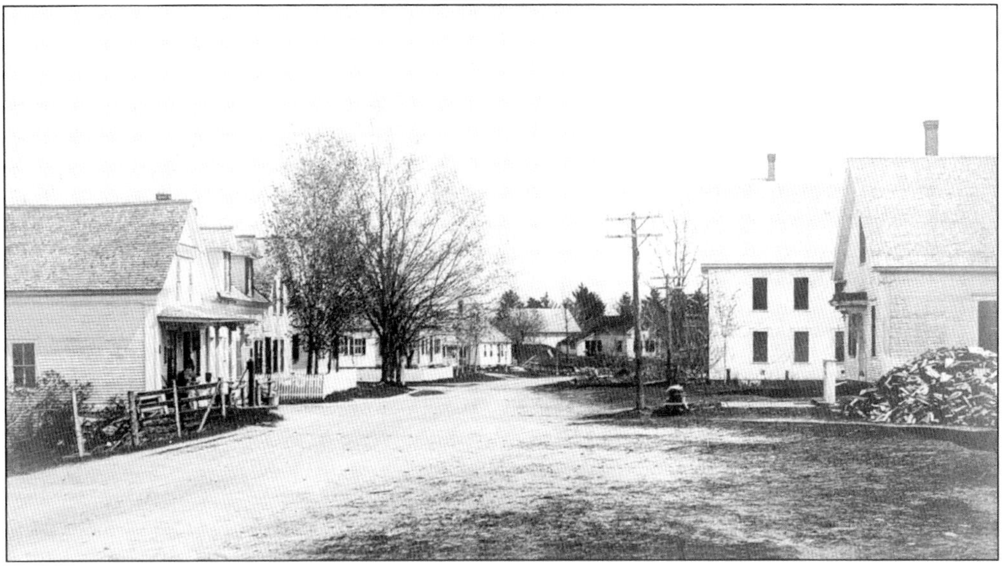

South Newbury village, shown here around 1905, has been home to Newbury families since the early 19th century. The main street, now Village Road, accommodated the church, schoolhouse, town hall, and Sunapee Lake Grange No. 112, one of the oldest active Granges in the state. The settlement was also served by a store, post office, blacksmith shop, and weigh station. (William Weiler.)

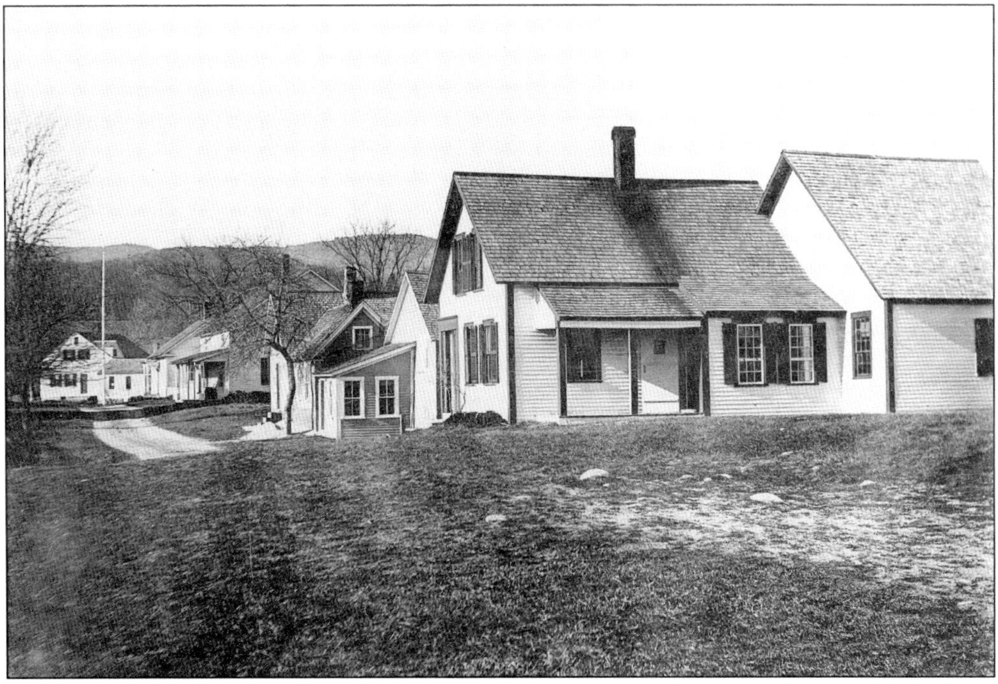

Sleepy Street in South Newbury has changed very little over the years. Florence Bly Perkins, in her book of reminiscences, *Grammie's Memories*, explains that it was home to elderly people who sat on their porches to chat with summer boarders out for a walk. One fine day a group of visitors stopped at the porch of Jane Perkins and asked the name of the street. It had no name, she replied, but "Sleepy Street—it's about all we do now-a-days." (Newbury Public Library.)

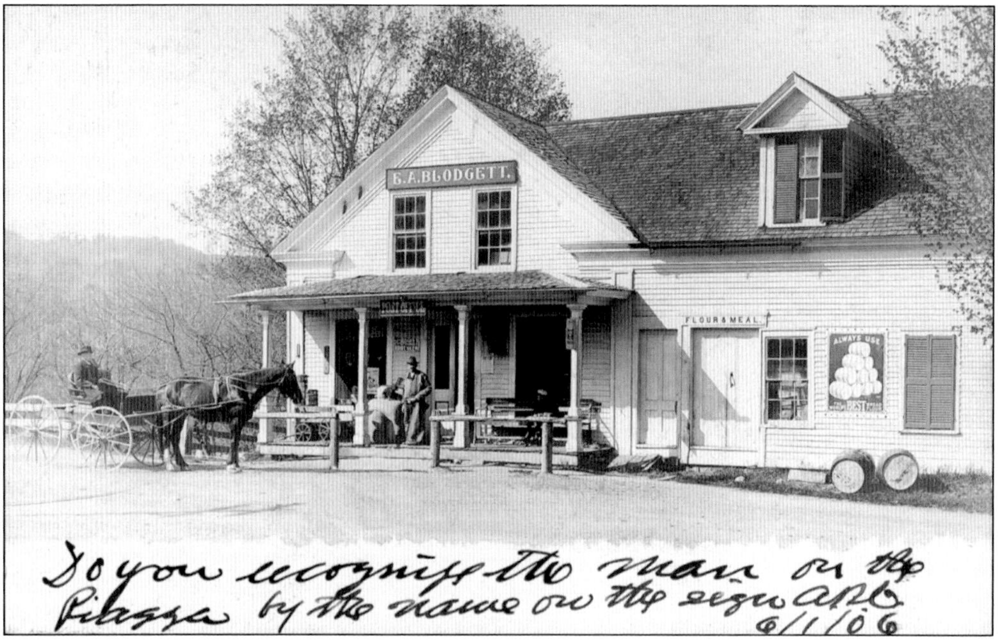

This landmark building in South Newbury operated as a store and post office under several ownerships from the late 1800s until 1960. Edwin A. Blodgett was proprietor and postmaster from 1900 to 1918, as well as town treasurer during that time. Here Blodgett is seen bringing a mailbag out to Hiram Gillingham, local mail carrier and stage driver. The store was later run by James Jepson and Wesley Cilley. (William Weiler.)

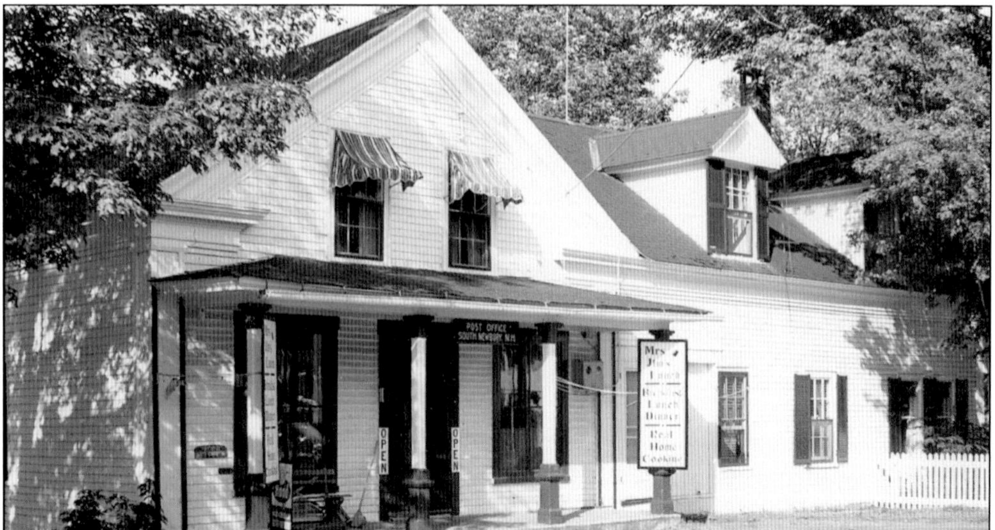

In the mid-1900s, Alice Jepson operated the South Newbury store as Mrs. Jim's Lunch. It continued to house the post office, but farming supplies were replaced with hearty noontime meals for village residents and the children attending the South Newbury school. The building was razed in 1960. Richard Perkins's wife, Dorothy, then ran the post office from her home until 1987, when postal service in South Newbury was discontinued. (Newbury Historical Society.)

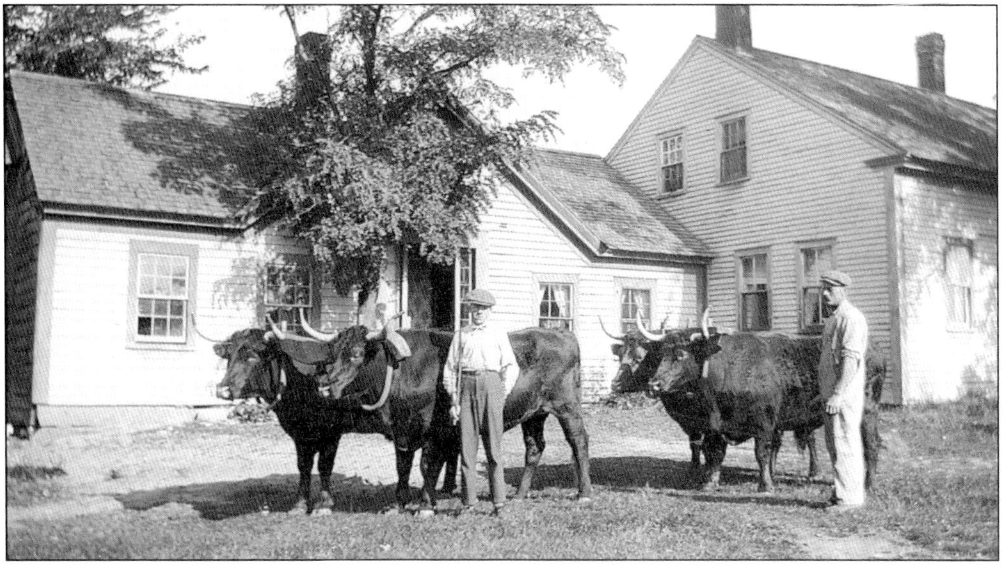

These handsome teams of oxen look as if they could supply plenty of power to the farmers on this South Road property. Oxen were a valuable asset in working the land, particularly in clearing felled timber and hauling rocks so that fields could be established for crops. (Sally Harris.)

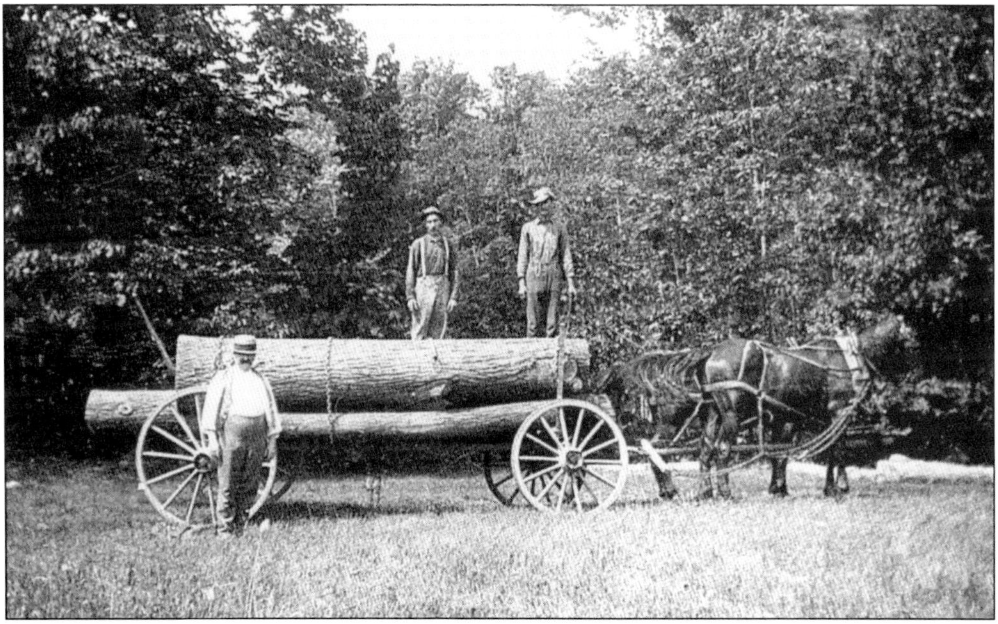

Mark Shultis and helpers transport some massive logs on his property while clearing fields. Wood was abundant on the Newbury hillsides and was a basic staple for the early settlers, who used it for building homes, barns, and furniture and providing heat during the long winters. Fire was a constant threat and all too often destroyed what had been so laboriously constructed. (Sally Harris.)

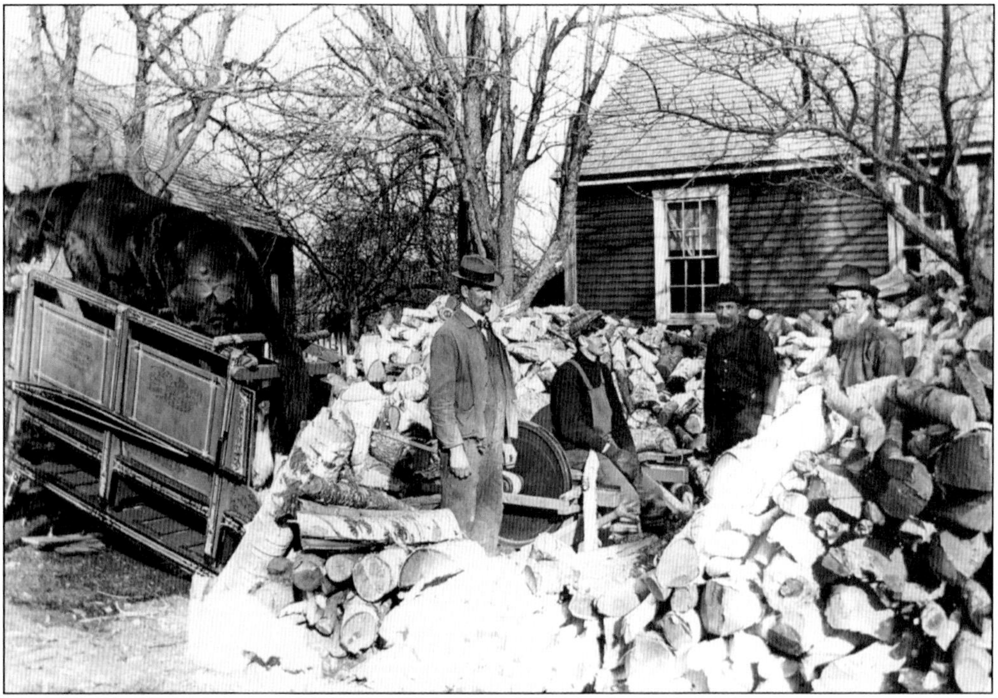

Cutting enough wood to feed the home fires was an ongoing chore often shared by friends and neighbors. Here one horsepower drives the saw (left) while neighbors do the stacking. Shown from left to right are Clarence Perkins, Forest Folsom, Sprague Morse, and possibly George Kidder. (Newbury Historical Society.)

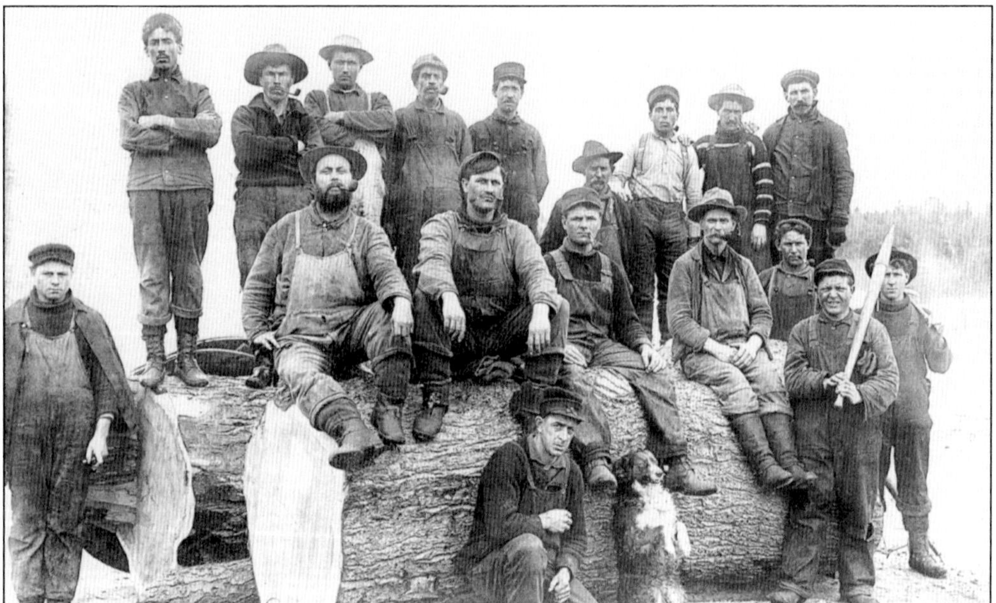

Loggers working for the Gove family, which owned land near the base of Mount Sunapee, pose for a picture atop massive newly cut logs. Some of the loggers enjoy a smoke as they rest, joined by Smutty, the Gove family's dog. (Paul Gove.)

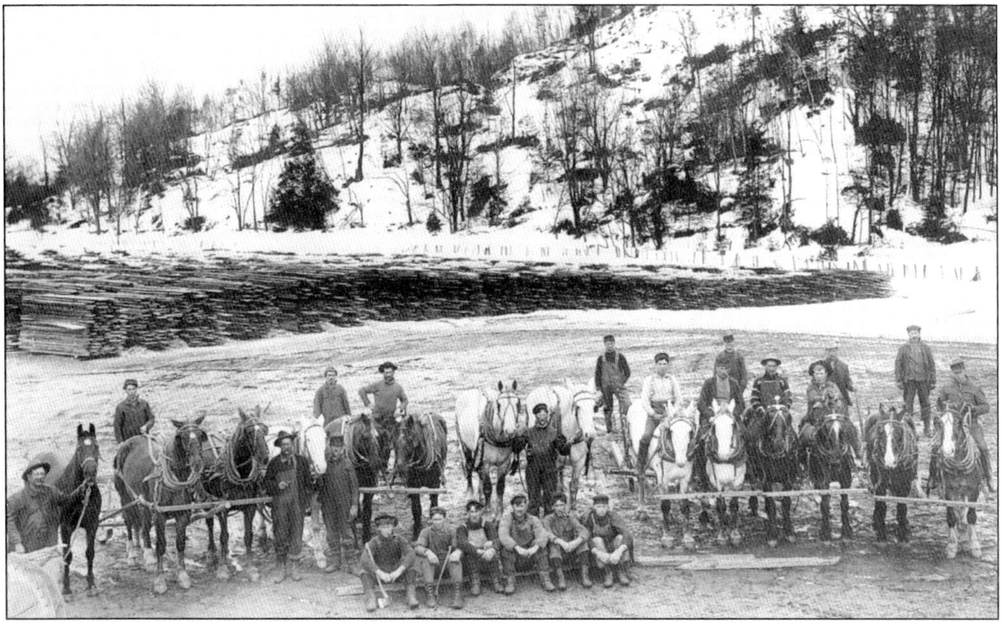

Pictured here is the logging crew and some of the lumber from the Draper Lumber Company sawmill, around 1910–1920. Formerly A. O. Gove's field, the property is now the base building and parking area at Mount Sunapee Resort. Heavy logging and clear-cutting on the mountain during this time led to local citizen action and the formation of the Society for the Protection of New Hampshire Forests. (Paul Gove.)

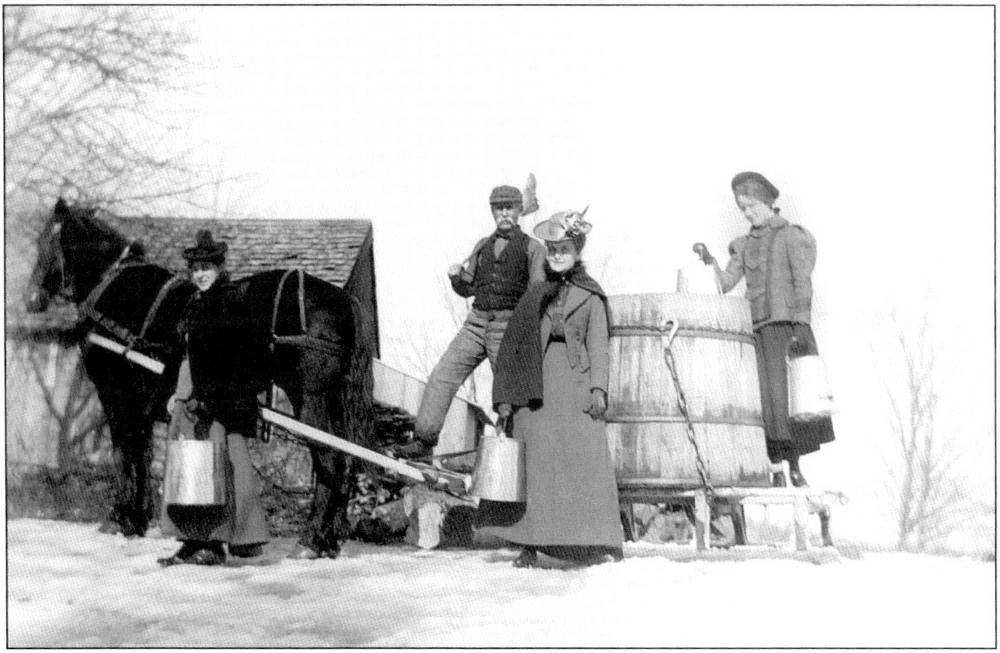

Ladies empty their maple sap buckets into the large vat drawn by sledge across the snow. Maple sap was gathered in the early spring, after freezing nights and gradually warmer days. It was transported through the woods in large vats to the sugarhouse, where it was boiled down. Maple syrup was a household staple, substituting for more expensive refined sugar. (Sally Harris.)

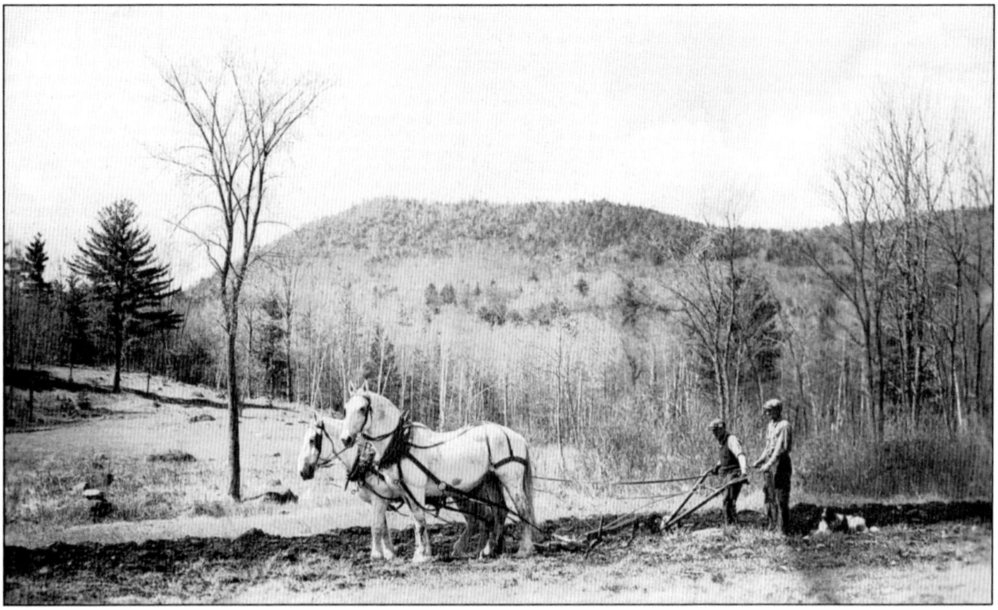

Spring plowing was the first step in assuring a successful crop, and the larger the tilled acreage, the more profitable the farm would be. A sturdy team of horses or oxen were needed to help break up the hard-packed earth. (Wayne and Judy LaPorte.)

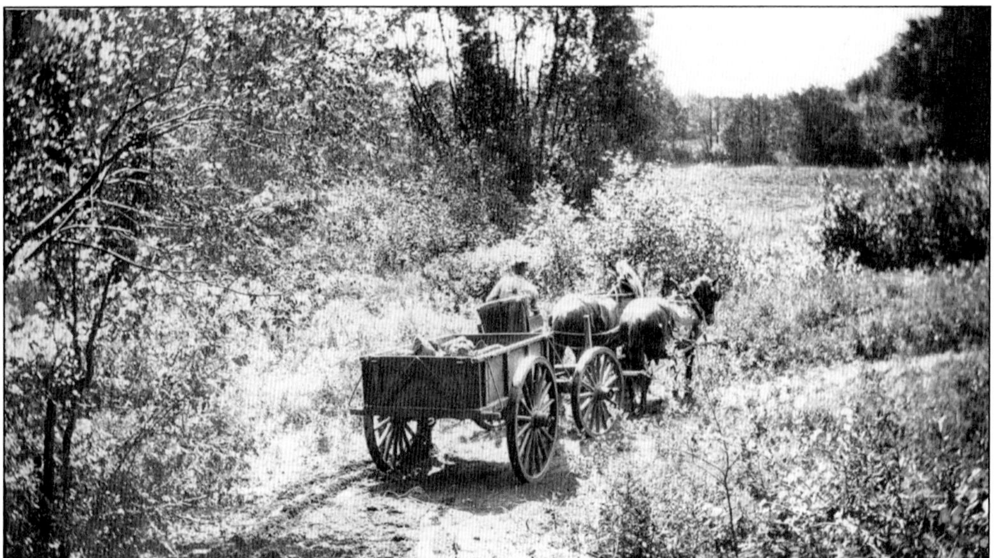

As fields were cleared, the ever-present rocks were laid bare. Moving them was back-breaking work, but stone by stone, they were moved to make cellar holes, stone walls, and other structures. This load is on its way to a new location. (Sally Harris.)

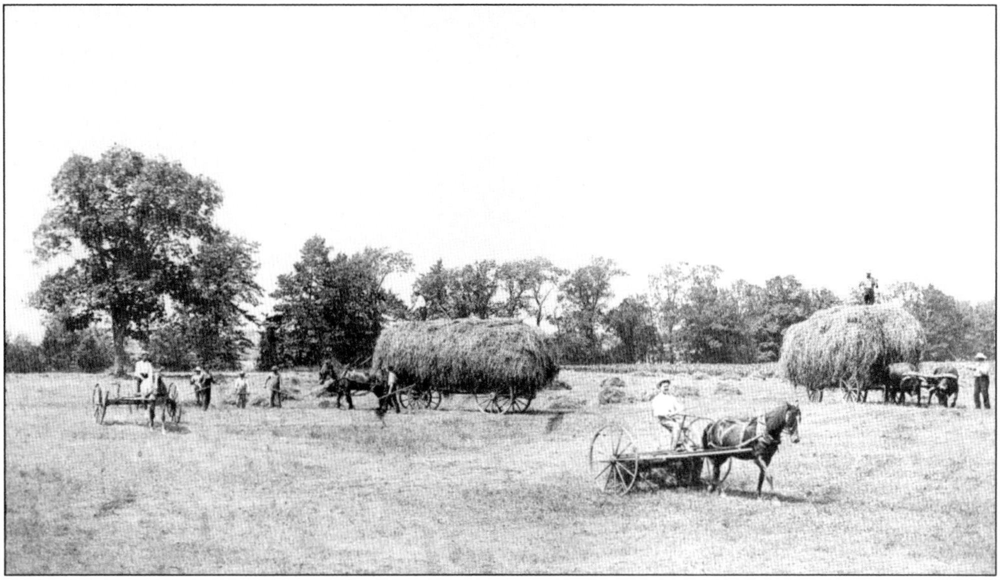

All hands turned out to harvest the hay crop. This picture shows hay rakes and farmhands forking mountainous loads of furrowed hay onto the wagons. Work had to proceed while the weather was fine, since a sudden rainstorm could spoil the cut crop. (Wayne and Judy LaPorte.)

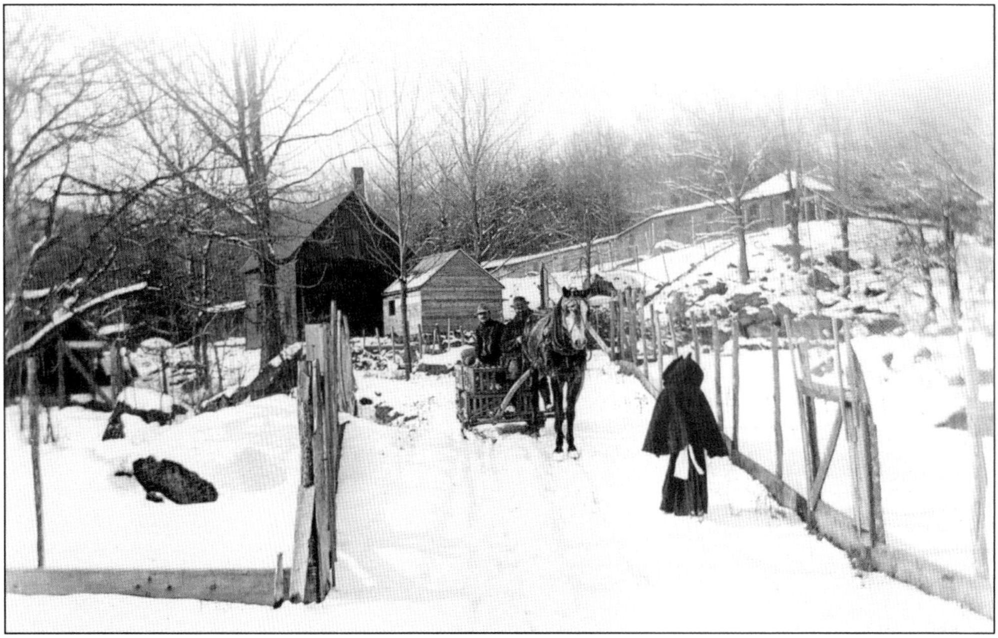

While winter brought relief from labor in the fields, it carried its own hazards for moving about in the cold and snow. By foot or by horse-drawn sledge, the chores had to be done. This winter farm scene is in South Newbury around 1903. (Sally Harris.)

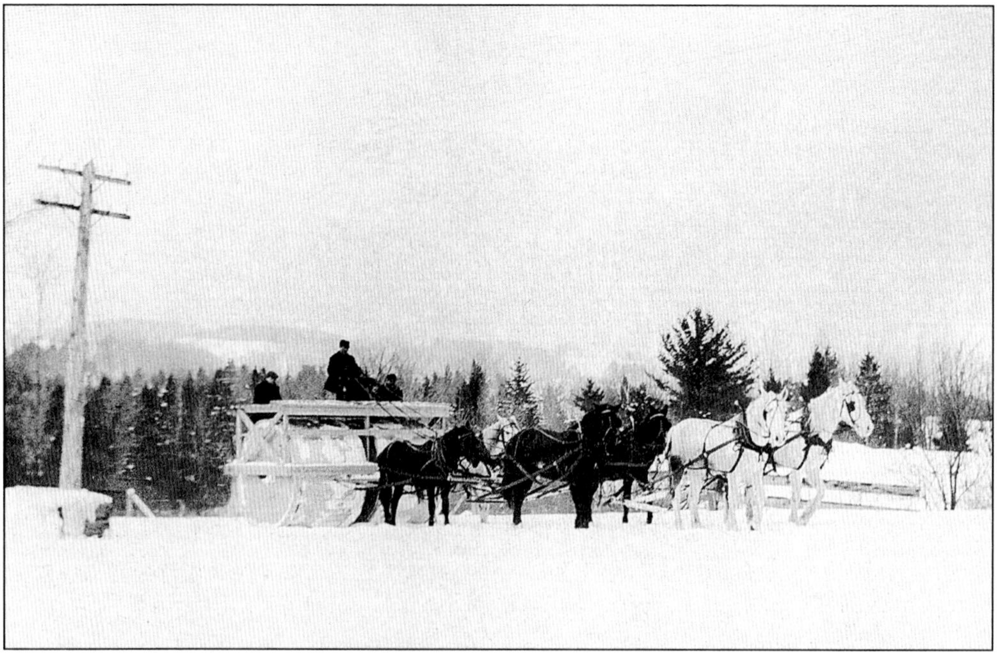

Heavy rollers were used to pack down the snow on town roads in winter. Breaking through the drifts and pulling the roller required lots of horsepower and was a tedious, time-consuming job in bitter weather. Russell and Forest Folsom are the drivers, with Russell owning the black teams and Forest the white. (Elizabeth Folsom.)

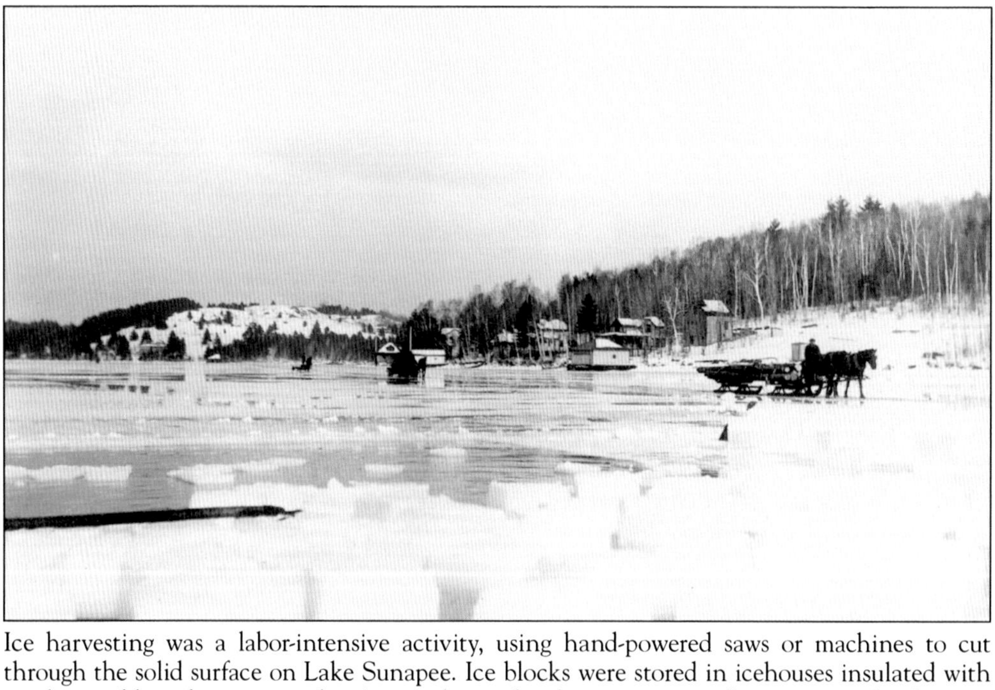

Ice harvesting was a labor-intensive activity, using hand-powered saws or machines to cut through the solid surface on Lake Sunapee. Ice blocks were stored in icehouses insulated with sawdust and lasted many months. An ample supply of ice was especially important for the inns and grand hotels that catered to summer guests. Pictured here, a horse and driver pick up a load of ice blocks from Sunapee harbor. (Newbury Historical Society.)

Three

Getting Together

By the 1790s, Province Road connected several area towns. Its passage at the end of Lake Sunapee, now Newbury harbor, made this a center for town activities. There the town's earliest still-standing building, the Cilley Tavern, served stagecoach travelers and local residents. Innkeepers Ezra and Moses Cilley provided food, spirits, and a place to gather and share news. The tavern was the site of a town meeting in March 1831, when the townspeople voted to tear down the 1790s Bly Hill meetinghouse, sell the timber, and erect a new building in the harbor area for religious use by private subscription.

In 1832, the Center Meeting House opened its doors. It contained timbers from the old Bly Hill structure, and its design reflected the influence of master architect Asher Benjamin. The interior arrangement, with a raised reverse pulpit, survives as one of only two such interiors in the state. It hosted several noted early ministers, including Elder George Buzzell Tewksbury, Dr. John Quackenbos, and evangelist Rev. Esther Smith. In the 1870s, town meetings were held there and various entertainments provided enjoyment for the community.

Children, too, had their gathering places. As early as 1791, the Baker Hill school district was established, followed by another dozen districts in the 1800s. Schoolhouses were one-room affairs heated by a wood-burning stove with crude desks, a blackboard, and possibly a map. Teachers boarded around with families of pupils. Young children attended the summer term, usually taught by a woman. When chores lightened in winter, the older boys attended, and it was thought prudent to have a male teacher to keep proper order. The scholars themselves ranged in age from 3 and 4 years old to young men in their 20s.

The quest for knowledge was also served by the library, first housed upstairs in Sherman Hall. A second library was established in the King's Daughters' Hall (now the Newbury Veterans' Hall) in the early 1900s. In 1963, these were consolidated into a new library built adjacent to the Center School.

Fairs provided a welcome opportunity for families to socialize and share their agricultural achievements. The Sunapee Lake Grange held annual fairs in the early 1900s and sponsored a winter carnival from 1915 to 1925. The Bradford-Newbury fair brought these two communities together in a hugely popular event that was a highlight of the year.

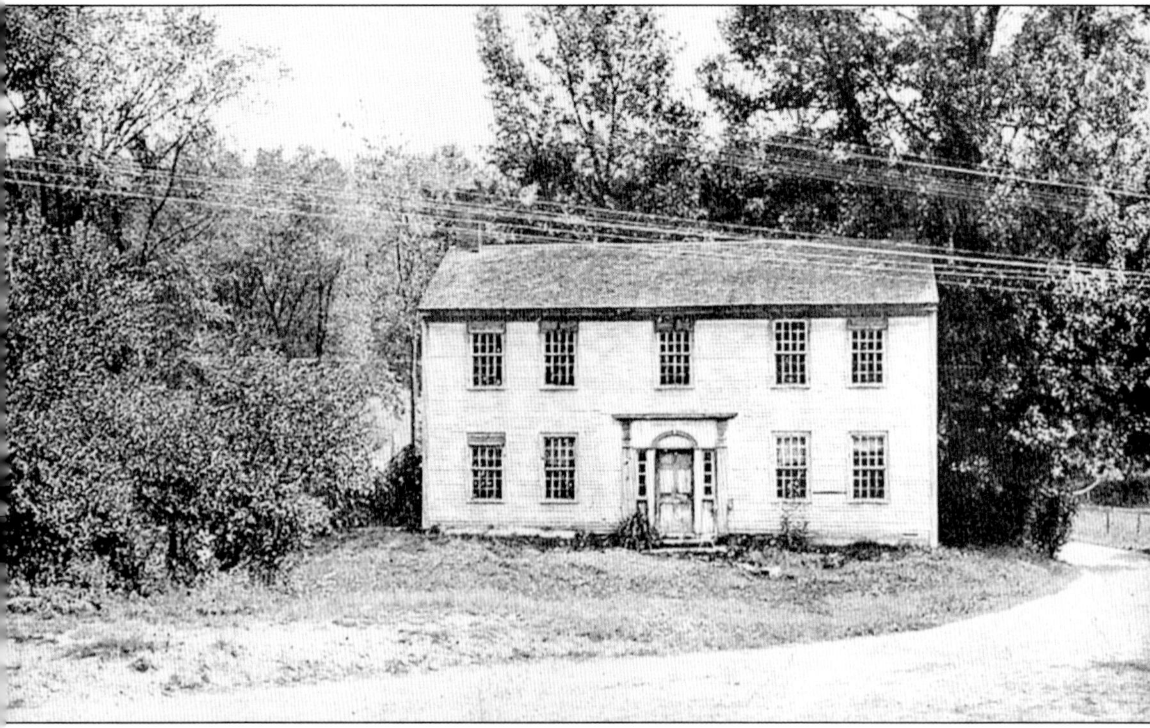

Built in the late 1780s to early 1790s, the Cilley Tavern is the oldest standing structure in Newbury. Located in Newbury center at the intersection of what are now Routes 103 and 103A, it was operated by brothers Ezra and Moses Cilley and served both residents and stagecoach passengers traveling on Province Road, which connected area towns. It was a haven for travelers and a focal point for town gatherings. After the railroad between Concord and Claremont was established in the 1870s, the tavern's function as a hostel became obsolete. It housed a store and later, with the arrival of the automobile, a gas station and garage. The building was rotated 90 degrees and moved back from Route 103A to allow better vehicle access. Sometime in the 1960s, a facade was added to create more work space, but tenants continued to live on the second floor and continue to do so today through the building's many transformations. (Tracy Messer.)

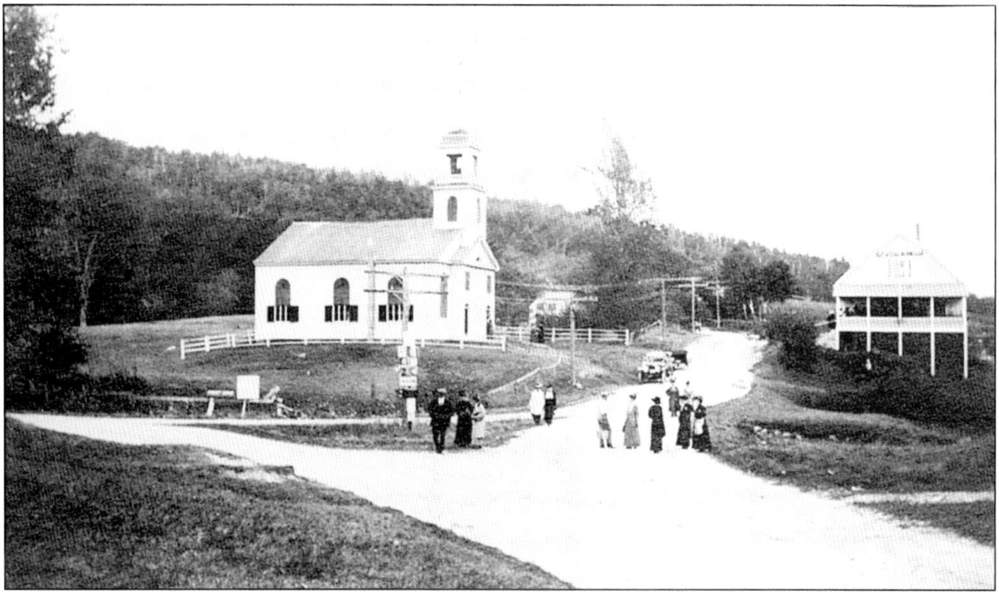

The Center Meeting House was built in 1832, following a town vote to erect a building for religious purposes across the intersection from the Cilley Tavern. Many old timbers from the Bly Hill structure were used in its construction, accomplished by a master builder in the Federal style. A reverse pulpit faces out over the interior, standing between the two entry doors with staircases on either side. The interior is one of only two examples of this arrangement in the state. The building is topped with an unusual weather vane and a steeple bell donated by John Hay. The meetinghouse hosted many community activities and noted preachers. A state nonprofit corporation was created in 1977 and trustees were charged with its historic preservation and protection. (Tracy Messer.)

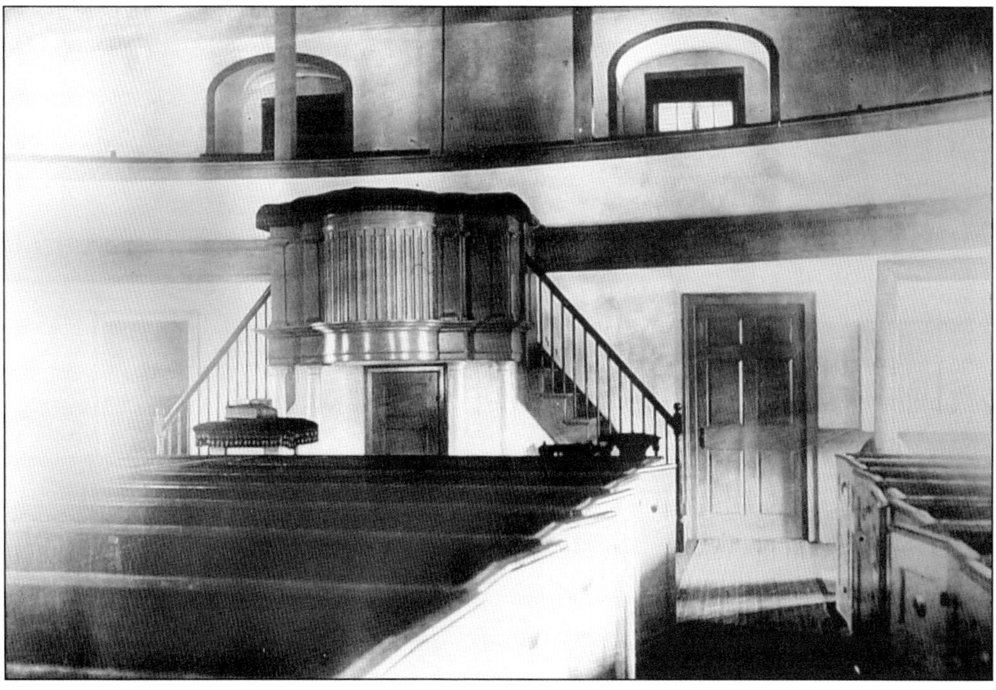

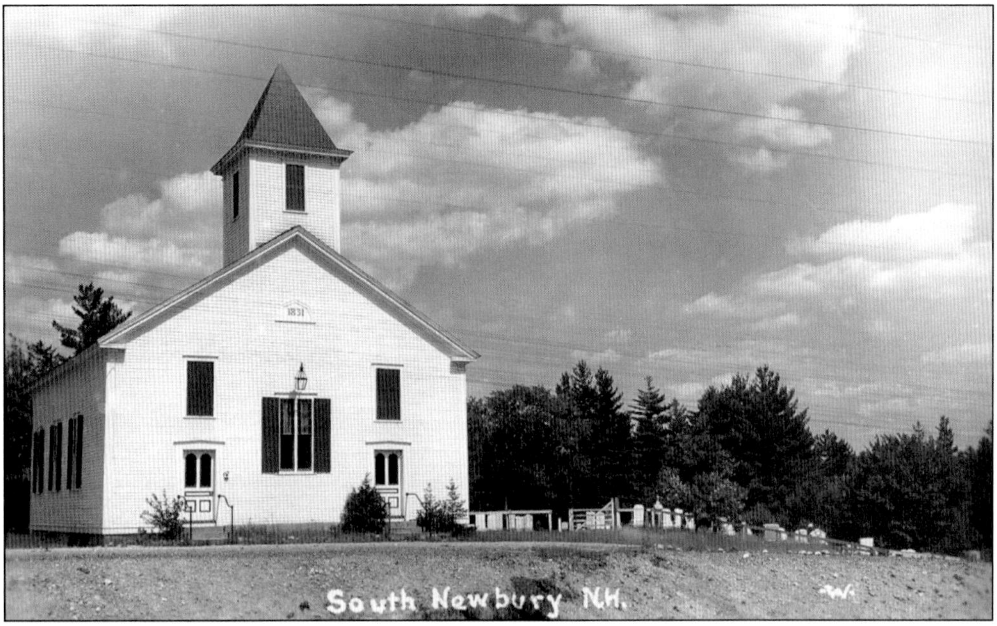

South Newbury Union Church was built in 1831 by Israel Putnam. A group of local residents raised money by selling pews and thus became proprietors. For many years, the church was distinguished by a mural painted by an itinerant artist. The church retains a strong membership and hosts services and several community events. The adjoining cemetery holds the remains of Newbury families dating back to Civil War times. (William Weiler.)

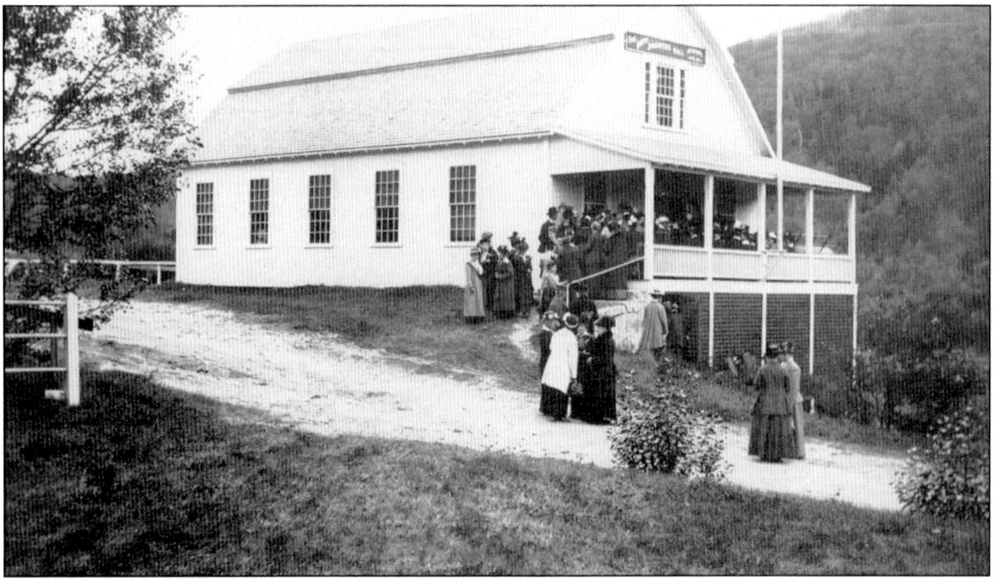

The King's Daughters' Hall was built in 1912 across from the Center Meeting House. This was the site of Matson's Hotel, which burned in 1909. The building held a small stage, seating for 200, a kitchen, and the town library. This religious and charitable association sponsored many town events until it deeded the building to the town in 1947. It is known today as the Newbury Veterans' Hall. (Tracy Messer.)

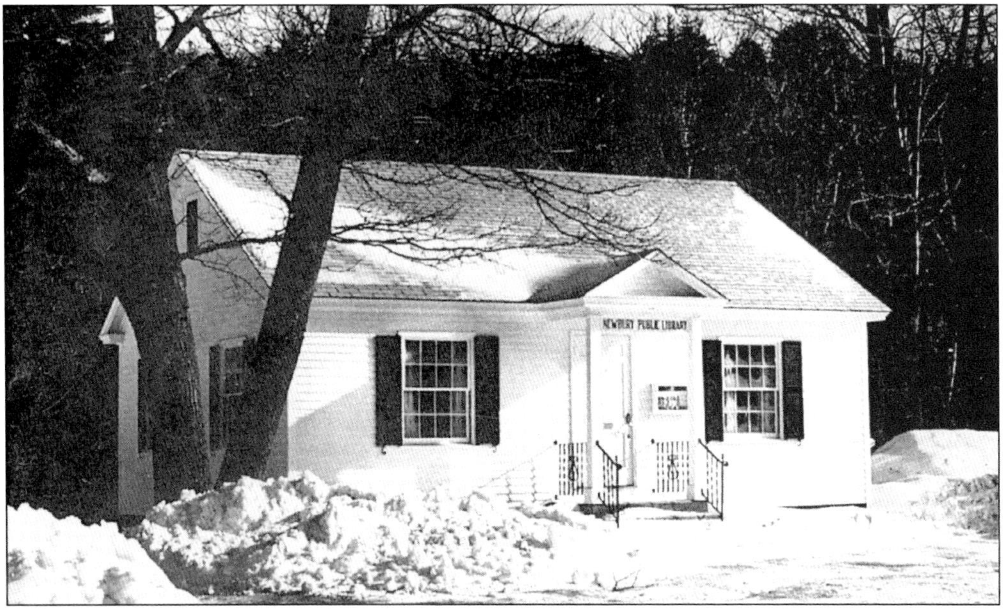

The Newbury Public Library found a home of its own next to the Center School in 1963, replacing small rooms formerly devoted to library use in South Newbury's selectmen's office and the Newbury Veterans' Hall. Bertha Rich and Helen Nye shared duty as librarians. Records indicate that the first library was in the home of Edwin A. Blodgett, established in 1892 with a $25 endowment from John Hay. (Town of Newbury.)

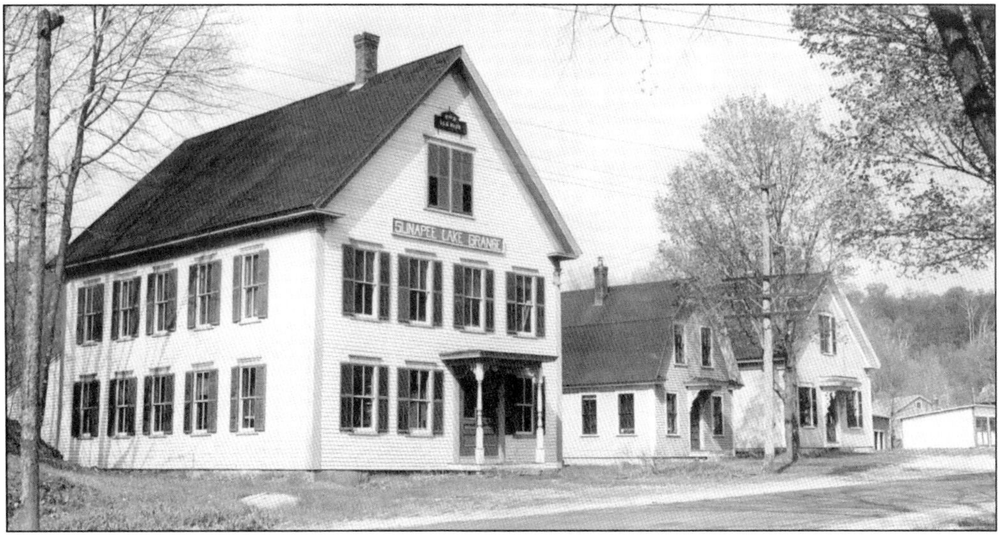

The Sunapee Lake Grange, Sherman Hall, and Newbury Town Hall stand in a row on Village Road in South Newbury. This was a center for town activities during Newbury's earliest days, and these buildings remain in use today under town ownership. (John Hutchinson.)

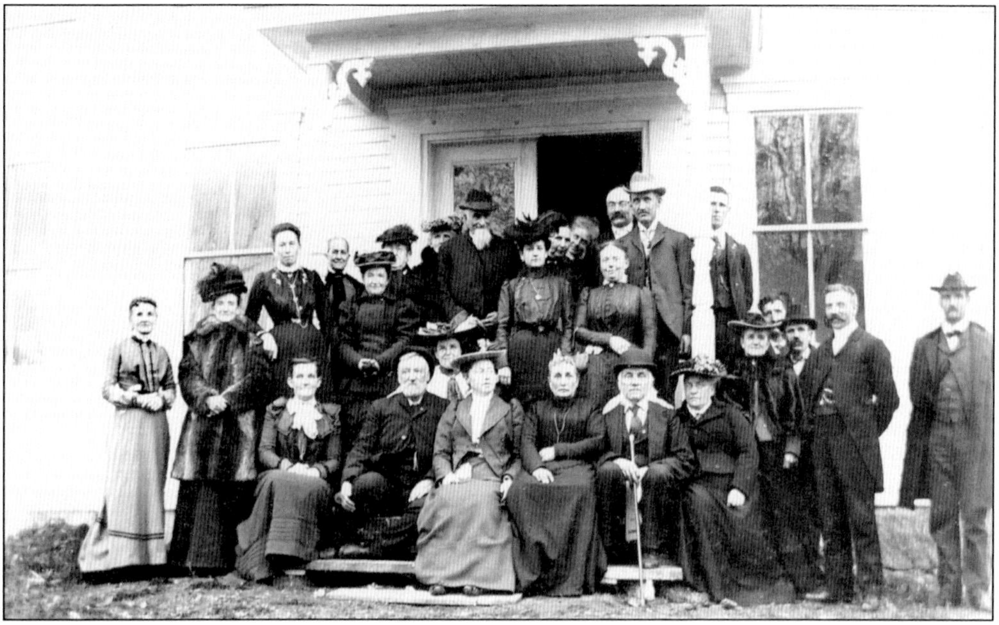

In October 1902, Sunapee Lake Grange members gathered in front of their new hall, built on land donated by Mark Shultis on the former site of Jason Perkins's blacksmith shop. Mary Cilley donated the furnishings from early Grange meetings in Cilley's Hall, upstairs in the South Newbury store. From its first meetings in the old town hall, the Sunapee Lake Grange has been in continuous operation since 1886. (Sally Harris.)

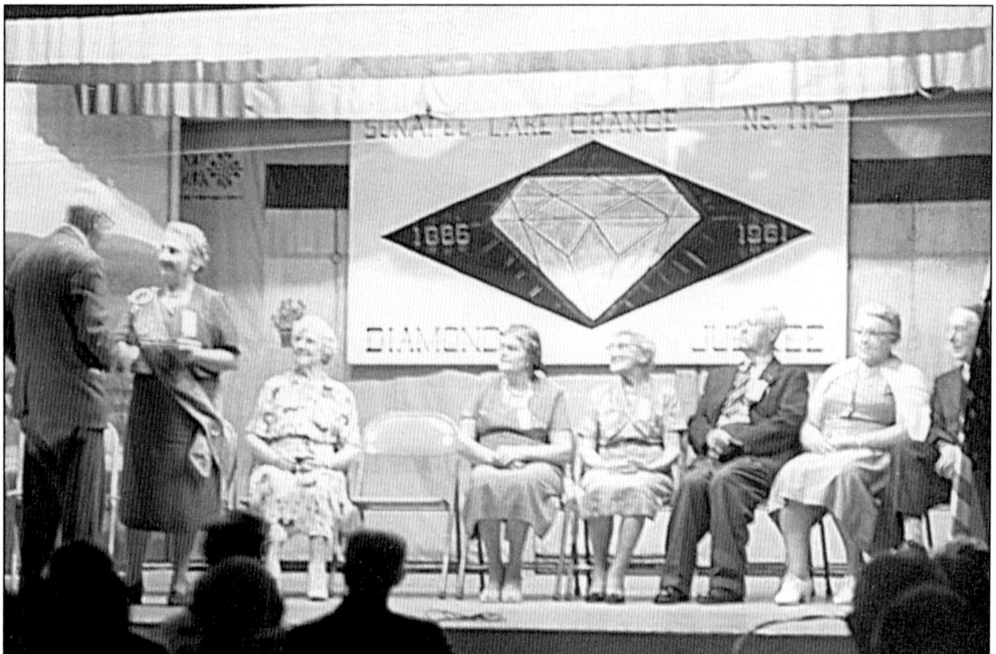

The Sunapee Lake Grange celebrated its diamond jubilee in 1961. Shown here are, from left to right, possibly James and Mary Farmer standing, possibly Ethel Craig, Edith Eaton, Mertie (Merrill) Rowe, Moses Bly, Bertha (Colburn) Rich, and Merle Rich. (Joyce Allen Cantu.)

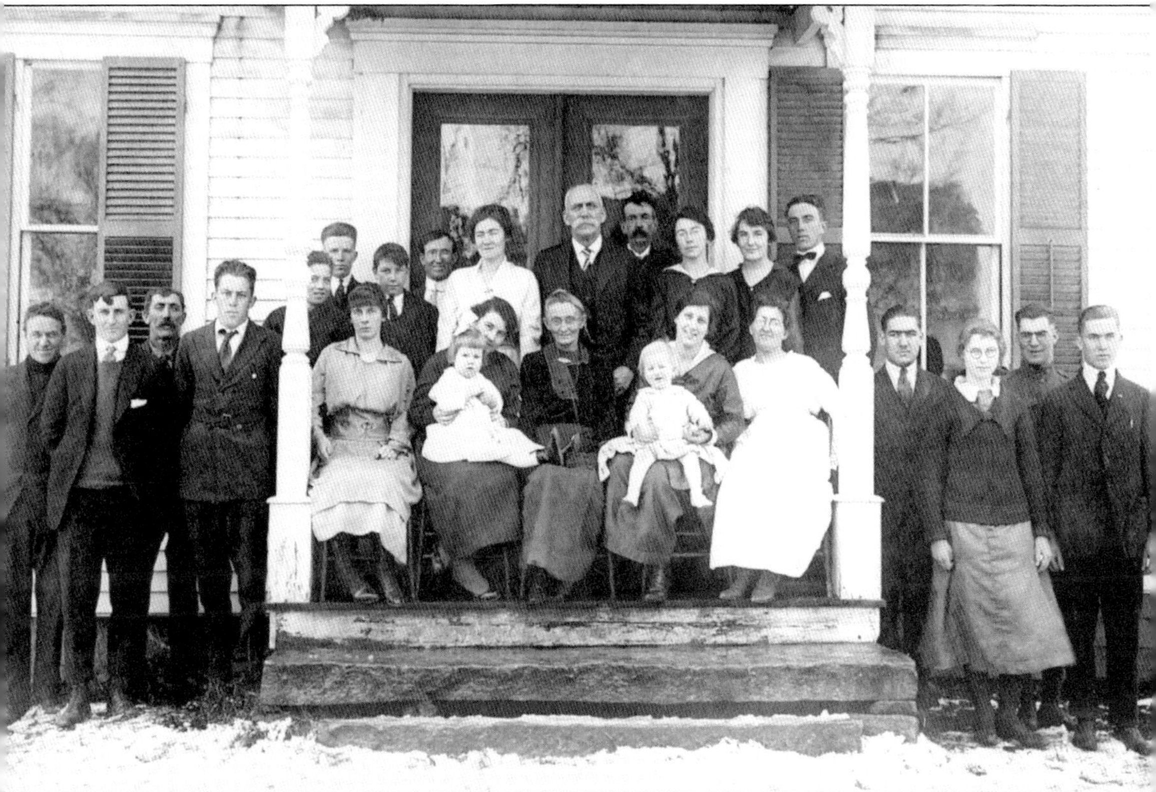

As growing families gathered to celebrate special occasions, they often required the extra space offered by public buildings. Here the Merrill family meets at the Grange for a Thanksgiving celebration in 1919. Guest of honor Jonathan Merrill (second row, center) was a member of the 2nd Regiment of the New Hampshire Volunteer Infantry, mustering in on June 7, 1861. Wounded at Gettysburg in 1863, he mustered out in 1864. After wintering in Florida for 14 years, this was the first time that Merrill stayed late enough in the season to celebrate with nearly all his extended family. Shown here are, from left to right, (first row) Florence (Spofford) Rowe, Mary Rowe with baby Barbara, Ida (Lewis) Merrill, Bessie (Marshall) Rowe with baby Marshall, and Mertie (Merrill) Rowe; (second row) Blane Hall, Harold Rowe, Sidney Merrill, Chester Merrill, Kenneth Bly, Laurence Bagley, Earl Rowe, Arthur Rowe, Evelyn (Whipple) Hall, Jonathan Merrill, unidentified, Dura J. Rowe, Effie Merrill, Evelyn (Rowe) Cheney, Harry Cheney, Ralph Whipple, Veda Whipple, David Whipple, and Perley Whipple. (Sally Harris.)

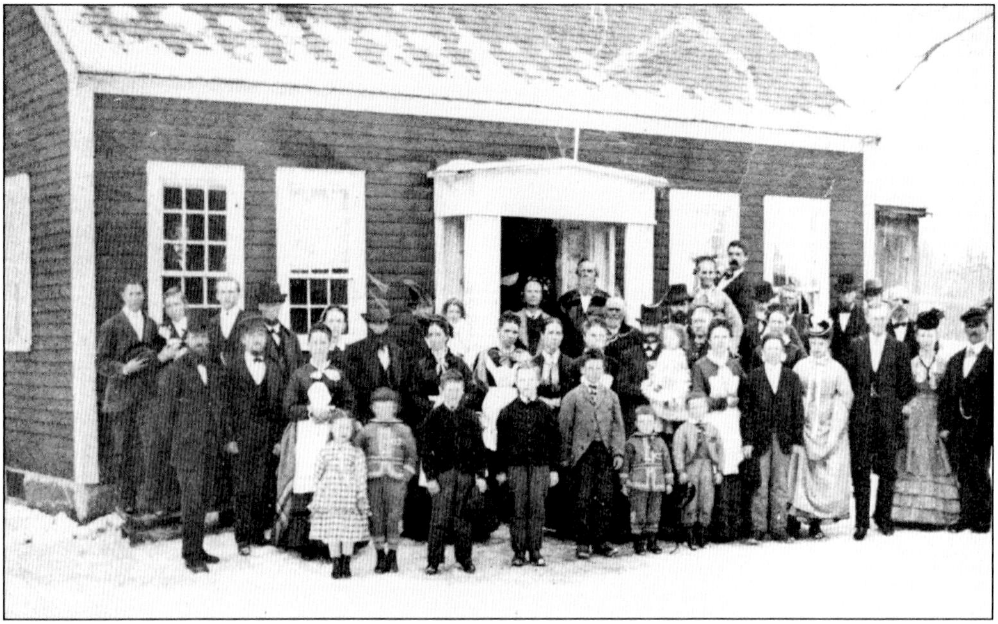

This keepsake picture of a Newbury family reunion in the 1880s or 1890s must have marked a special occasion, such as Thanksgiving or Christmas. Several generations are present, dressed in their best attire. (Newbury Historical Society.)

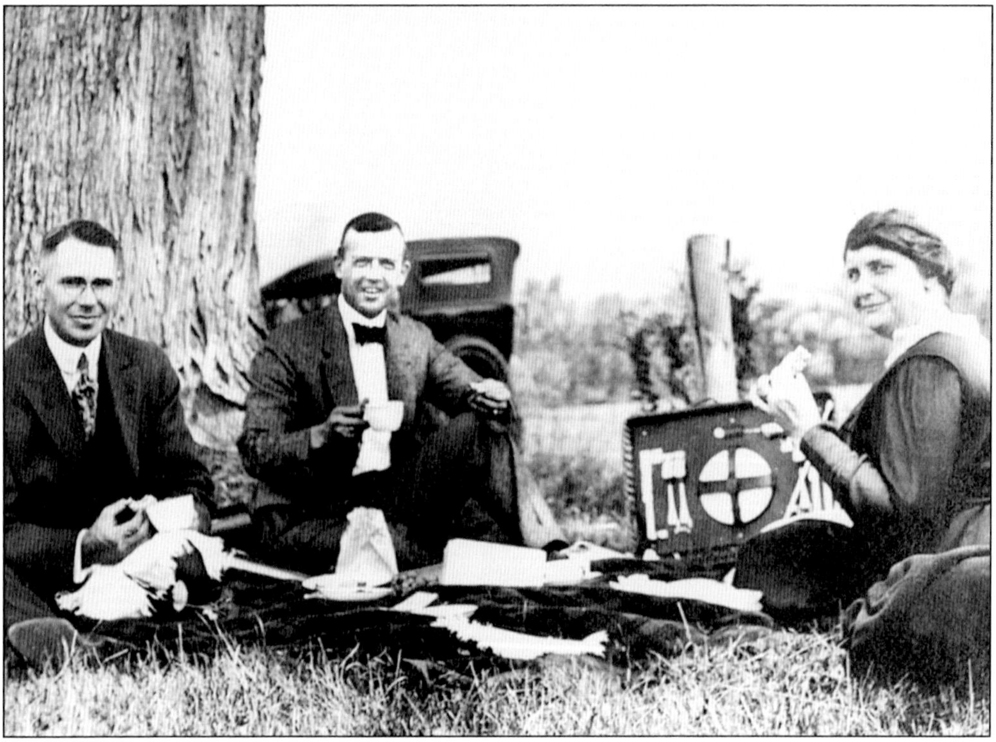

It looks like a fine day for a picnic as some of Newton Shultis's friends enjoy a vantage point on his property. Such occasions were rare for hardworking farmers, but as automation and automobiles arrived, life became a bit easier. (Sally Harris.)

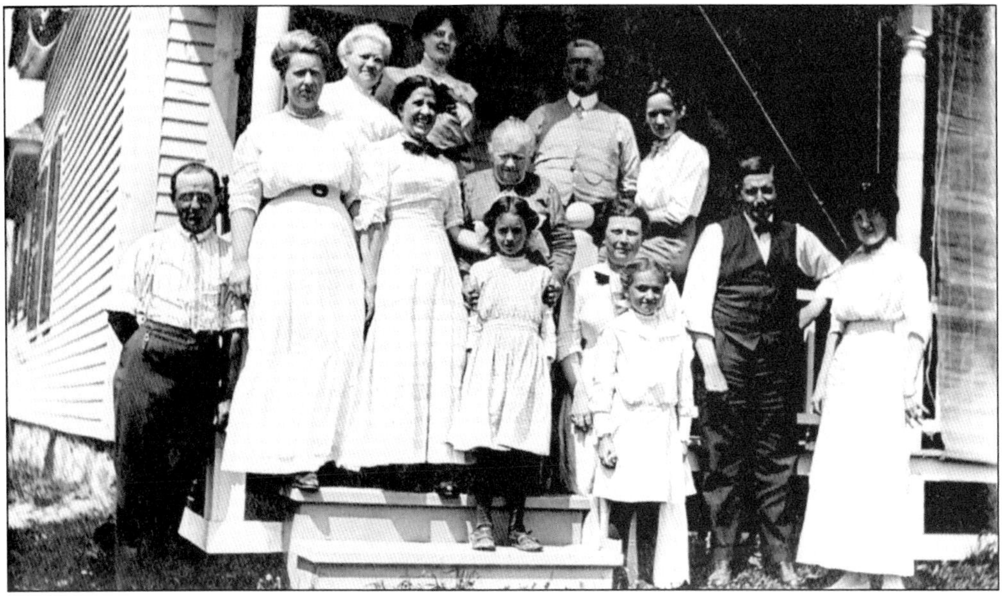

Shown here are members of the McElroy family posing on the steps of Archie Gove's house on the present-day Mount Sunapee parking lot area. Pictured are, from left to right, (first row) Edward Curtice, Sarah Curtice, Gertie McElroy, Ellen Price, Edith Price, Dorothy Gove, William McElroy, and Ruby McElroy; (second row) Mary McElroy Holt, Mildred Price, Eliza McElroy Price, William McElroy, and Elsie Gove. (Wayne and Judy LaPorte.)

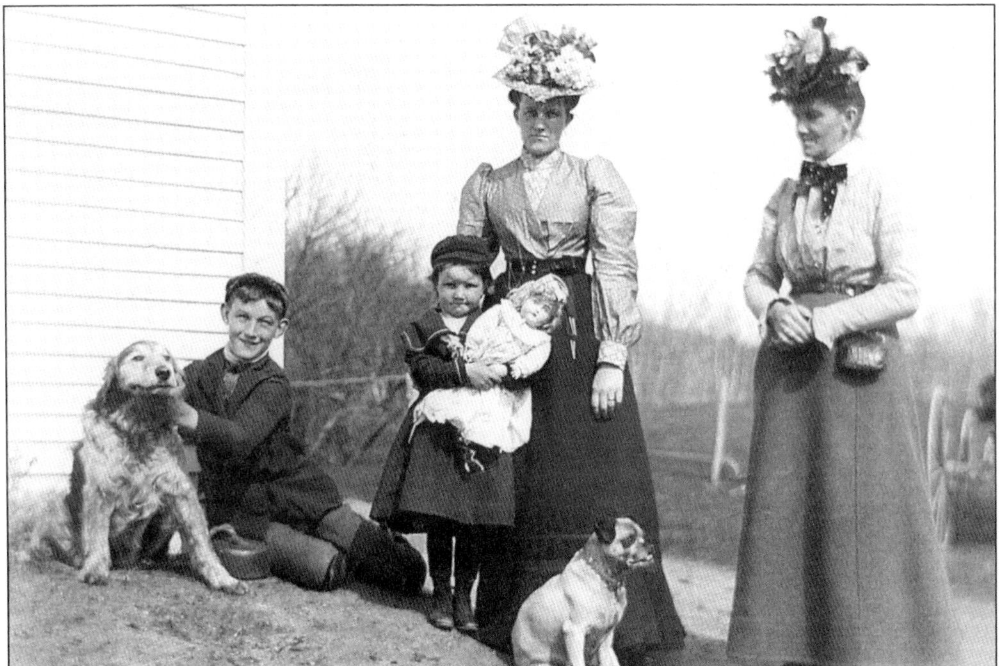

Decked out in their best bonnets, Estella (Gillingham) Russell (standing at left) and Lura (Farmer) Gillingham pose with their children, Arthur Gillingham and Bernice Russell, at a 1902 family gathering. Arthur grew up in Newbury and served in World War I, dying in France in 1918 at the age of 29. (Dorothy Beckner.)

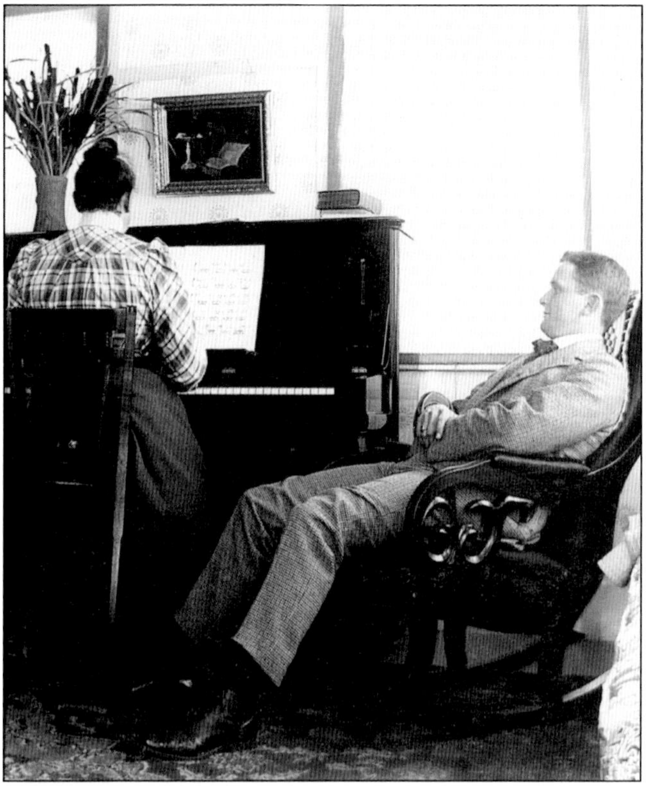

Blanche and Newton Shultis enjoy an evening's musical diversion at home around 1900. Those blessed with a talent for singing or playing an instrument were called upon to provide entertainment for relaxing moments at home or for livelier social gatherings. (Sally Harris.)

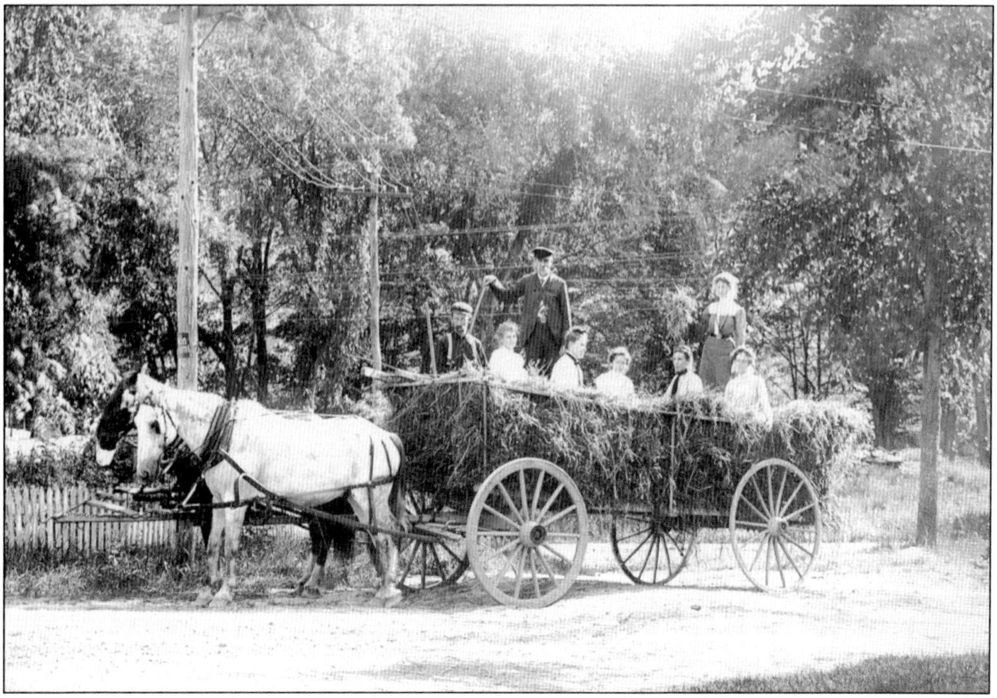

These young ladies are out for a pleasant hayride as they socialize on a summer's afternoon. The gentlemen will make sure that the team does not lead them astray. (Wayne and Judy LaPorte.)

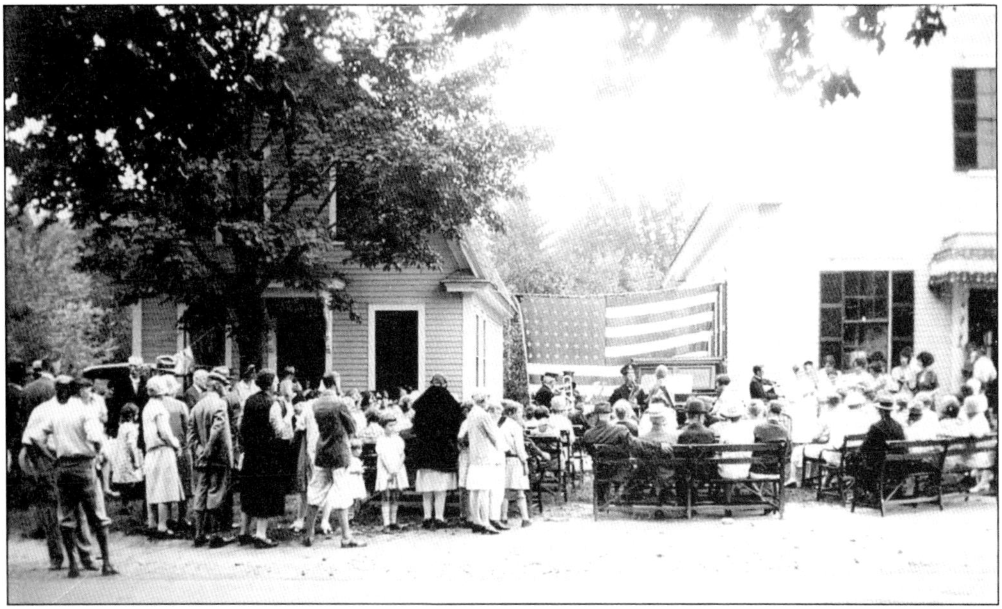

From 1915 until the 1950s, the annual Sunapee Lake Grange fair in South Newbury attracted large crowds to admire livestock and poultry, garden and field produce, and food, flowers, and needlework. (Newbury Public Library.)

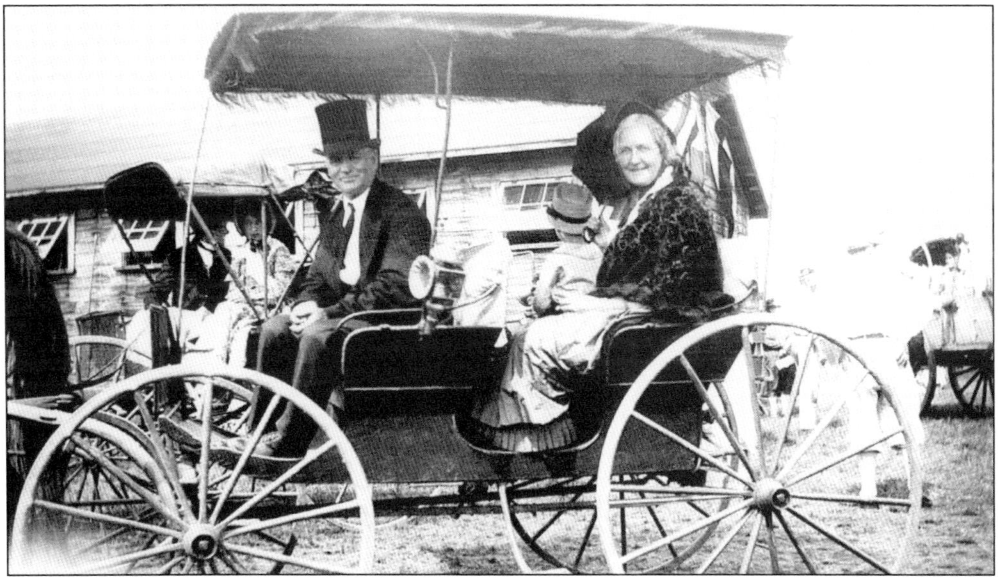

A happy couple travels to a local outing in its surrey with fringe on top. The event may have been an agricultural fair, but the finery suggests that it was a more formal gathering. (Bradford Historical Society.)

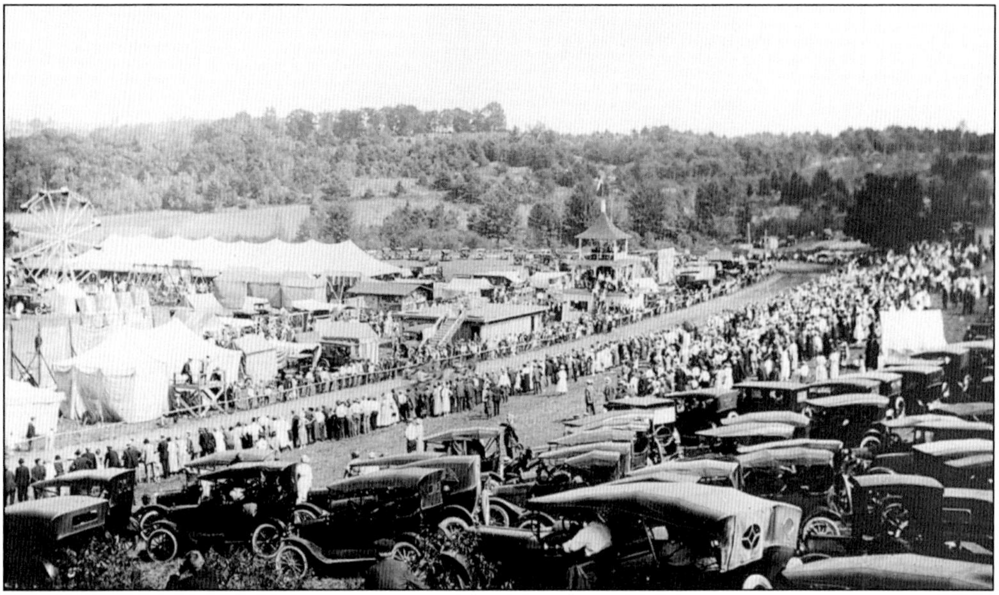

The annual Bradford-Newbury fair drew thousands of attendees. It was organized in the 1870s by Col. Mason Tappan of Bradford and Ezra Cilley II of Newbury. J. Albert Peaslee of Bradford donated 20 acres of land for the venture. The first fair was held in the fall of 1875. Over the next 20 years, it grew in popularity as exhibits and entertainment became more elaborate. After a 17-year lapse, the fair resumed in 1920 with additional buildings for farm and home products. It was so successful that additions to the large exhibition building and stock sheds were required. In 1922, a 25-by-40-foot platform was built for outdoor entertainment, including vaudeville acts. Crowd pleasers included a racetrack, band concerts, parades, horse-pulling contests, baseball games, balloon ascensions, 4-H demonstrations, and a "Mile of Midway." The last fair was held in 1927. (Bradford Historical Society.)

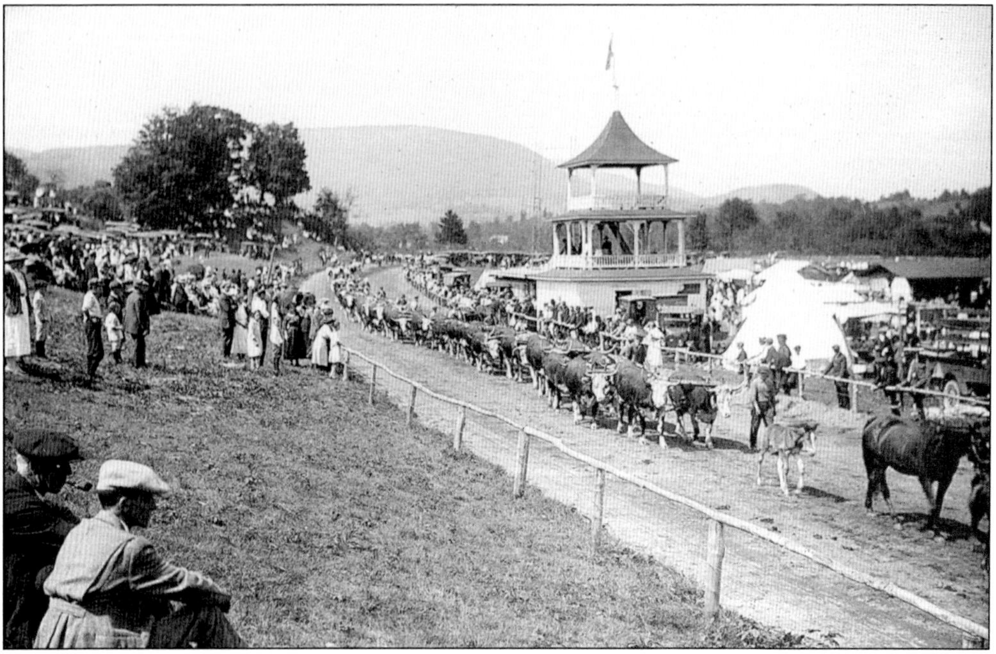

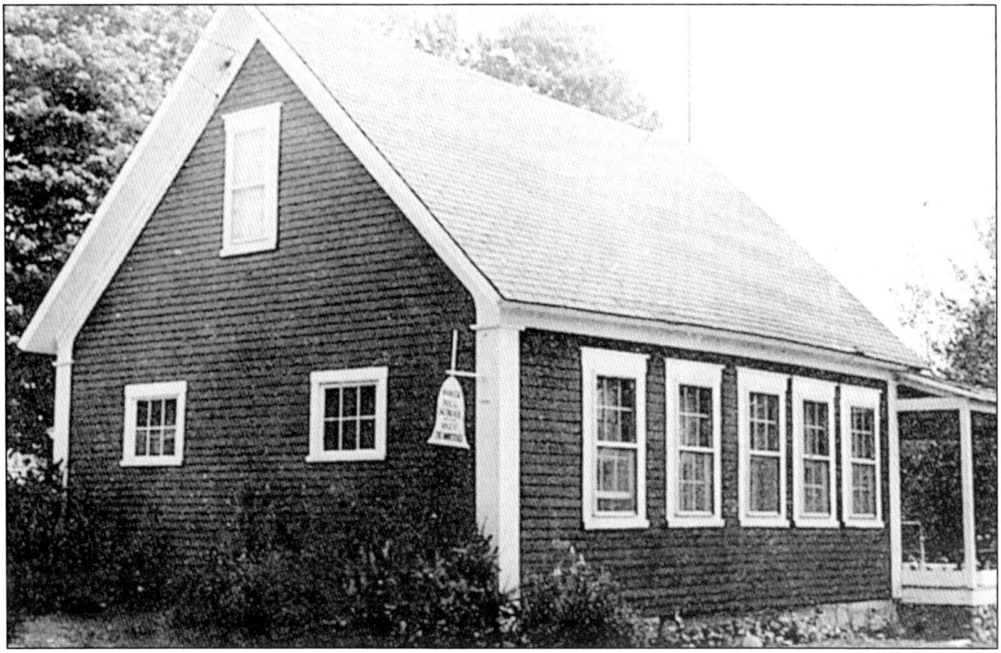

Several of Newbury's old one-room schoolhouses are still standing, including the first, Baker Hill School, built around 1800 on land donated by John Peirce. Julia Wood taught there in the early 1900s, followed by Clara Cressey and Mary Farmer. Clara Cressey earned $8 per week and boarded with the neighboring Messer family. Teacher Frances Stevens was found dead in the schoolhouse in 1938. The building is now a private residence. (Town of Newbury.)

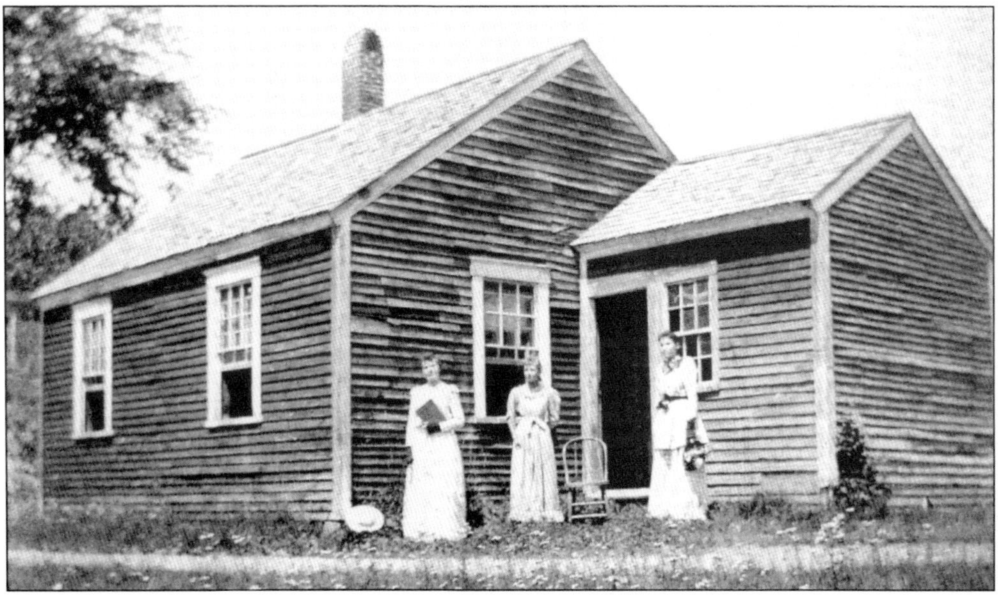

The Box Corner schoolhouse was part of the Union School District run cooperatively with Bradford. It was annexed to Newbury in 1850. Throughout the years, there were at least 13 school districts in Newbury, although not all were in session every year. Schools were ungraded, and pupils wishing to go on to higher education had to take placement exams. Many Newbury students went to the Warner high school via the train; others went to Newport. (Elizabeth Folsom.)

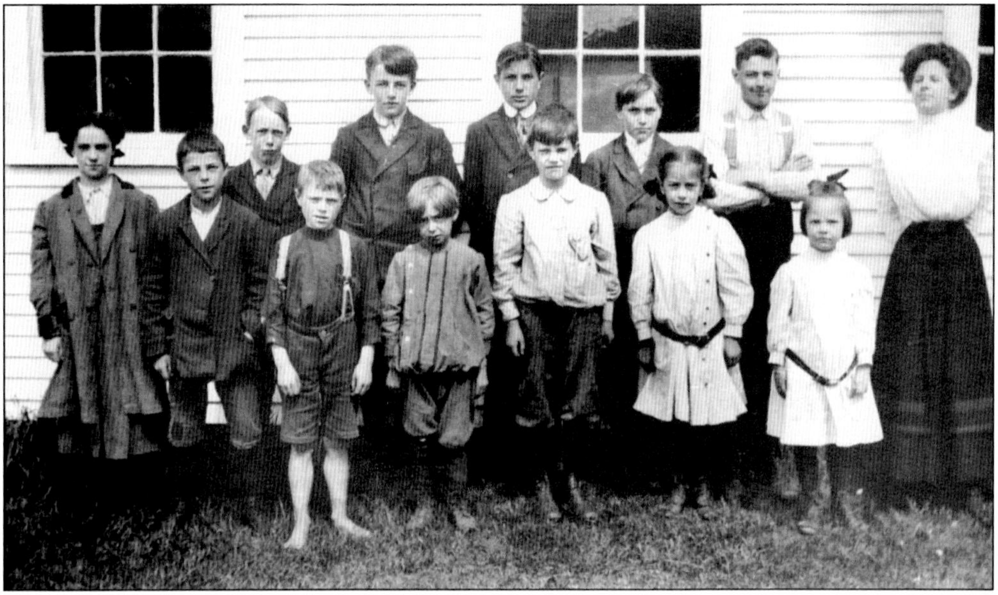

These students are at the Mount Sunapee School on Province Road, around 1910. The subjects are, from left to right, (first row) Minnie Fortune, Lawrence Fortune, Franklin Fortune, ? Blake, Jack Johnson, Hope Johnson, and Polly Johnson; (second row) Merle Rich, Hamilton Creamer, possibly Joseph Fortune, Harold Gove, John Fortune, and teacher Jessie Rowe. Teachers had to be flexible and multitaskers to simultaneously teach children ranging widely in age. (Virginia Hancock.)

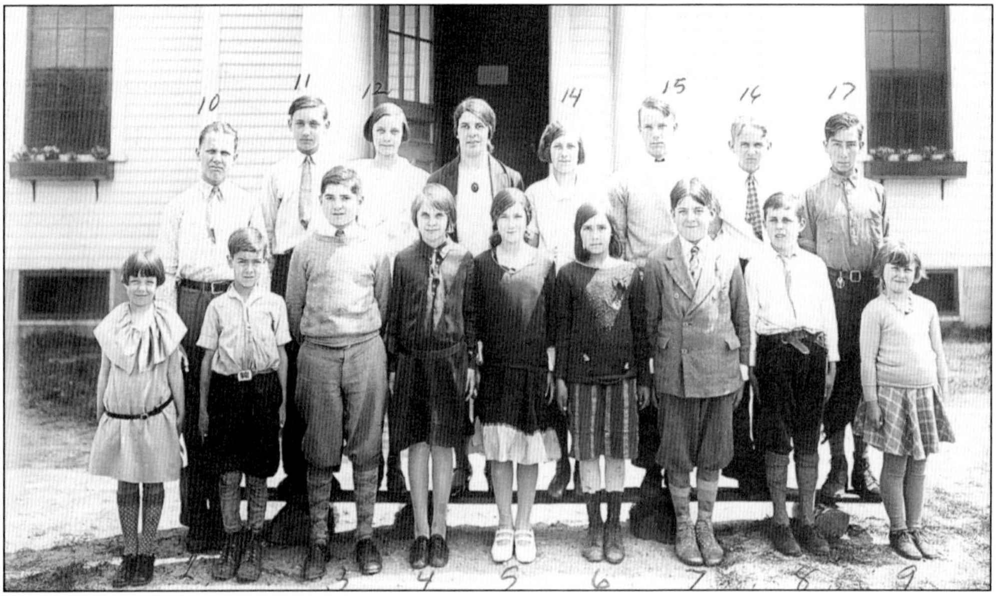

The Center School was opened in 1927 with a Mrs. Symonds as teacher. She was followed by Edith Watson in 1929, who taught for 31 years. Students pictured here in 1929 are, from left to right, (first row) possibly Lucille Fortune, Walter Croteau, possibly William Maxfield, Janet Maxfield, Alice Croteau, Mimi Croteau, Roland Hall, Edwin Maxfield, and Jean Plumeridge; (second row) Arthur Bushway, Walter Rogalski, Adele Rogalski, teacher Edith Watson, Margery Muzzey, Henry Bushway, Robert Kean, and James Bernard Croteau. (Norman Purple.)

Four

UNDER MOTION

Railroad fever hit New Hampshire in the early 1800s, fueled by the power of steam and the promise of economic growth. As track went down and trains rolled through towns, they were met by excited throngs, bands, and political dignitaries celebrating the occasion. By 1850, the Concord and Claremont Railroad provided service between Concord and Bradford, but the route beyond Bradford was blocked by the formidable Newbury Summit, a long, steep granite barrier. It would be 20 years before the way west was opened by blasting the massive ledge to remove 10,000 cubic feet of rock.

During the summer of 1871, a crew of 50 men worked around the clock, seven days a week. The project drew a stream of onlookers, with entire families making an outing to the site after Sunday services. Despite setbacks and accidents, the Newbury Cut was finished in September 1871, and one year later, the track was completed in Claremont. This vital link brought new business to Newbury, carrying the first wave of summer visitors from Boston, New York, and distant points to Lake Sunapee.

Trains arriving at Newbury and Lake Station were met by steamboats waiting to deliver travelers to summer homes and hotels around the lake. Brothers Dan, Frank, and Elias Woodsum built and operated half a dozen steamships on Lake Sunapee from the late 1870s through the early 1900s. Their flagship, the *Armenia White*, was 101 feet long and accommodated 650 passengers. A boiler explosion on the *Lady Woodsum* killed Elias in 1877, and his brothers invented a new safety control used on the rebuilt boat and later additions to their fleet.

Several grand hotels, inns, and boardinghouses welcomed the steamboat passengers. In Newbury, the Sunapee Mountain House, built on the mountain some 500 feet above the lake in 1873, anticipated the completion of the railroad and subsequent influx of travelers. After it burned in 1875, the Johnson family took in boarders. The Forest House, also known as Blodgett Lodge, hosted visitors to the Spiritualist conventions at Blodgett's Landing, and Pine Cliff Inn attracted a colony of prominent Concord families, including Nathaniel and Armenia White, backers of the Woodsum brothers' enterprise.

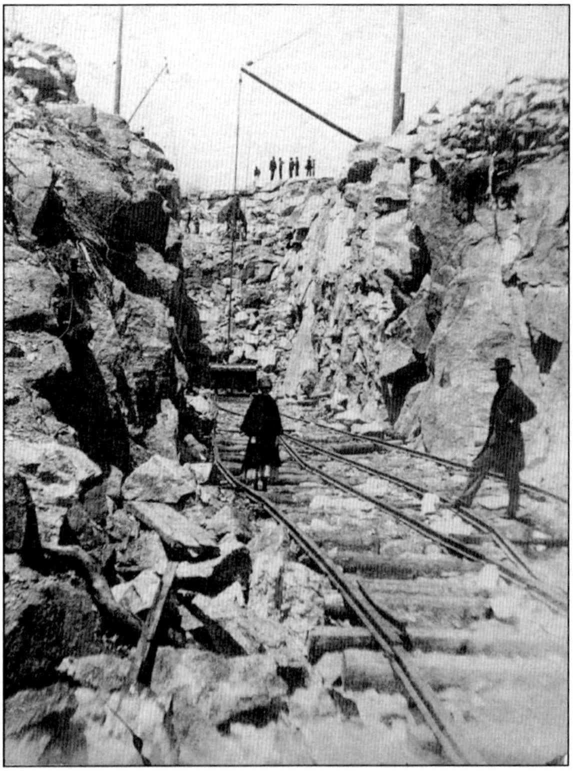

By 1850, the Concord and Claremont Railroad provided service between Concord and Bradford, but the way to Claremont was blocked by Newbury Summit, a granite barrier climbing at a grade of 100 feet per mile. It took 20 years of determination and fund-raising to attack the formidable summit. In August 1870, blasting contractor August Floyd applied the most modern technology available: a steam drill and 10-pound charges of black powder to blast a path through the ledges. Work began on the southern (Bradford) approach. A 2.5-inch bit drove forward at a rate of 9 feet in 50 minutes, shaping holes for the charges of black powder to be set and exploded, blasting away 10,000 cubic feet of granite rock. The debris was used for fill along the line. (Left, Bruce Davison; below, John Hutchinson.)

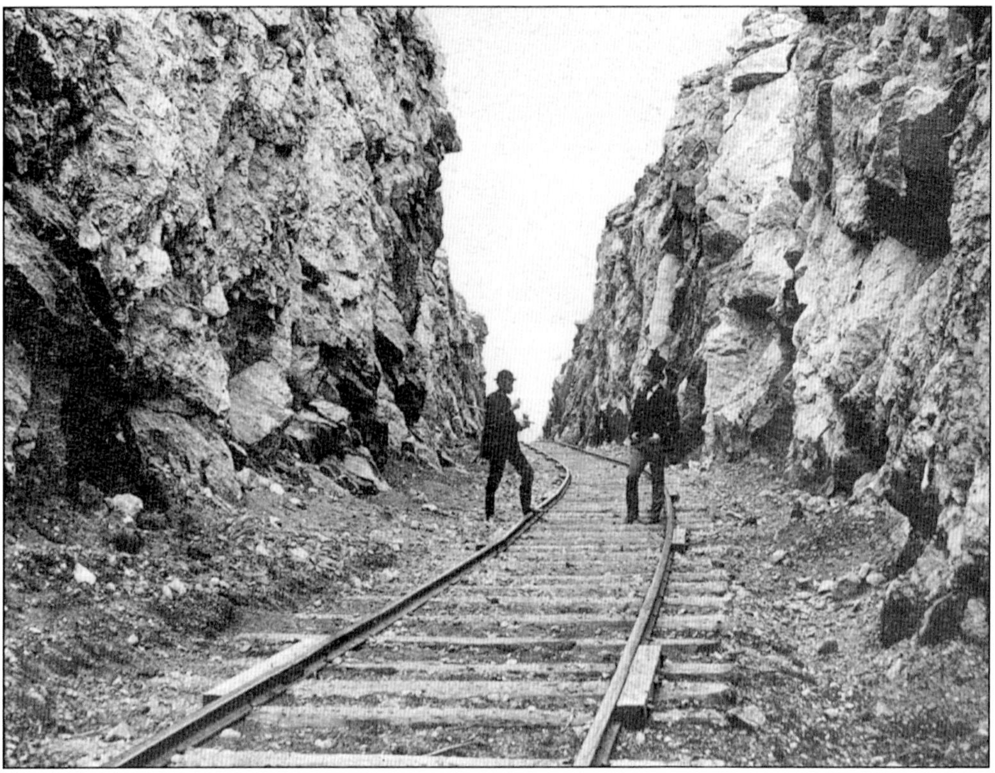

When the track was laid, people came to marvel at the feat that enabled the railroad to continue from Bradford through Newbury and onward to Claremont. The completion of the Newbury Cut in 1871 and the connection to Claremont a year later brought profound changes to Newbury, making it accessible for moving goods and passengers and opening up the area to a future flourishing tourist trade. (John Hutchinson.)

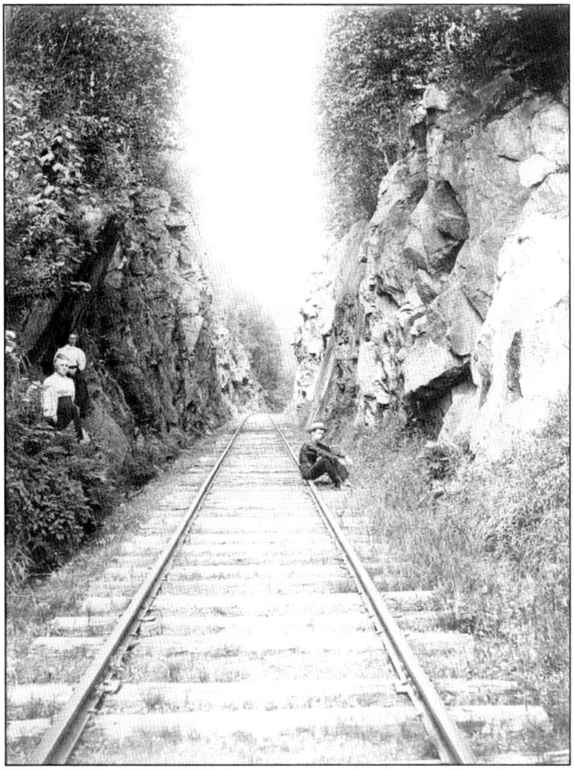

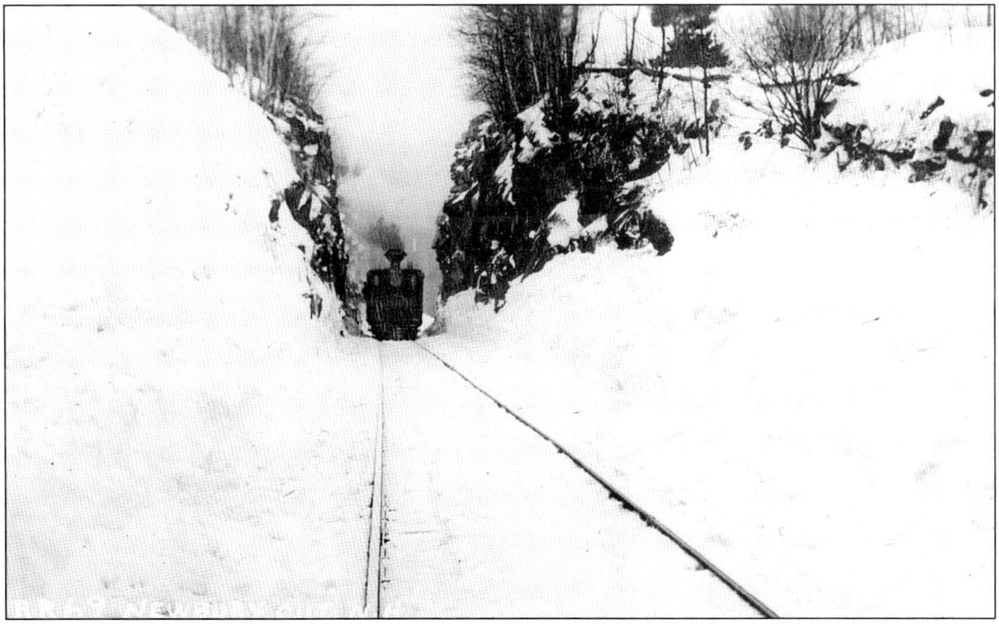

Winter snowstorms often filled the Newbury Cut with drifting snow. Despite the efforts of wooden snowplows on the lead locomotive and crews armed with shovels, snowstorms could delay trains and sometimes stop them altogether. The trip from Bradford became perilous, sometimes requiring the train to stop at the cut, keeping the engines going until the storm abated and the train could continue or, in some cases, back down the track to Bradford. (William Weiler.)

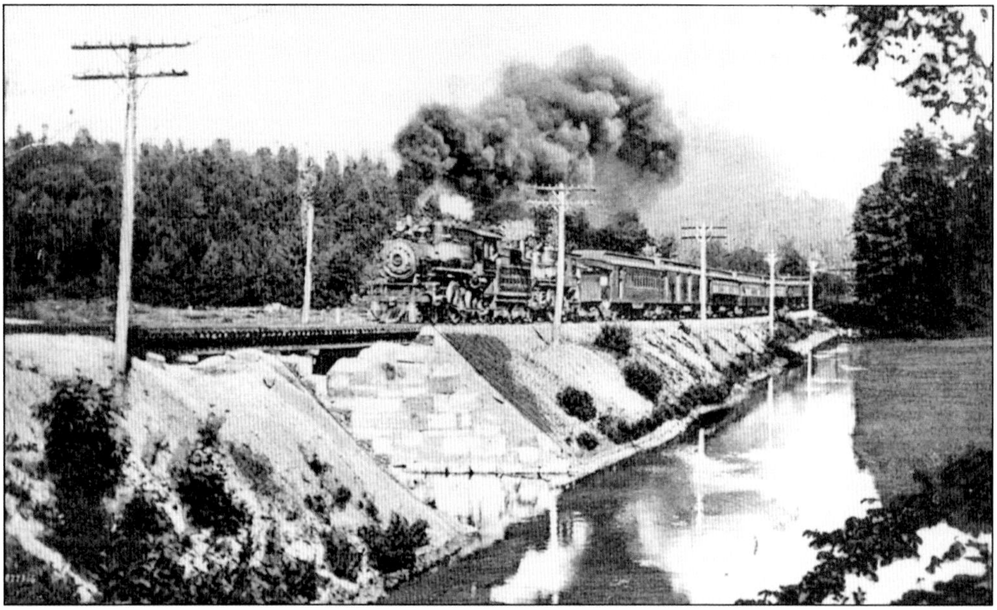

Leaving Bradford, the train traveled across Lake Todd on a causeway, billowing smoke and disturbing the quiet waters. At the end of the railroad era, the track was removed and the causeway became the foundation of what is now Route 103. (William Weiler.)

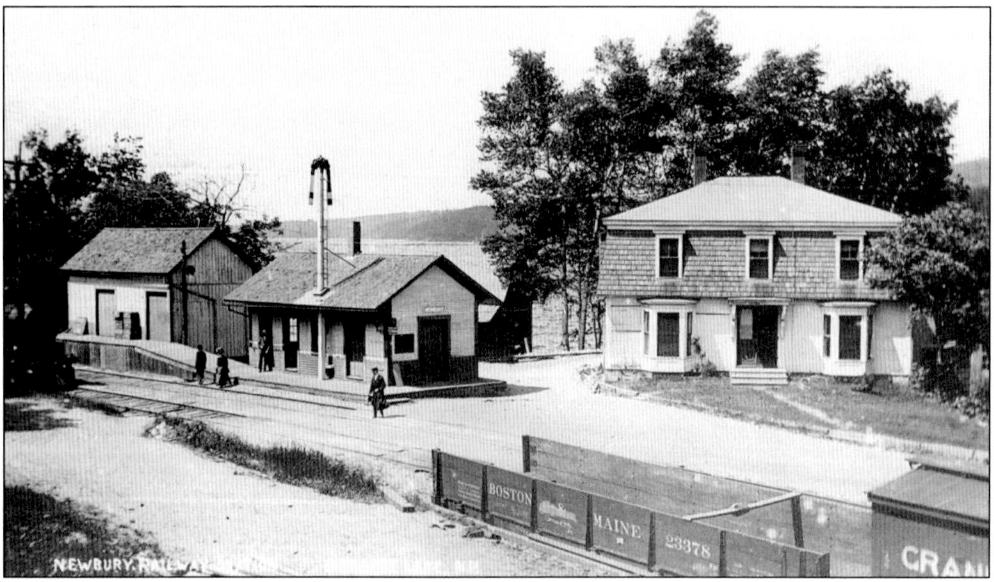

The train station in Newbury was located at the southern tip of Lake Sunapee. The freight building (left) is no longer standing, but the station has been restored and is now owned by the town. The building on the right is the Durgin House, a guesthouse conveniently sited for travelers. The town gazebo now stands on that location. (Davis Cabins.)

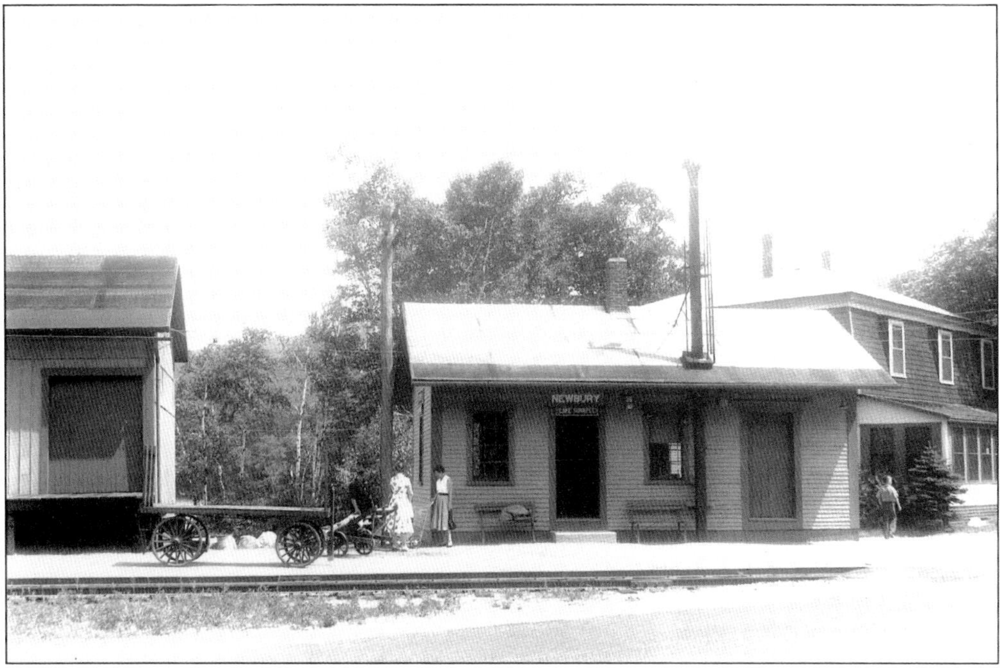

This is another view of the Newbury station with freight and baggage carriers as well as passengers waiting for the arrival of a train. This depot handled 600 pieces of baggage a day during the summer season. (William Weiler.)

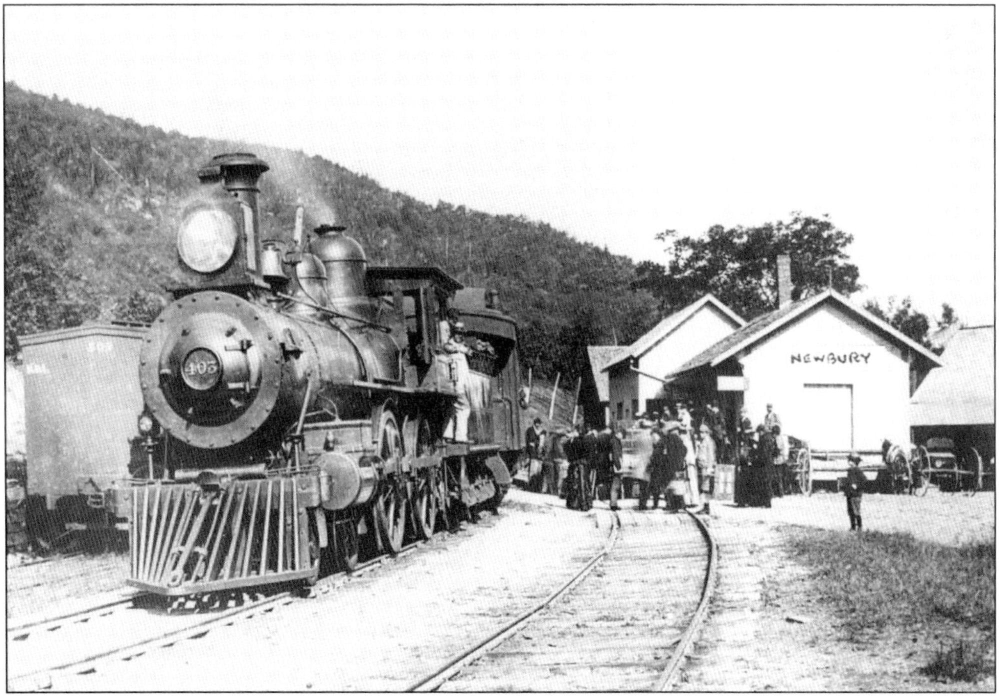

This train is leaving the Newbury station heading for Bradford and points south. Ten trains a day ran through Newbury between Claremont and Concord with local stops along the route. (Nancy Marashio.)

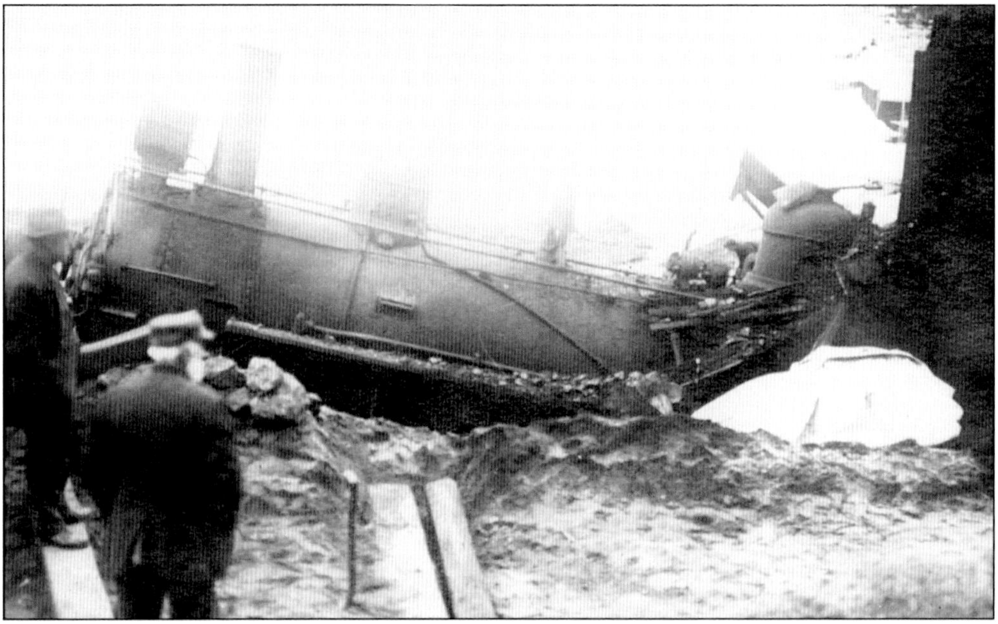

The worst recorded accident on the Claremont branch line occurred on April 12, 1922. Freight train No. 1979 piled into a gully caused by heavy rain and a washout between the Lake Sunapee and Edgemont stations. The tender dropped into a 50-foot-wide cavity, followed by five heavily loaded cars that pushed the tender into the cab. Three men in the cab were killed: George Atwood, engineer, found sitting at his post with his hand on the throttle; fireman Ralph Ching, his body crushed; and brakeman Edward Kelley, whose body was recovered when the wrecking crew lifted the tender and found him. The freight consisted of coal, box boards, and bales of wool, some of which can be seen in the pictured debris. (Above, Brent Michaels; below, John Hutchinson.)

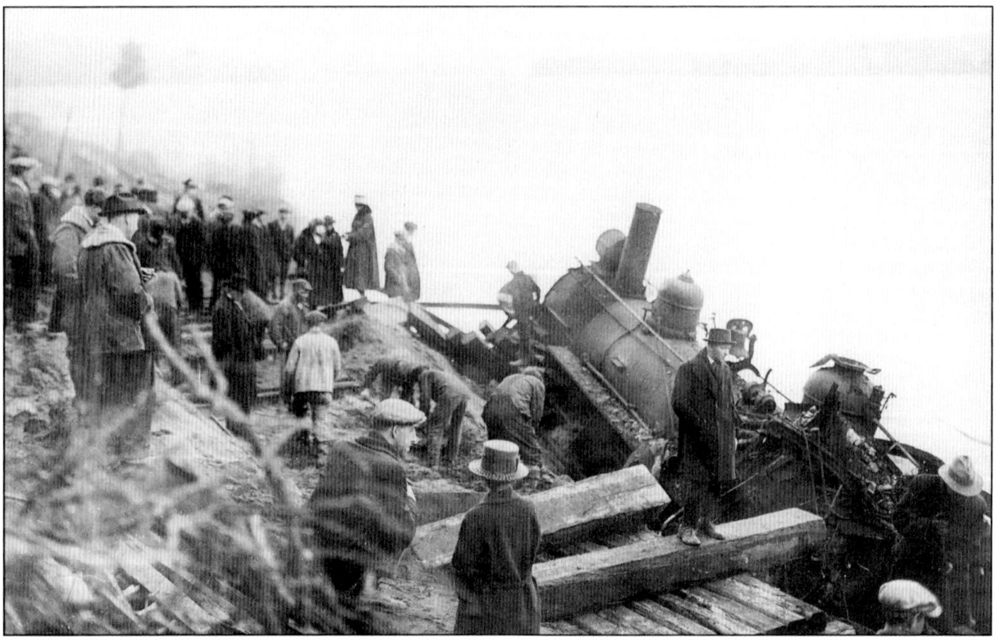

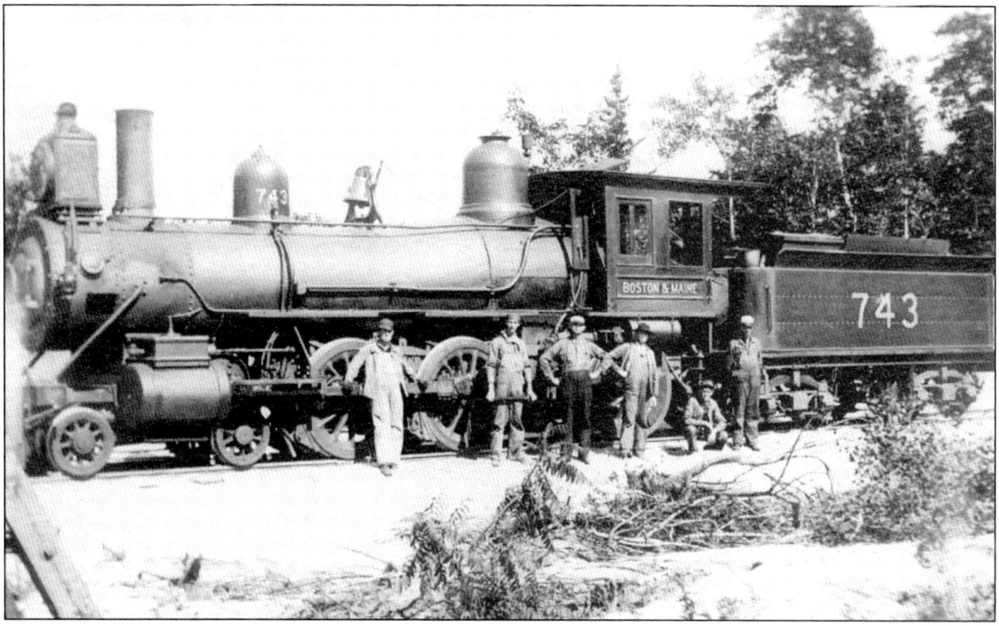

The crew of the Boston and Maine Railroad takes time out for a group photograph. The Boston and Maine bought out the Concord and Claremont Railroad in 1890 and suffered financial losses until World War II, when there was a resurgence of service. After the war, the railroad again declined, and by 1952, the branch line was losing $100,000 annually. Despite private efforts, the line was closed in the mid-1950s. (Brent Michaels.)

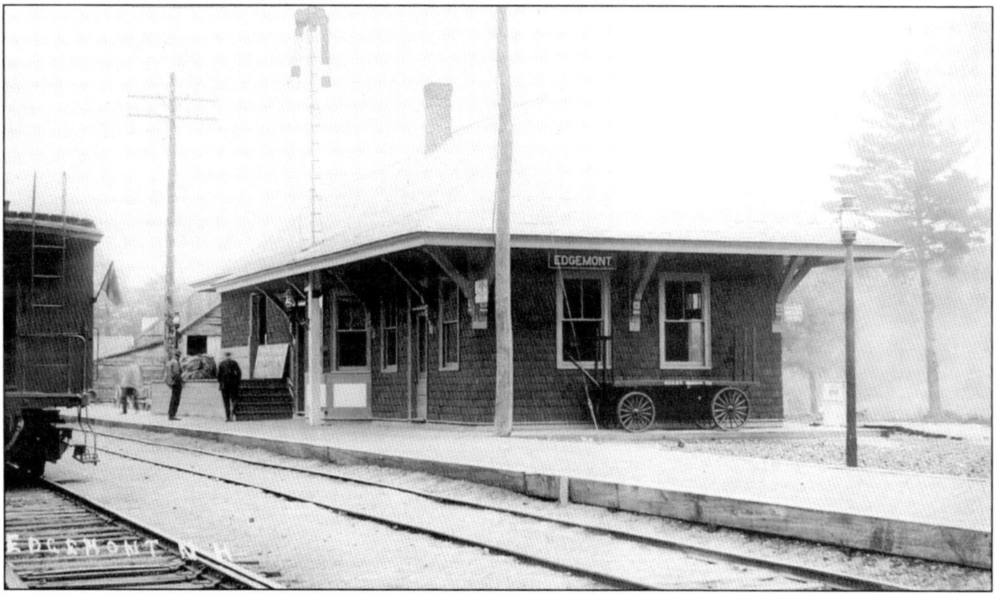

The Edgemont station at the base of Mount Sunapee served the Bay Point area. Visitors arriving by rail at this quiet spot, once known as Chandlersville, gave Edgemont new life and vitality. There was a 50-foot right-of-way on either side of the track, which ran between the lake and the shorefront, making it necessary for property owners to cross the tracks to get to the water. (Brent Michaels.)

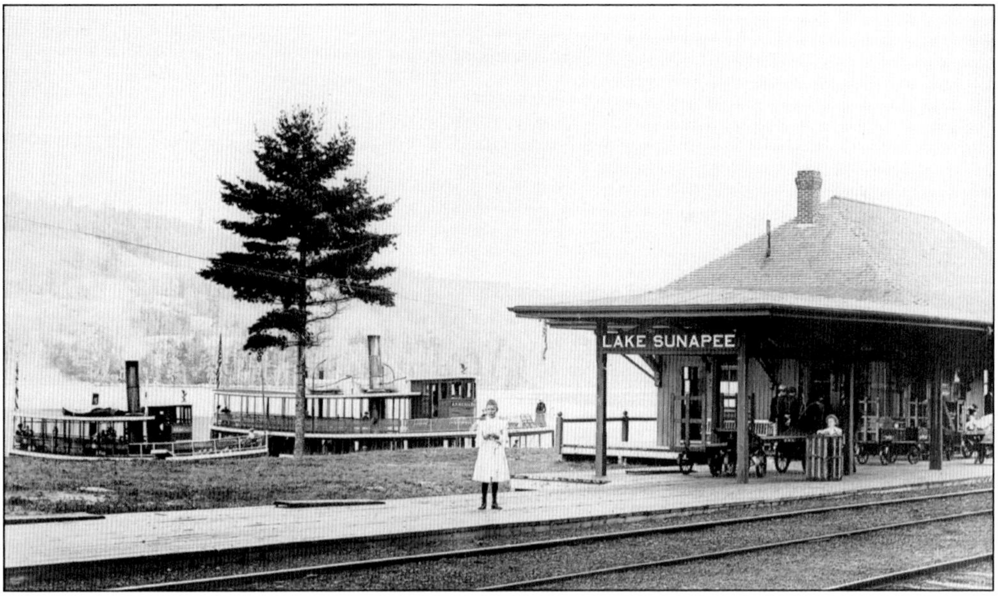

The Lake Sunapee station was a major railroad stop for travelers headed to their summer homes or the grand hotels around the lake. This was the location of the landing that was home port for the Woodsum fleet of steamboats that would ferry them to their final destinations. The train could be delayed as long as half an hour while scores of trunks and baggage for passengers were unloaded. Friends and family waiting to meet passengers thronged the station, and those who were departing waited patiently to start home at the end of their holiday. (Above, John Hutchinson; below, Town of Newbury.)

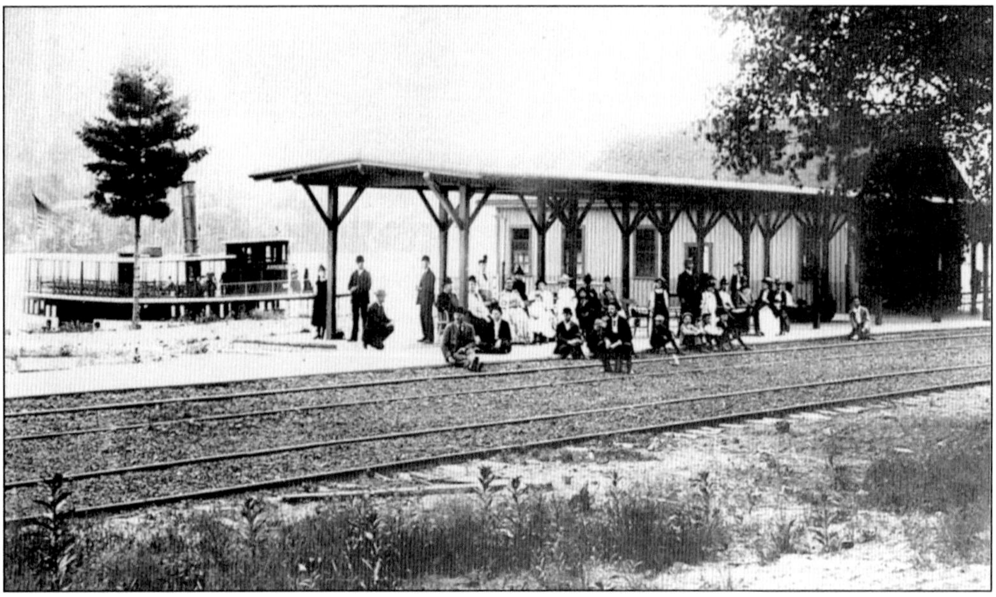

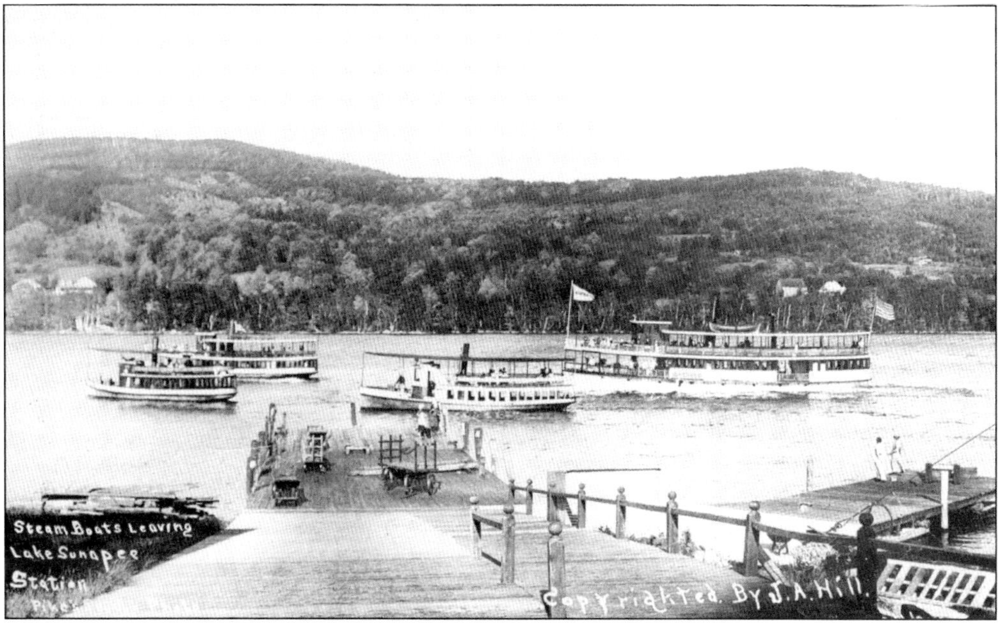

Lake Station depot and steamboat landing were teeming with activity throughout the summer. Many families arrived for the season accompanied by servants, trunks, children, and pets. While some were met by private launch and transported to their summer homes, most boarded one of the great steamboats that plied the lake between the grand hotels and the railroad stations. The steamers began their rounds at 6:00 a.m. and completed their trip around the lake in about three hours, making regular stops at a dozen or so lakeside landings. Individual residents who needed transportation signaled for service with a white marker hoisted on a dockside pole. (Above, John Hutchinson; below, Town of Newbury.)

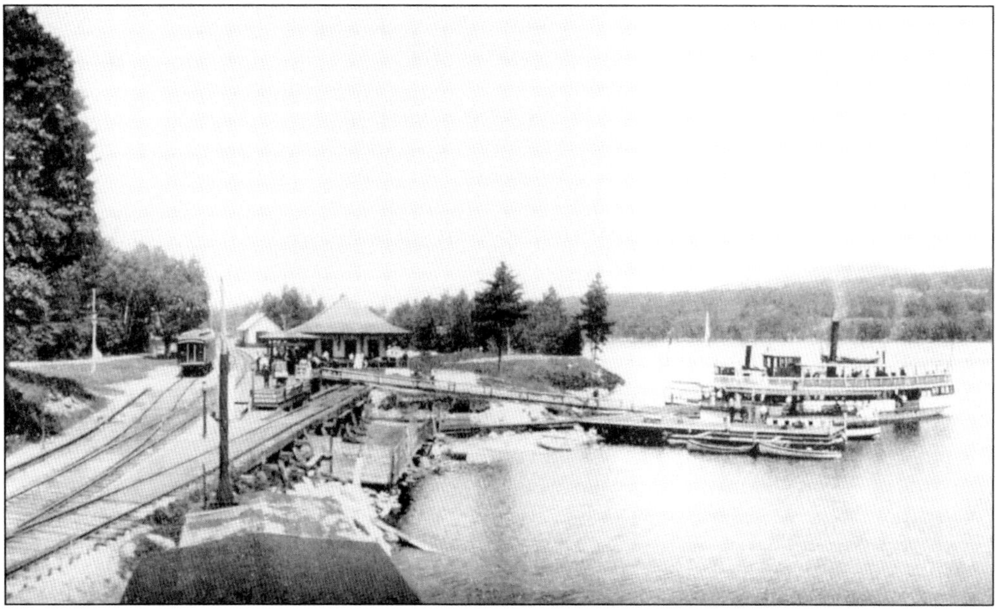

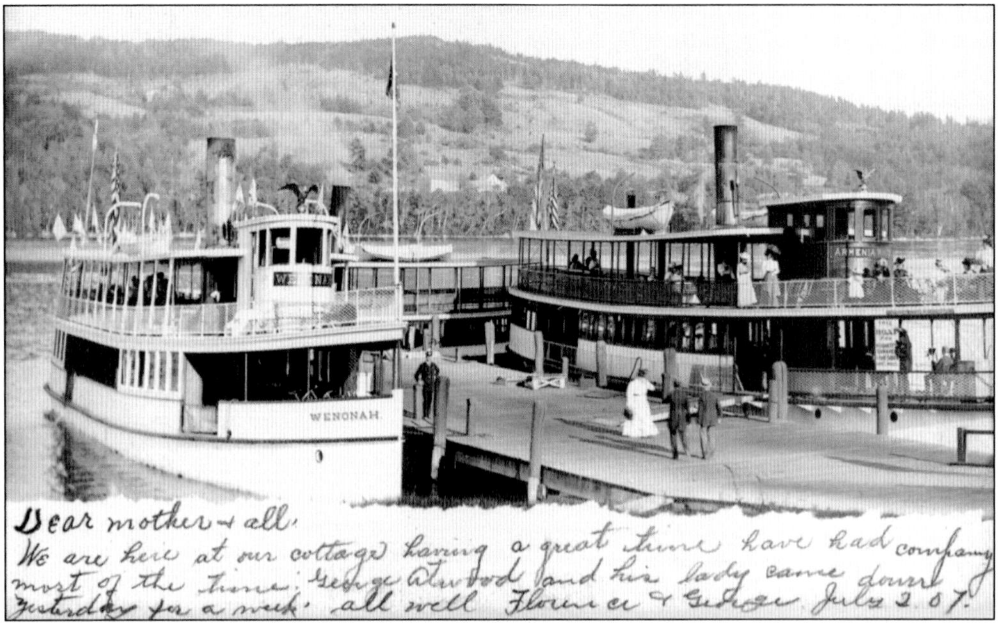

Passengers appear eager to board the *Armenia White* (right) as the *Wenonah* stands by. Notice the extent to which the hillside across the lake has been cleared for farmland. (John Hutchinson.)

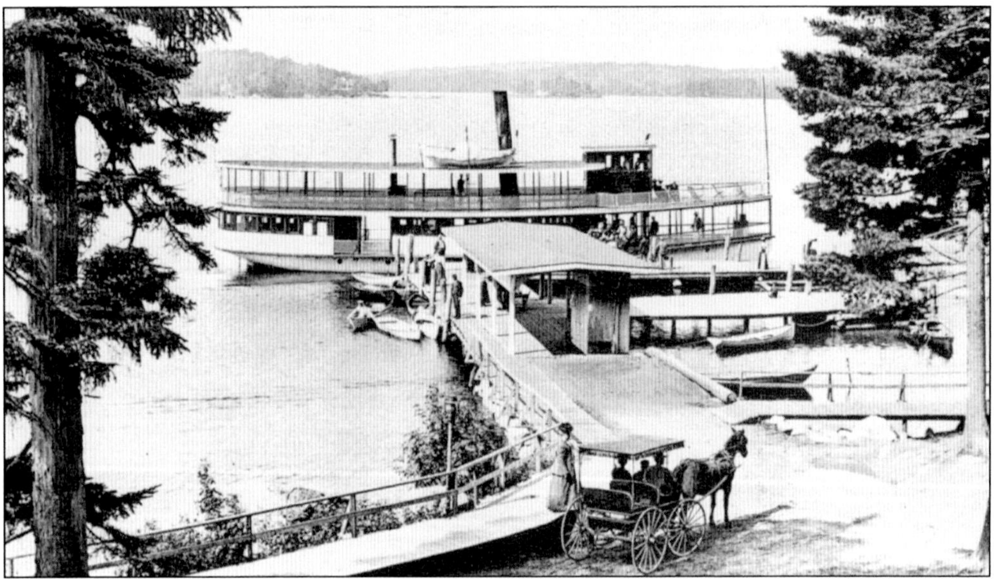

Small craft pull up along the dock at Blodgett's Landing as the *Armenia White* makes an arrival. The horse and buggy in the foreground is waiting to greet a summer visitor. (Town of Newbury.)

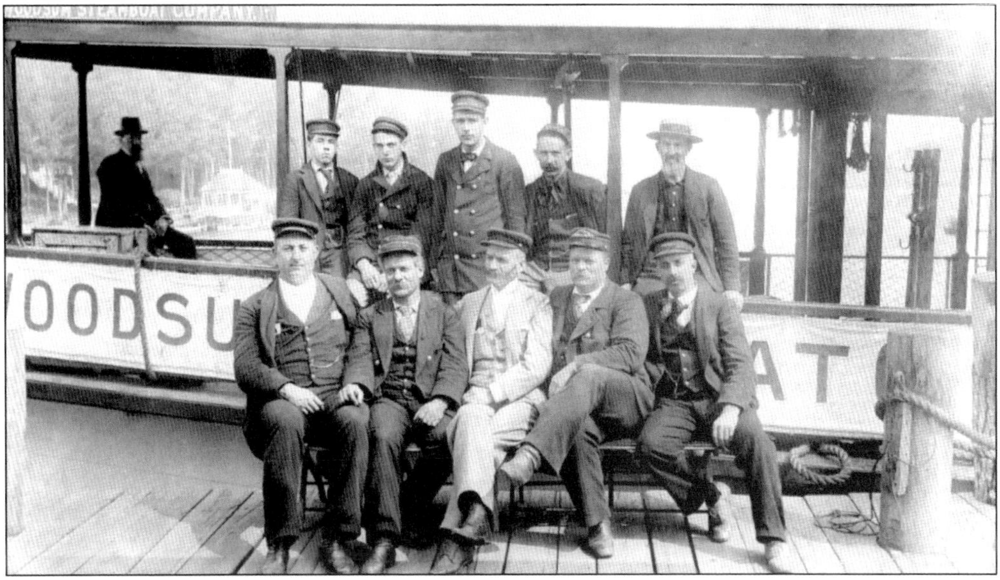

Seen here is the Woodsum crew, only a few of whom are identified. From left to right are (first row) Perley Fitch, Dan Woodsum, unidentified, Frank Woodsum, and unidentified. The names of the men in the back row are unknown. In addition to the captain, crews could include an engineer, fireman, purser, ticket agent, baggage master, seaman, and candy and paper boy. (John Hutchinson.)

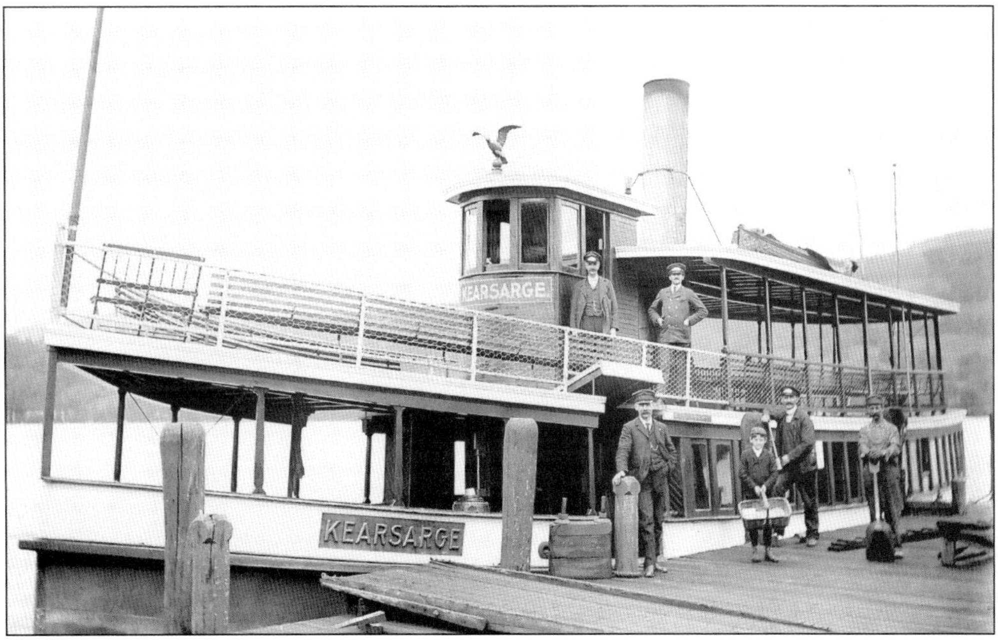

The *Kearsarge* was the third steamboat built by the Woodsum brothers and the last to operate on Lake Sunapee. Launched in 1897, it carried 250 passengers. After plying the waters of the lake for nearly 40 years, it was sold to the Ben Mere Inn and then to Davis Cabins. It was scrapped in 1939. The pilothouse was salvaged and is now restored and on display at the Sunapee Historical Society. (Newbury Historical Society.)

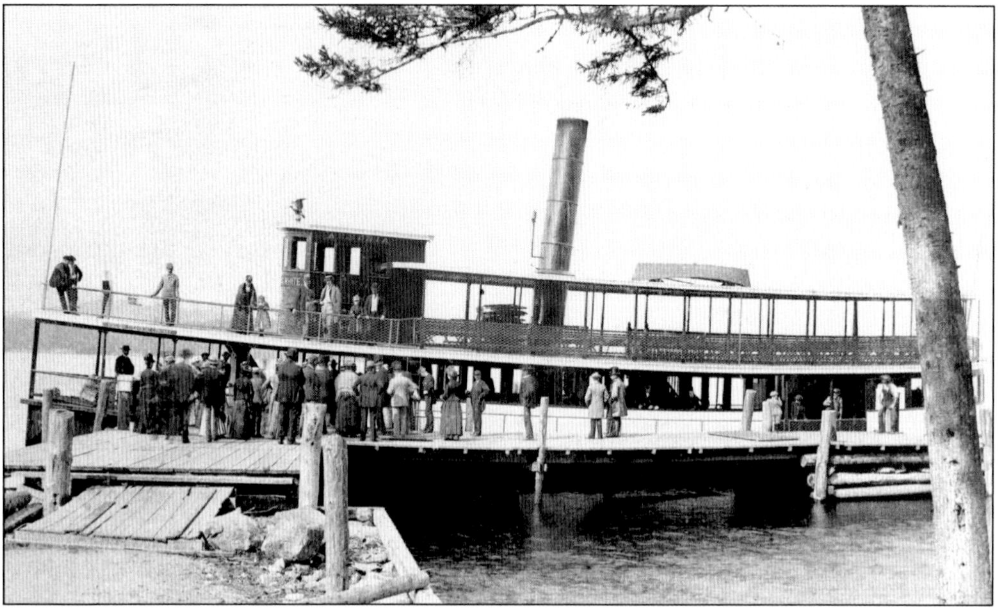

The *Armenia White* was the Woodsum brothers' flagship. Built in 1887 at a cost of $17,000, it was 101 feet long and could accommodate 600 passengers and a seven-man crew. It was named after a prominent stockholder from Concord who summered at Pine Cliff. The steamer retired at Georges Mills in 1917 and was sold for scrap in 1939 for $100. (Joe and Beverly Digilio.)

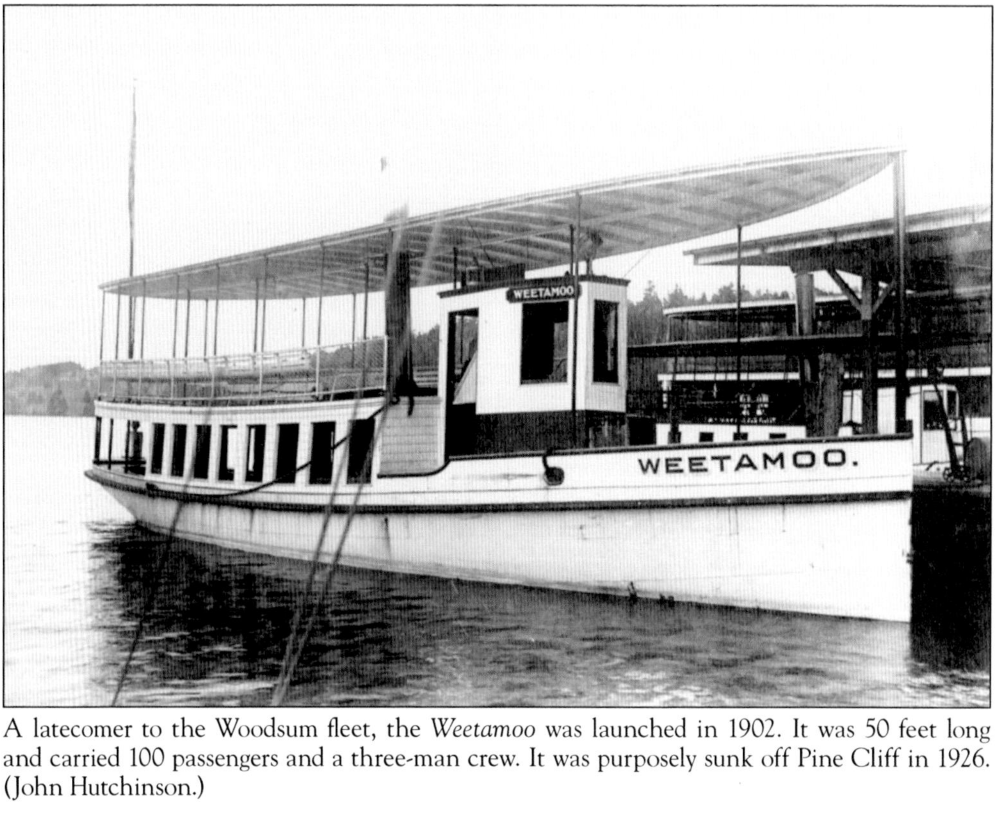

A latecomer to the Woodsum fleet, the *Weetamoo* was launched in 1902. It was 50 feet long and carried 100 passengers and a three-man crew. It was purposely sunk off Pine Cliff in 1926. (John Hutchinson.)

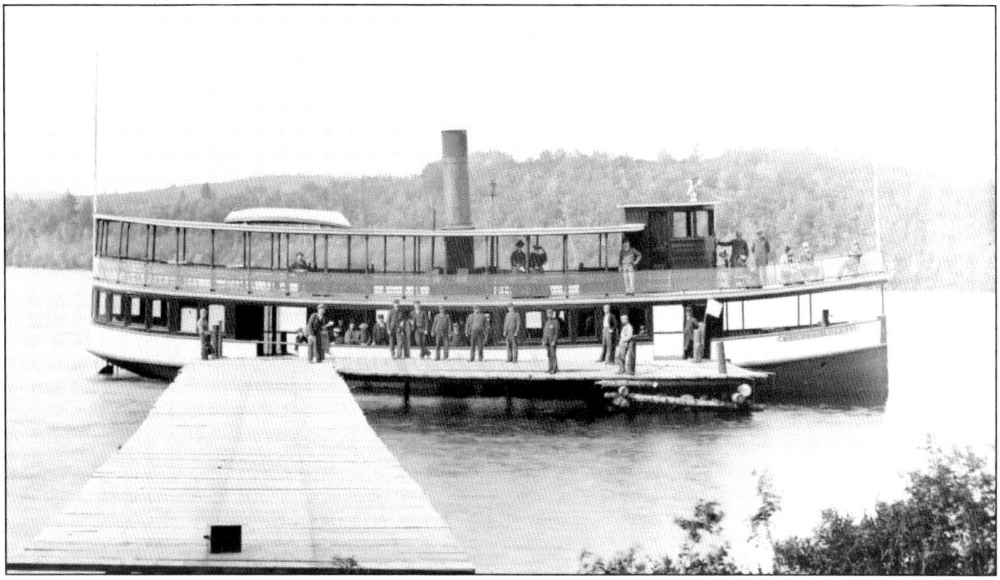

The *Edmund Burke* was the only steamer on Lake Sunapee in competition with the Woodsum brothers' operation. It was built in 1885 by a group of businessmen from Newport. It was 87 feet long with a double deck and carried 500 passengers. In 1887, the *Edmund Burke* was enlarged to compete with the *Armenia White* by increasing capacity to 650 passengers. On one August day that year, it carried more than 1,500 travelers around the lake. It was later sold to George Blodgett, who renamed it *Wenonah*. The *Wenonah* caught fire at Blodgett's Landing on July 4, 1908, burned to the waterline, and sank. (Above, Newbury Historical Society; below, Ron Garceau.)

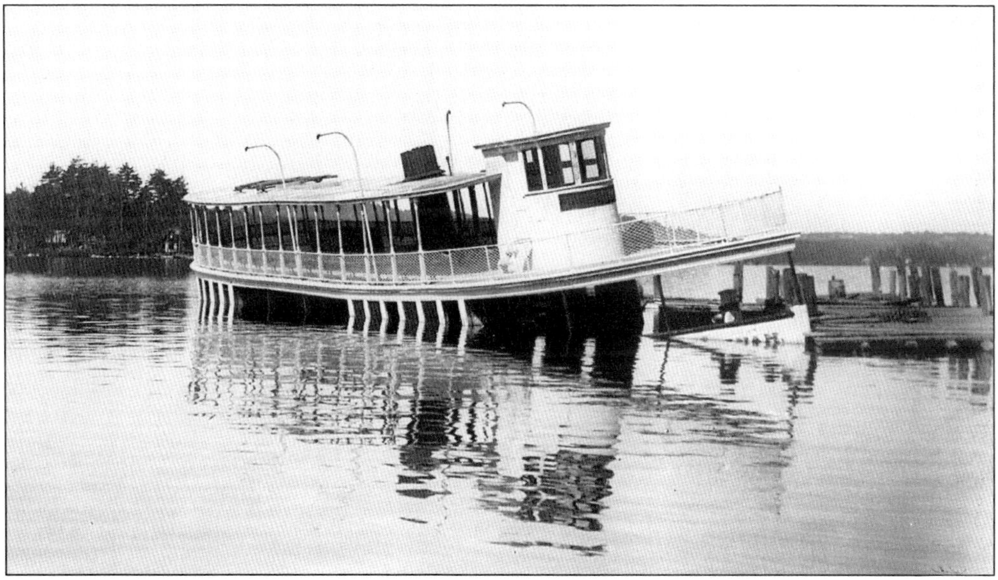

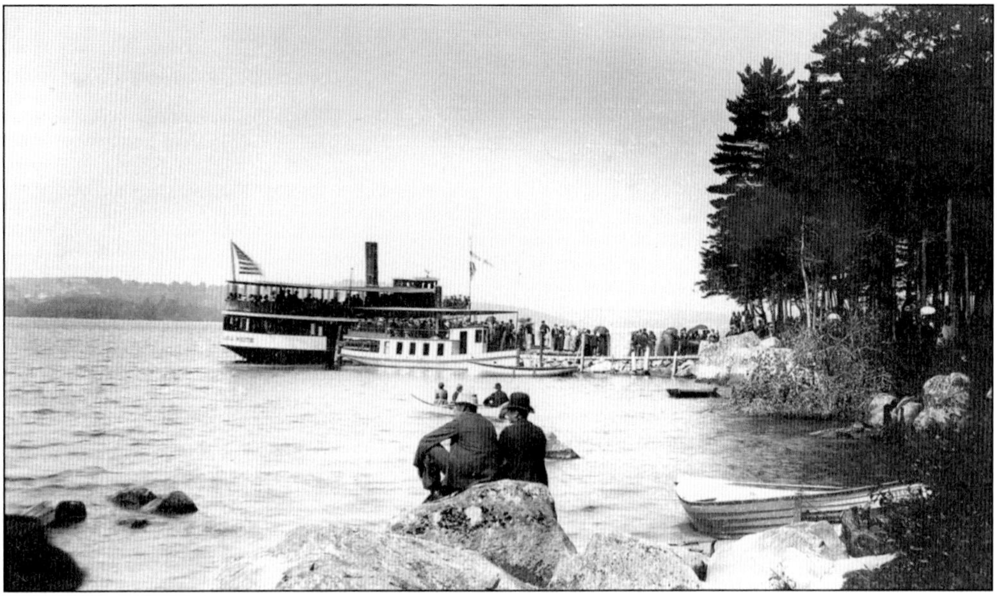

Onlookers watch the *Armenia White* picking up passengers at the Great Island dock. Summer residents on the island were dependent on the steamboats and other watercraft for transport to points in Newbury, where they could replenish necessities for their summer sojourns. (John Hutchinson.)

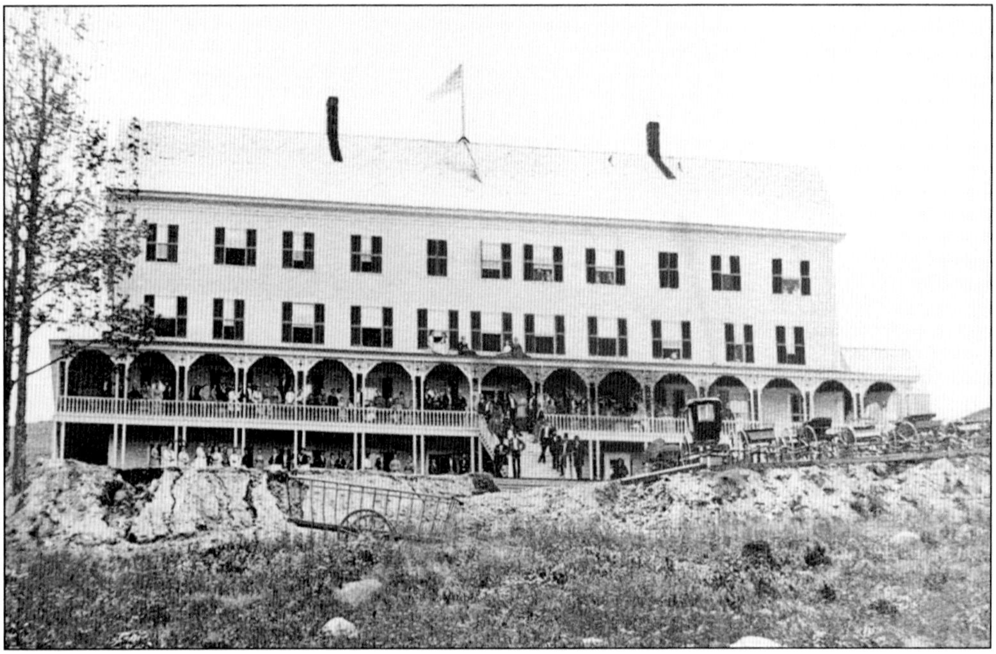

Newbury's only grand hotel, the Sunapee Mountain House, was built by Nathan Johnson and David Coggswell. Johnson first built a large farmhouse, barn, and sawmill on Mount Sunapee beginning in 1864 and added the hotel in 1873. The site offered majestic views and healthy mountain air. After two successful seasons, the hotel burned in 1875. The Johnson family continued to farm the land and take in boarders for another 30 years, leaving the mountain in 1906. (John Hutchinson.)

Five

Area Attractions

Carved by glaciers and largely spring fed, Lake Sunapee offers more than six square miles of exceptionally pure water. It is distinguished by eight islands, many inlets, and three lighthouses. In the 1920s, the Lake Sunapee Fish and Game Club built hatcheries and released salmon, lake trout, and brook trout into the lake. These joined the indigenous species to provide outstanding fishing. With the arrival of summer visitors, pleasure boats joined fishermen on the lake, and water sports of all kinds grew in popularity. The watershed teems with wildlife, including moose, deer, bears, foxes, beavers, and fishers. The lake and watershed have been monitored since 1898 by the Lake Sunapee Protective Association.

Looming above the lake is Mount Sunapee, once attracting local families for skiing and hiking and now a premier ski resort. It was saved from excessive lumbering operations at the beginning of the 20th century. In 1909, local residents and the Society for the Protection of New Hampshire Forests acquired 656 acres, including the summit, Lake Solitude, and the north face of the mountain. By 1934, the society had acquired 1,185 acres, which were turned over to the state in 1948. That December, Mount Sunapee opened the North Peak area with a single chairlift, three trails, and two rope tows. In the 1960s, more equipment was added and the base and summit lodges were built. In 1966, the North Peak double chair was converted into a gondola for rides to the summit. Newbury children enjoyed the mountain's ski school when skiing became part of the school curriculum during the mid-1900s.

Close by is the Fells, summer home of statesman John Hay, secretary of state under Pres. William McKinley and Pres. Theodore Roosevelt. Between 1883 and 1900, Hay purchased 1,000 acres of lakeshore farmland for a retreat for his family and friends. Hay died at the Fells in 1905. His son, Clarence, and Clarence's wife, Alice, transformed the grounds from rocky pastures into a series of formal lawns and gardens. In 1960, Clarence donated 675 acres to the Society for the Protection of New Hampshire Forests. Sixty-three acres, including the house and gardens, now comprise the Fells and are open to the public for hiking, tours, educational programs, and special events.

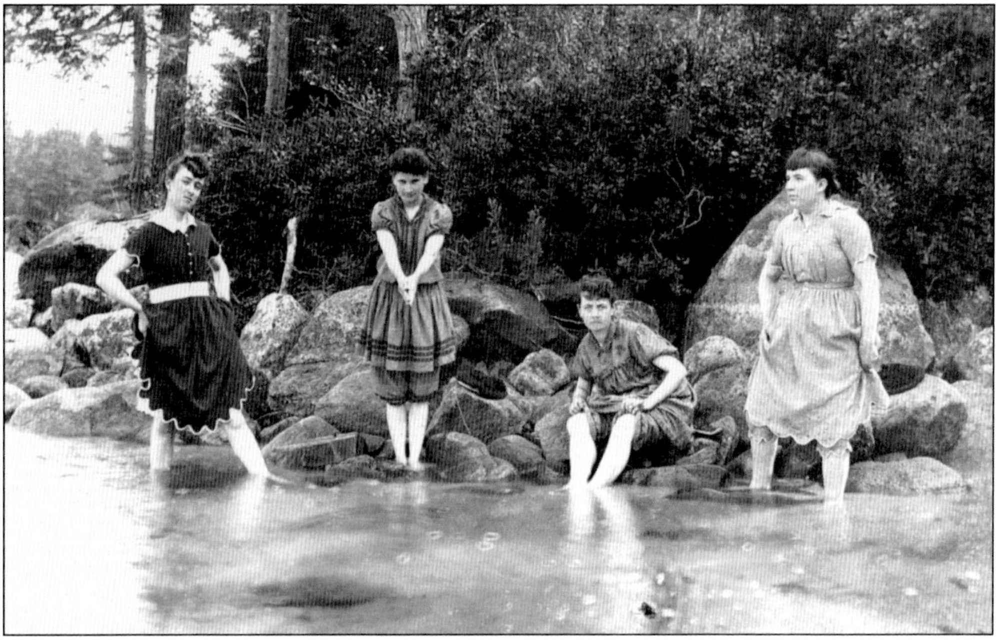

Lake Sunapee's crystal clear water and numerous beaches have drawn people to its shores for centuries. These young ladies look eager to take a plunge, although their approach is cautious. Rock formations provide great places to explore and cool off on a hot summer day. (Newbury Historical Society.)

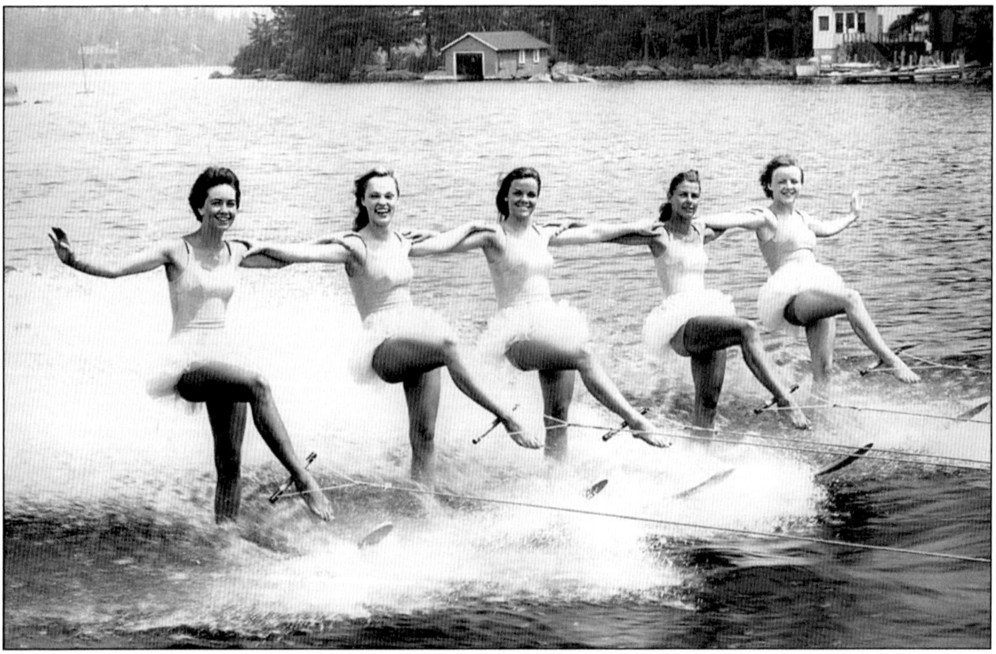

Water-skiing on Lake Sunapee was hugely popular in the 1950s. Spectators enjoyed watching the skilled maneuvers of the skiers during public performances. Seen here, from left to right, Harriet Mahoney, Marianne Benoit, Katheryn Holmes, Dottie Morse, and Janet Wiggins show off impeccable form. (Katheryn Holmes.)

A water-skier traverses the wake as she passes the Mount Sunapee Sporting Center at Edgemont. This store rented supplies for a variety of water sports and offered motorboat rides around the lake. (Nancy Marashio.)

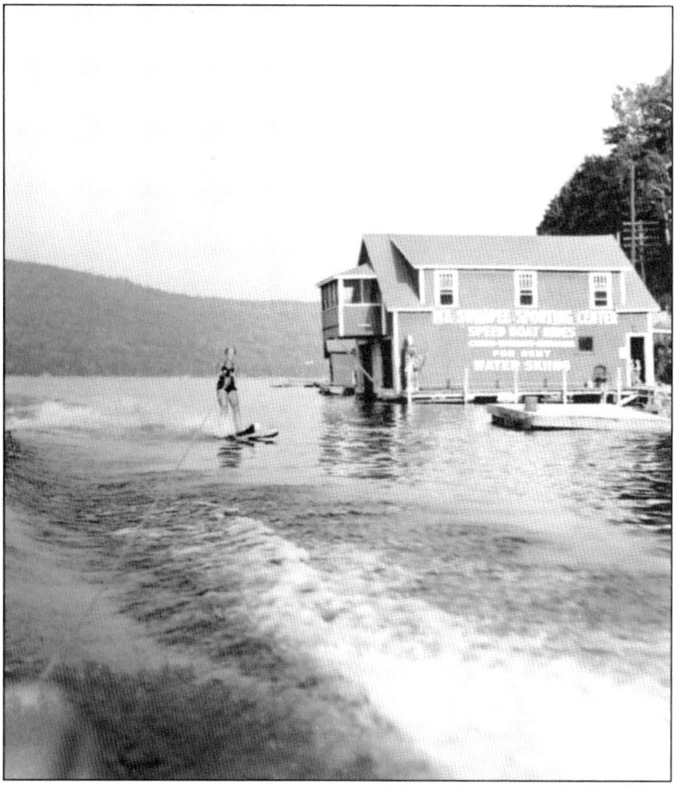

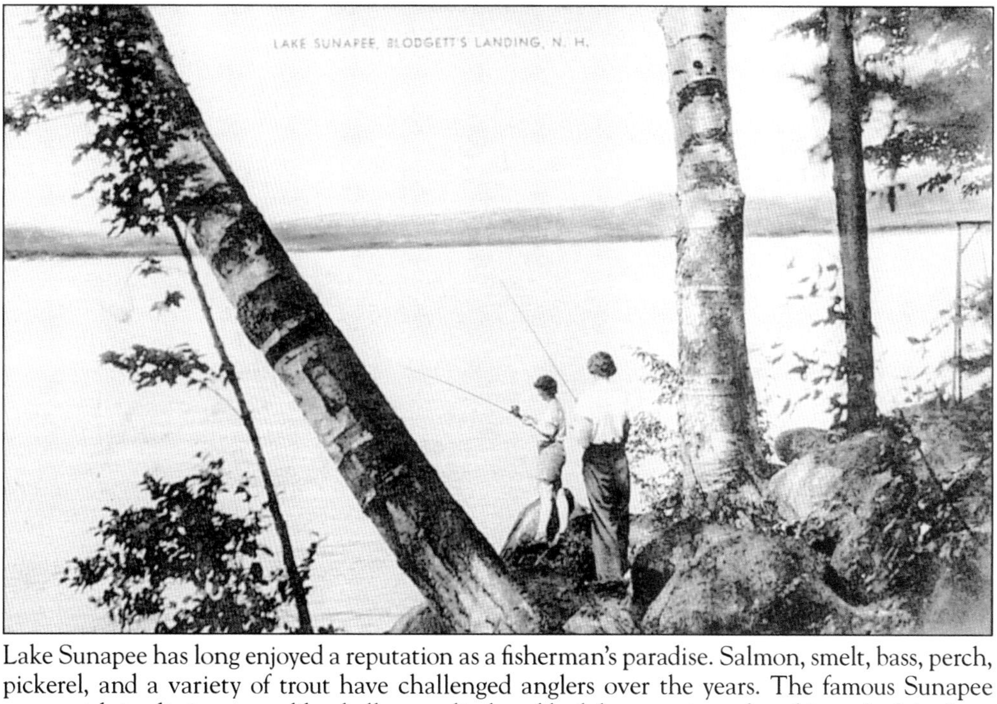

Lake Sunapee has long enjoyed a reputation as a fisherman's paradise. Salmon, smelt, bass, perch, pickerel, and a variety of trout have challenged anglers over the years. The famous Sunapee trout, with its distinctive golden belly, was displaced by lake trout introduced into the lake from hatcheries and has not been seen in these waters since the mid-1950s. (William Weiler.).

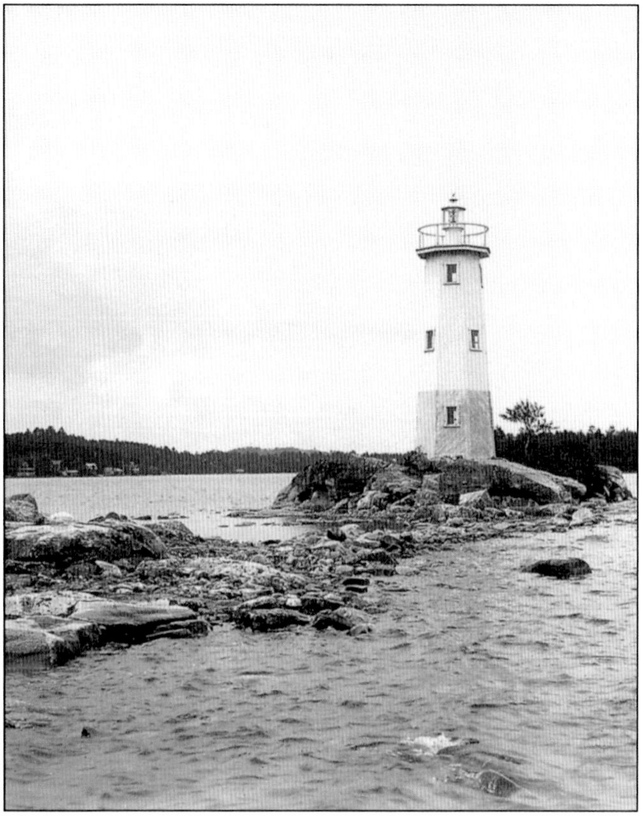

Loon Island Lighthouse, one of three on Lake Sunapee, was built in 1893 by the Woodsum brothers after the *Edmund Burke* struck an underwater ledge at the site. Some years later, while being repaired by local firemen, the lighthouse caught on fire. They used buckets of lake water to put out the blaze. The tower was struck by lightning in 1960 and burned to the ground. It was rebuilt with private funding. Today the lighthouse is owned by the state and maintained by the Lake Sunapee Protective Association. (Ron Garceau.)

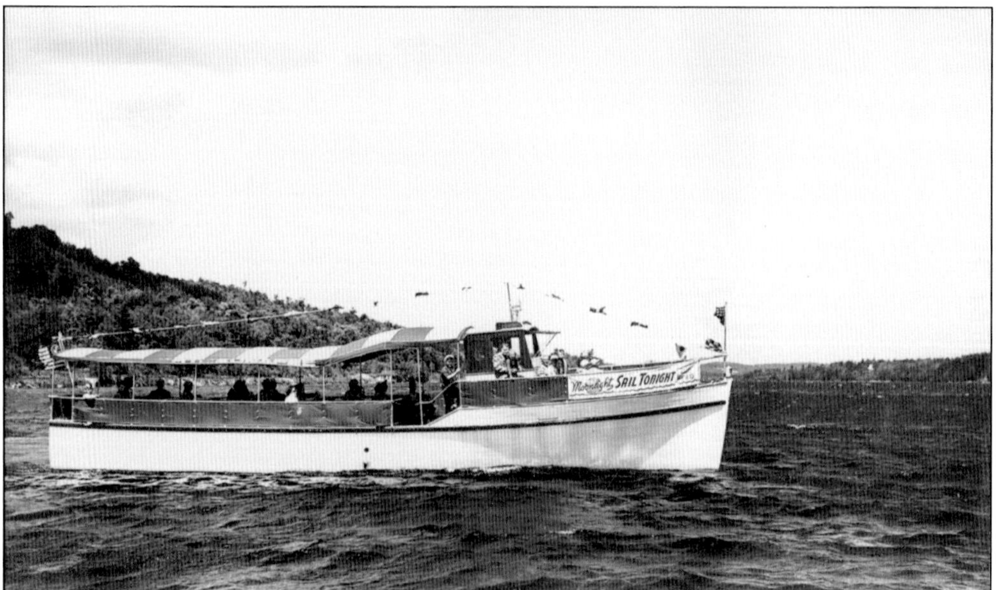

MV *Mt. Sunapee* made its maiden voyage in 1950, carrying area visitors around the lake on a narrated tour. This boat was originally called the *Susie Q* and came to Lake Sunapee from a stint as a rumrunner in Damariscotta, Maine. The boat was replaced by a steel-hulled boat in 1965 and now operates as the MV *Mt. Sunapee II.* (William Weiler.)

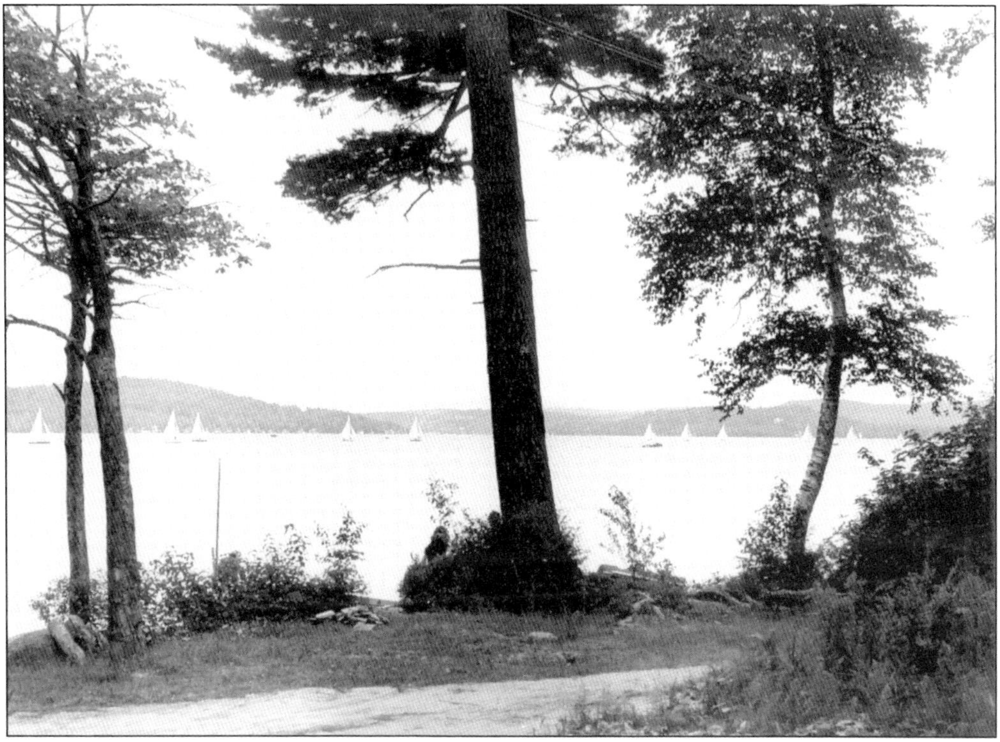

Lake Sunapee is well suited for a variety of boating, and one of the most popular over the years has been sailing. There is almost always an ample breeze to fill the sails, and regular races for various classes of sailboats have been held for decades. Here a regatta is viewed from Idlehurst, adjacent to Blodgett's Landing. (Sally Kassman.)

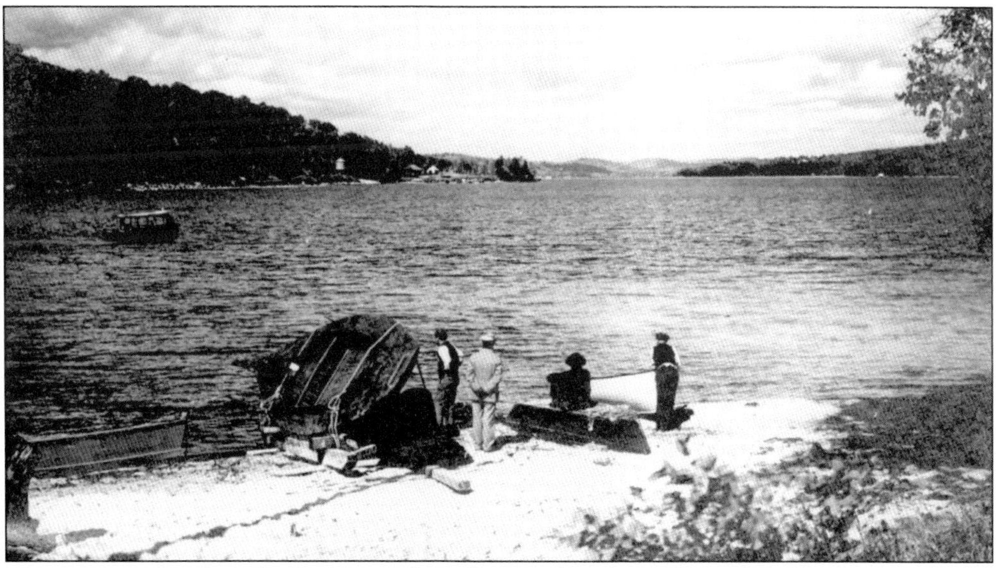

These men at Newbury harbor's waterfront have gathered to admire the sweeping view north and the surrounding range of hills. A large sailboat is secured at the rough landing, predating the building of the esplanade, and a small launch steams toward the eastern shore. The water tower at Lake Station stands out among the trees in the distance. (William Weiler.)

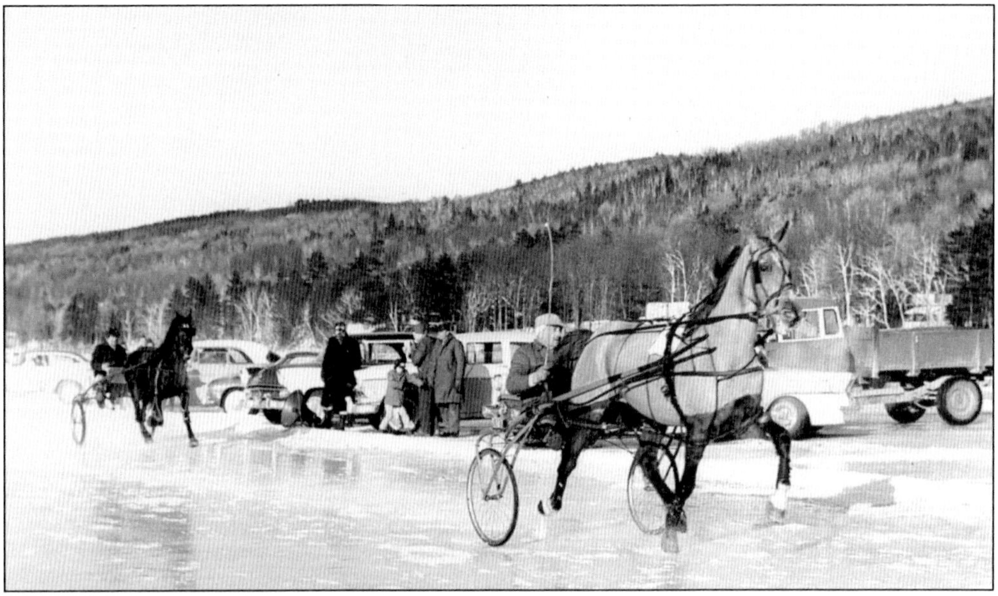

Winter activities abound on Lake Sunapee, although ice racing with horses has passed into history. In the 1960s, Newbury's Harbor Club sponsored these races, which featured outstanding sulky trotters from the summer fair circuit that loved to run in any weather. For ice racing, they were shod with specially tooled metal spikes called corks to help them keep their footing. Leon Bushway and his trotter, Mighty Ben, receive a warm welcome from the crowds at these cold windswept events. (William Weiler.)

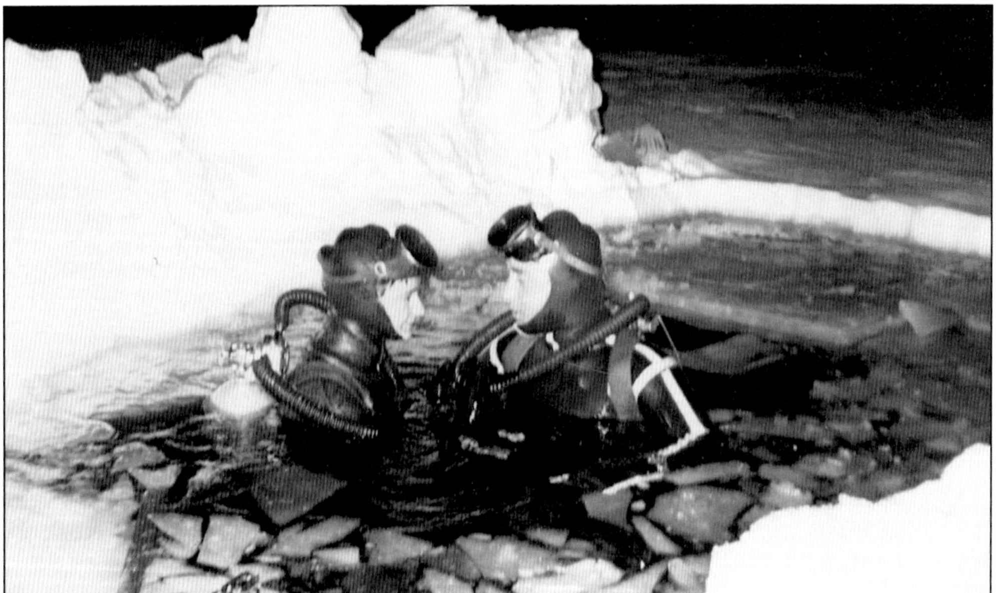

Winter sports on the lake offer something for everyone—although this practice may not be as popular as ice-fishing and skating. Professional divers Wayne and Judy LaPorte make a tradition of bringing the New Year in under the ice. Here in the late 1950s, they take the plunge off Newbury's dock. Over the years, friends and family have joined them in the ritual, numbering as many as 16 divers for the occasion. (Wayne and Judy LaPorte.)

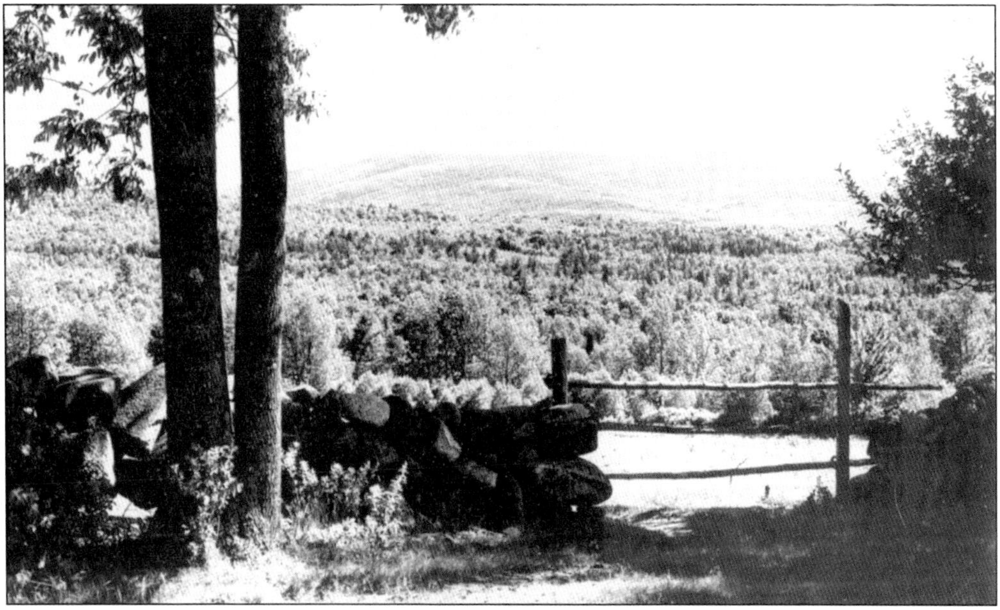

Outstanding views of the lake and mountain from Newbury's hillsides have drawn visitors to the area since Newbury's earliest days. Many have returned to establish homes where they can enjoy the beautiful vistas throughout the changing seasons. Here Mount Sunapee is seen from a pasture on Baker Hill, formerly Digilio property and now home to a golf course. (Sally Kassman.)

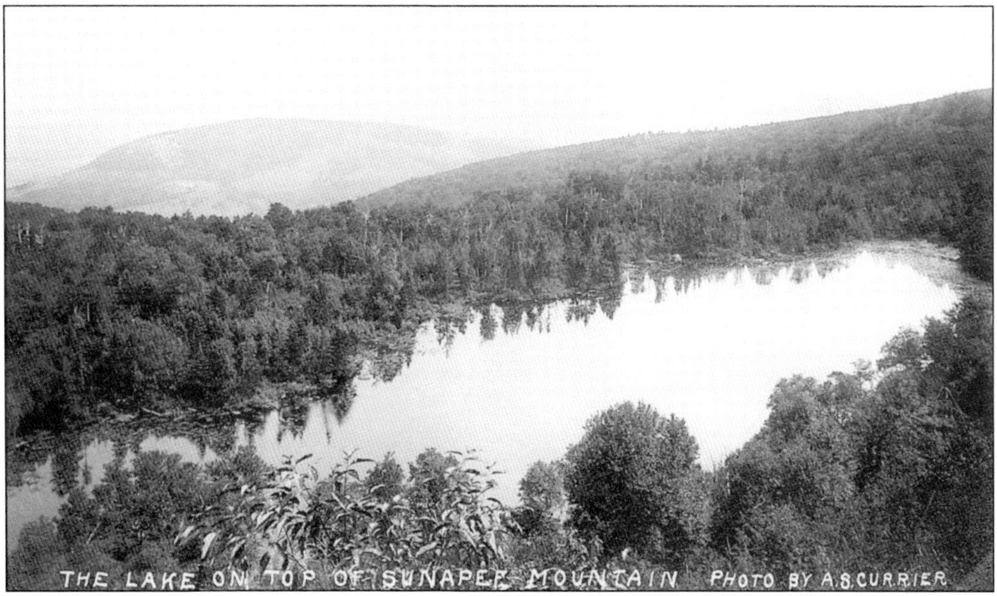

Mount Sunapee hikers find a treat when they discover Lake Solitude with its sweeping views and ledge-formed caves. Herbert Welsh, an early proponent of preserving the forested mountain, spent many happy hours here and built a log shelter and fireplace for overnight camping. The efforts of summer residents and the Society for the Protection of New Hampshire Forests to curb logging resulted in the society's purchase of 1,185 acres on the mountain by 1934. (Ron Garceau.)

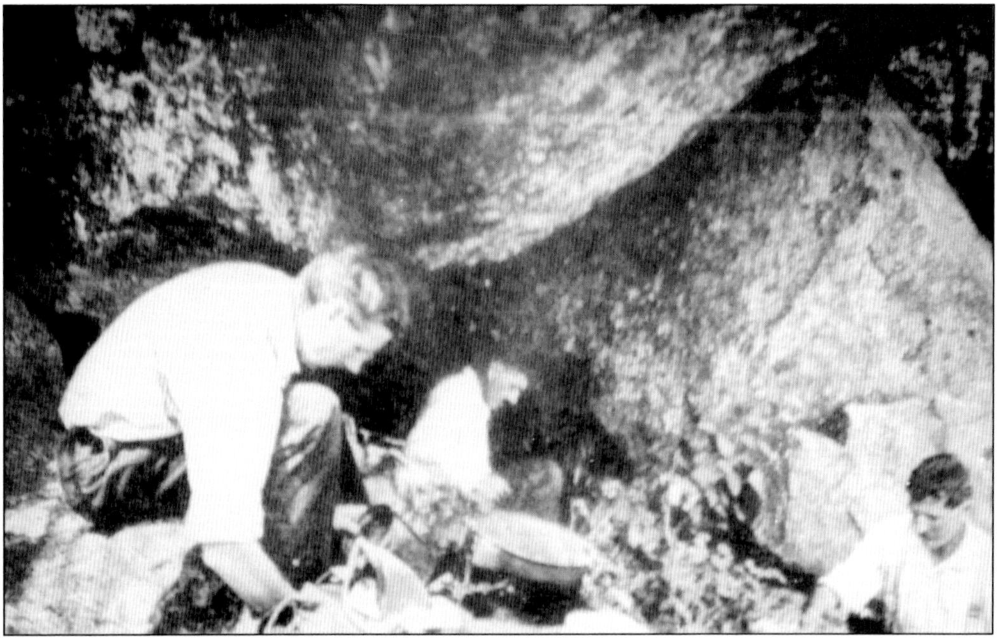

Explorers at Lake Solitude examine the ledges and cave formations to see if they will yield up treasure. The rocks contain abundant minerals, and the area is also known to harbor several rare and endangered plant species. (Newbury Public Library.)

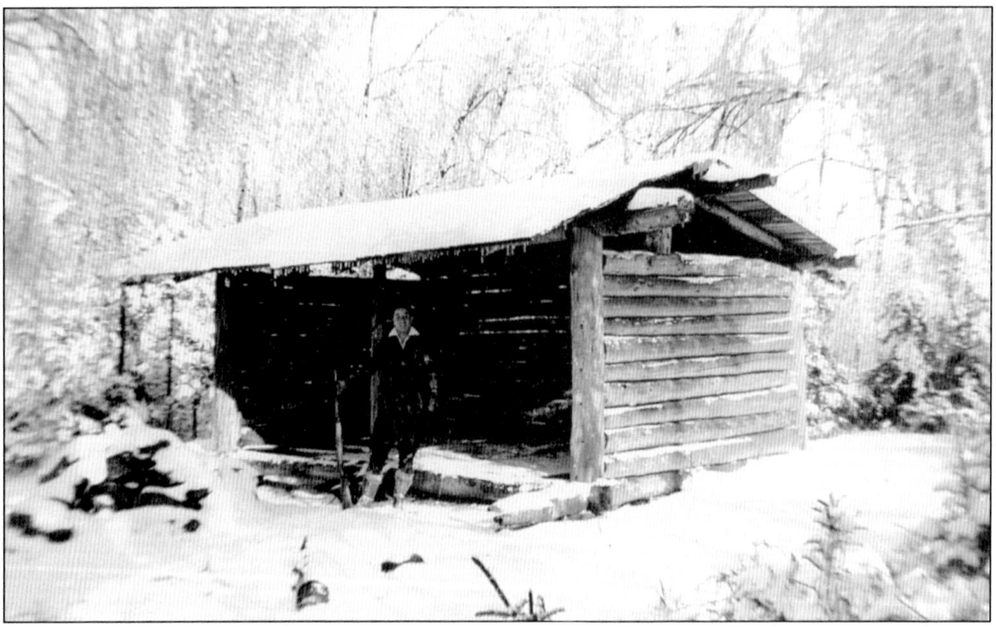

During the 1930s, trails on Mount Sunapee were expanded and wooden maps were installed at the base of each trail. Summer explorers made use of campsites. This shelter, seen in 1949, was at Lake Solitude where hikers used the Andrew Brook Trail to bring provisions to camp overnight. A spring of fine water was located nearby. In winter, young men hunting porcupine for bounty took refuge here. (Wayne and Judy LaPorte.)

The State of New Hampshire named Mount Sunapee a state park in 1948, and late that year the North Peak area was opened for skiing with a single chairlift, three trails, and two rope tows. This picture of the original chairlift was taken looking back at the newly built North Peak Lodge. Skiing excursions were an instant hit with area families. (William Weiler.)

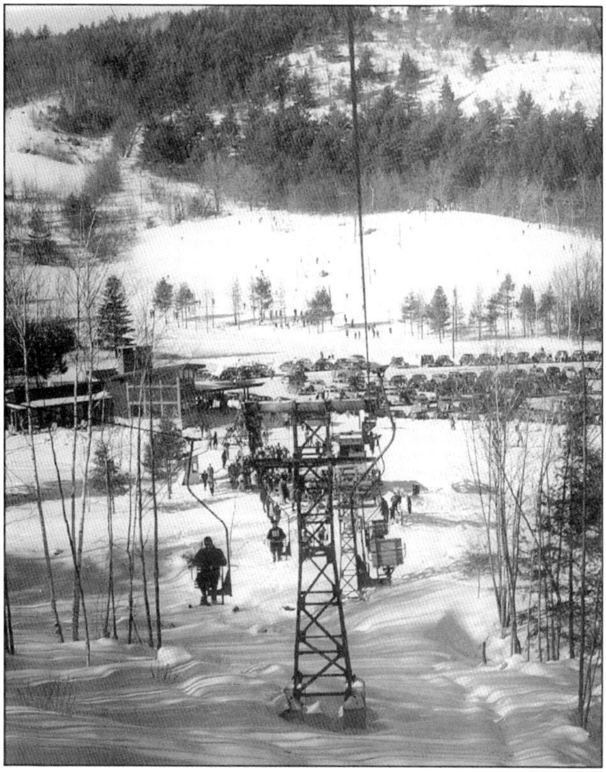

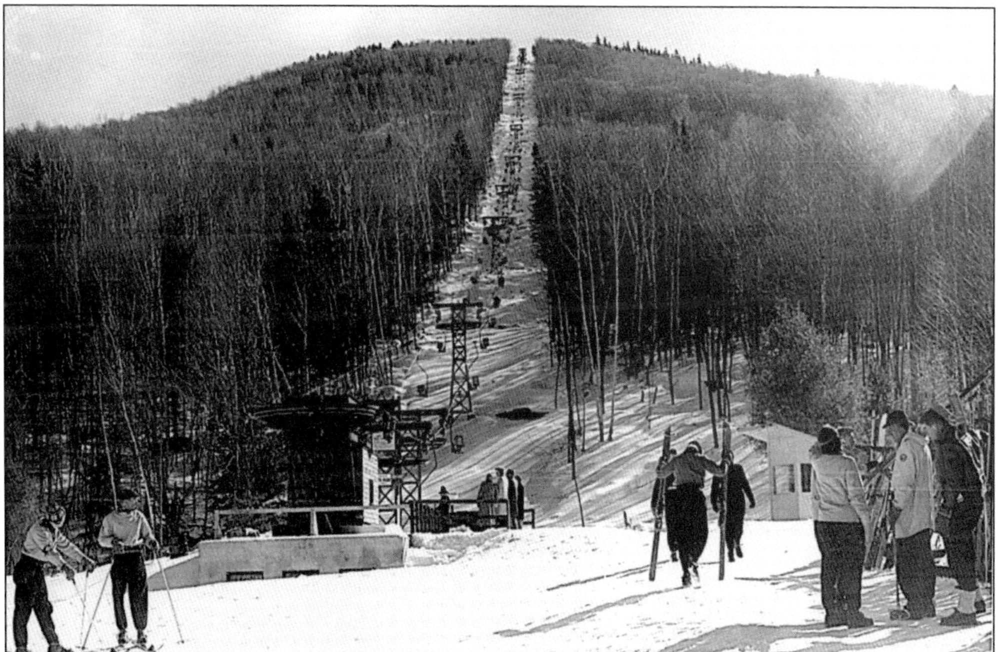

This is another view of the chairlift at Mount Sunapee, taken from the base and looking up the 3,300-foot North Peak run, around 1949. In 1957, a Poma lift was added, and by the 1960s, a double lift, T-bar, and J-bar lift were installed. (John Greenwood.)

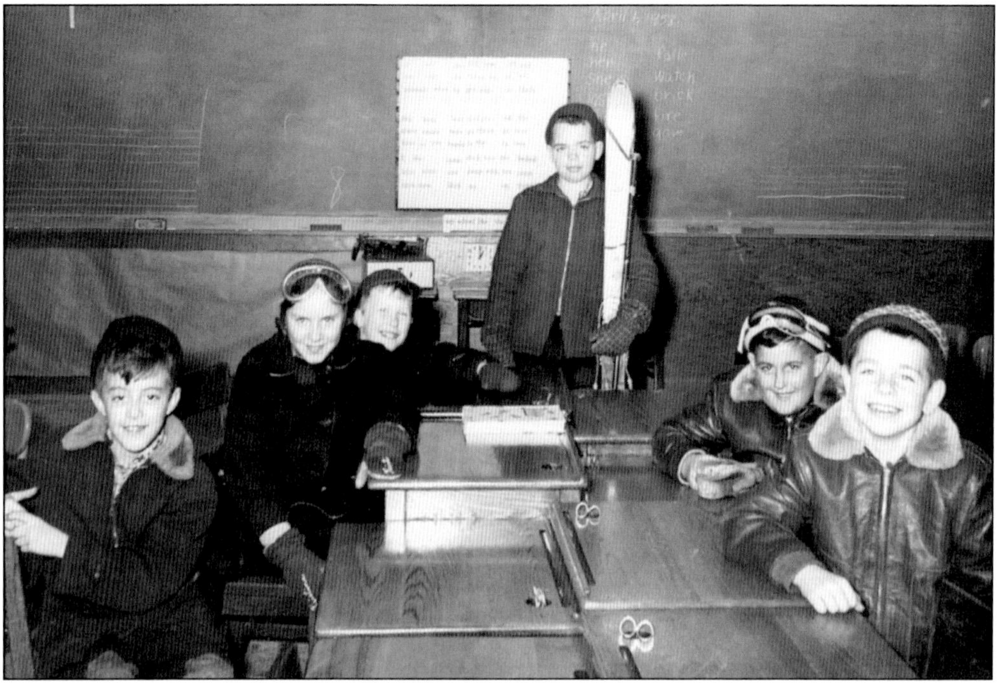

By the 1950s, skiing had become enormously popular. Newbury families flocked to the mountain, and a ski school was established. During the winter season, skiing became part of the school curriculum, and once a week eager students were transported to Mount Sunapee for lessons in the great outdoors. They were often joined by mothers or family members who wanted to sharpen their skiing skills. In the photograph above, students from the Center School get ready for their weekly excursion. Pictured are, from left to right, Ronnie Ansart, Grace Mitchell, Rusty Perkins, Bruce Croteau, Howard Eaton, and Richard Folsom. Below, Center School students line up with their gear ready to head to the mountain. (Elizabeth Folsom.)

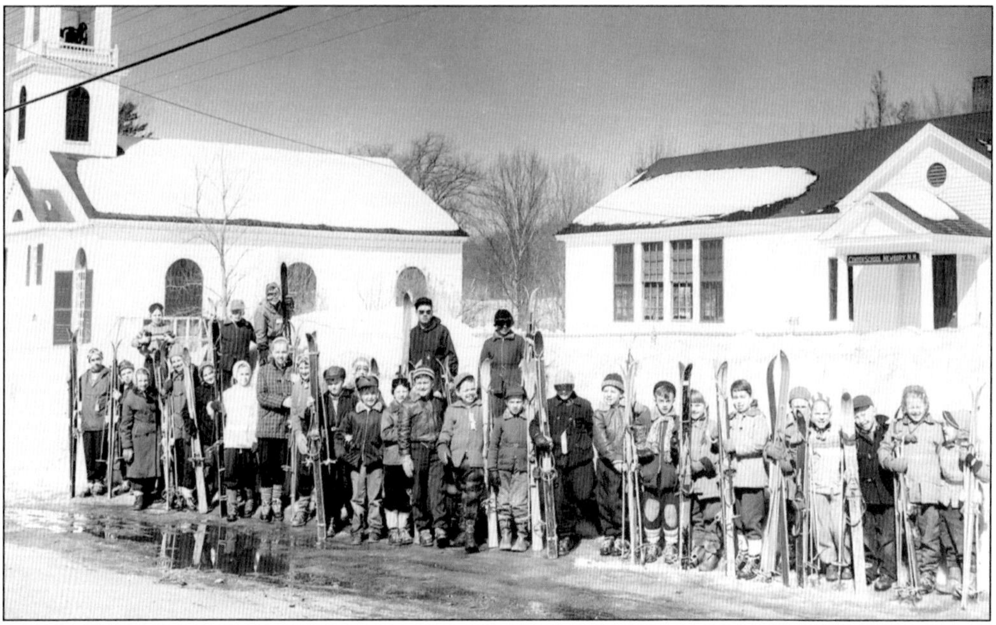

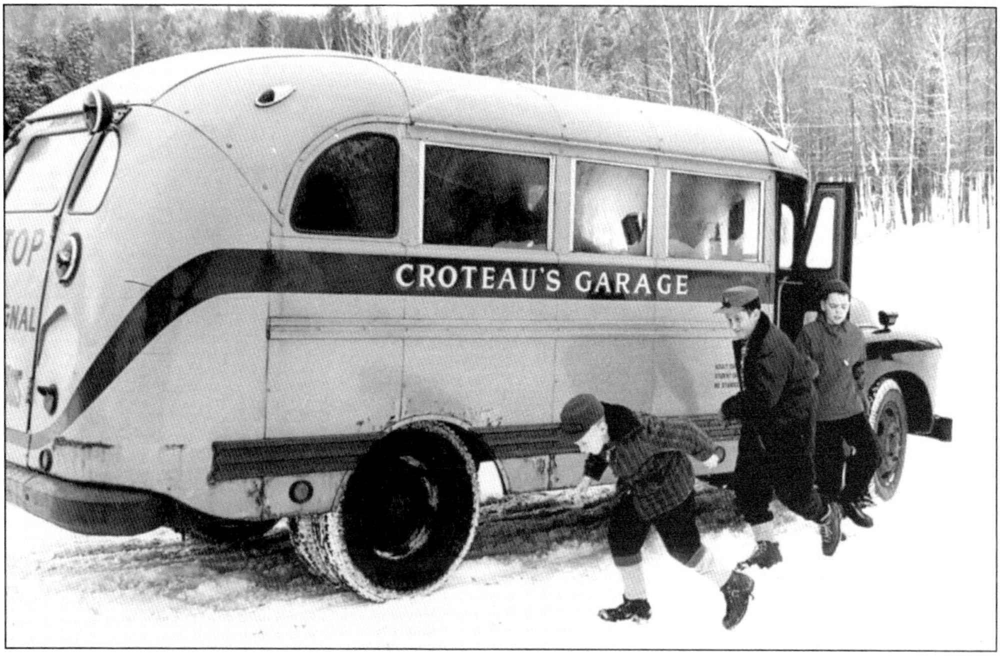

The state expanded ski operations on Mount Sunapee during the 1950s and 1960s. More chairs and lifts were added, trails were extended, and lodges were built at the base and summit. In 1966, the North Peak double chairlift was converted into a gondola for rides to the top. The expanded operation drew crowds to the mountain from around the state and as far away as Boston. Newbury schoolchildren enjoyed their weekly excursions into the 1970s. In the photograph above, from left to right, Bruce Croteau, Howard Eaton, and Rusty Perkins head for the slopes. In the photograph below, a group of students learns the right moves at the Mount Sunapee ski school. (Elizabeth Folsom.)

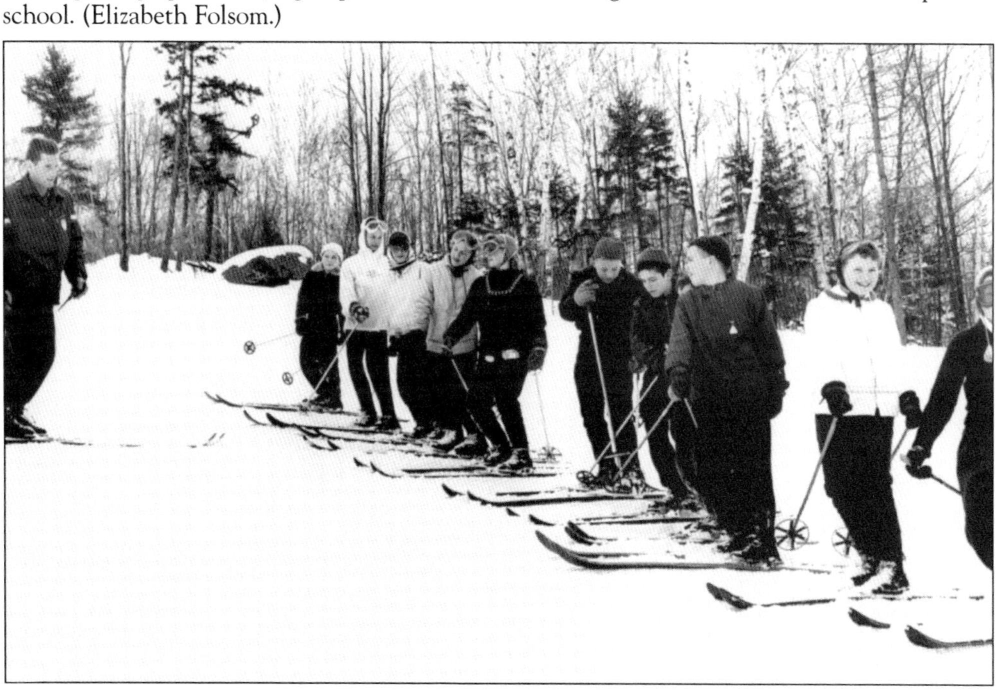

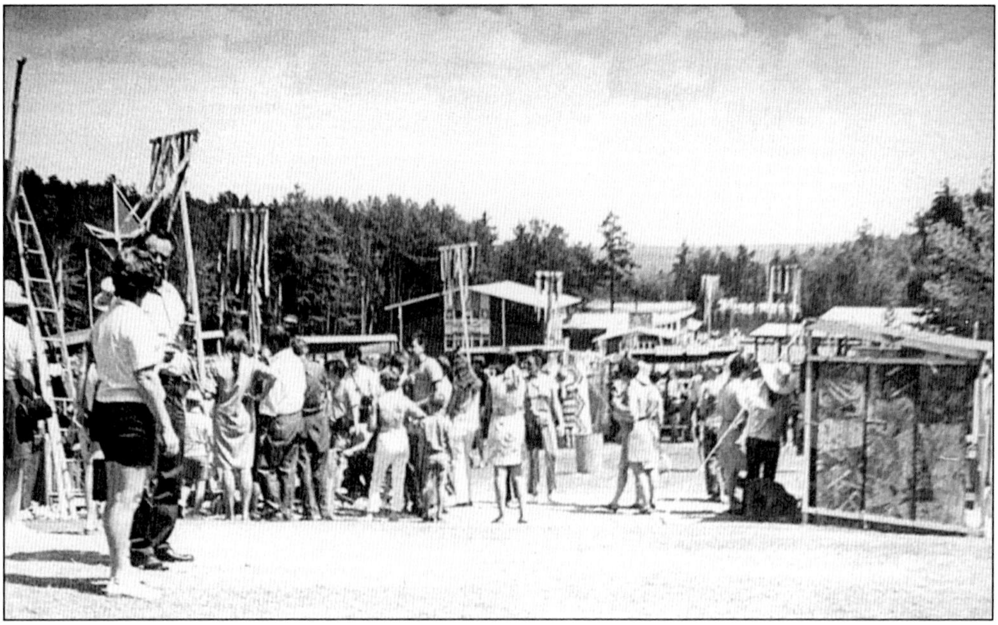

A summer highlight is the League of New Hampshire Craftsmen's fair, an annual weeklong event drawing thousands of attendees to Mount Sunapee. The oldest fair of its kind in the country, this event showcases the finest examples of a wide range of crafts. The fair was first held in Crawford Notch in 1933 and, after moving to various venues throughout the state, has made Mount Sunapee its home since 1964. (Newbury Public Library.)

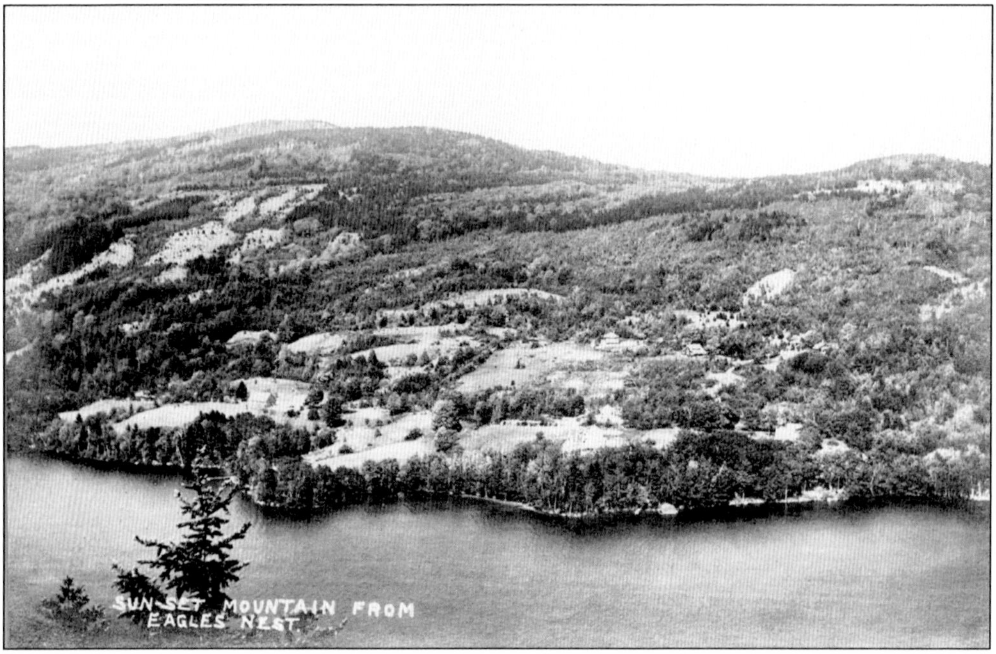

Sunapee lake and mountain offer beautiful scenery everywhere one turns. Here Newbury's Sunset Hill, seen from the west side of the lake, shows some early farmland reclaimed from the forested hillside. Over the years, the forest has again encroached, and hiking trails on this hill offer spectacular views of the sunset, lake, and surrounding countryside. (John Hutchinson.)

Lakeside docks and landings provide points of interest to travelers on the lake. Walkways such as this one at Brightwood, near Bay Point on the west shore of Lake Sunapee, attract the eye with colorful open gazebos. (Newbury Historical Society.)

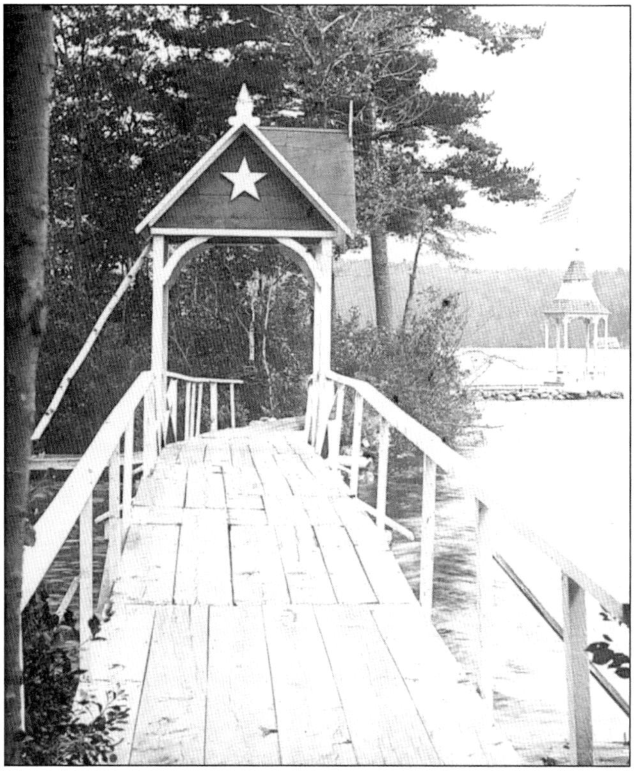

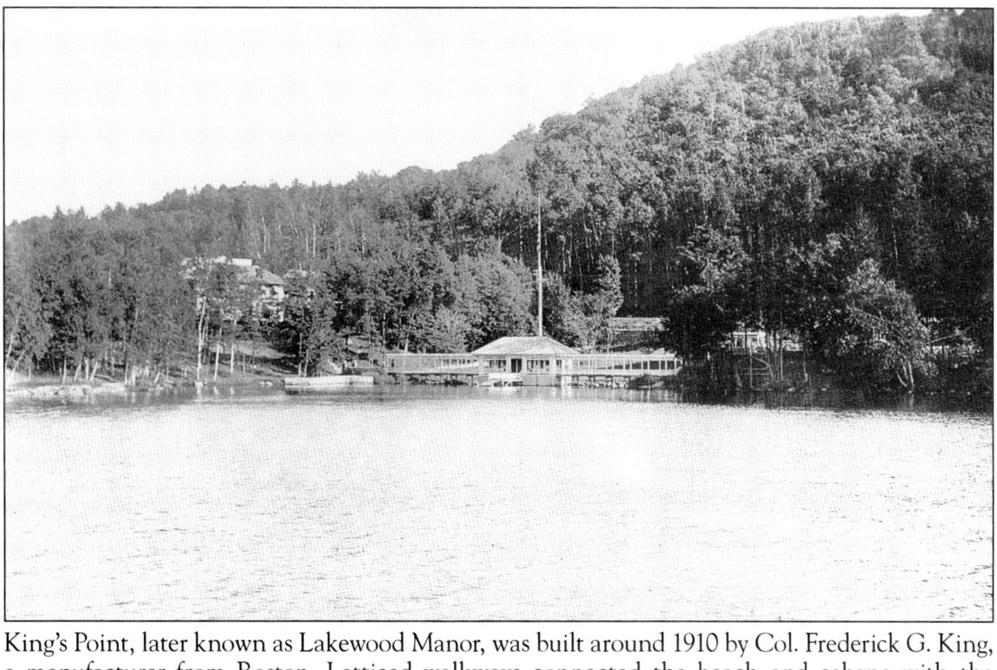

King's Point, later known as Lakewood Manor, was built around 1910 by Col. Frederick G. King, a manufacturer from Boston. Latticed walkways connected the beach and cabana with the boathouse and led to the grand main house with its massive fireplace and balconies and porches. King died by suicide in 1927, leaving the property to his wife, ex-wife, and would-be wife. The estate was sold to settle his affairs. (William Weiler.)

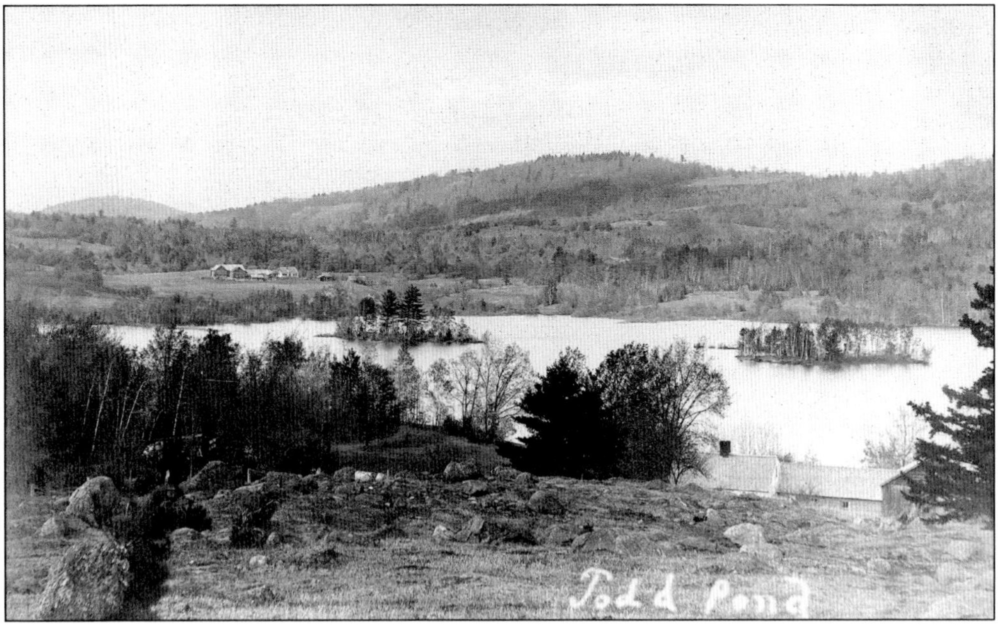

Lake Todd, located in South Newbury close to the Bradford town line, is a peaceful reservoir of 168 acres. It is popular with fishermen and small-boat enthusiasts. It is ringed with cottages, some of which are permanent homes and others summer retreats or rental properties. On the north end of the lake, visible from Route 103, is the original James Gillingham property. (Elizabeth Folsom.)

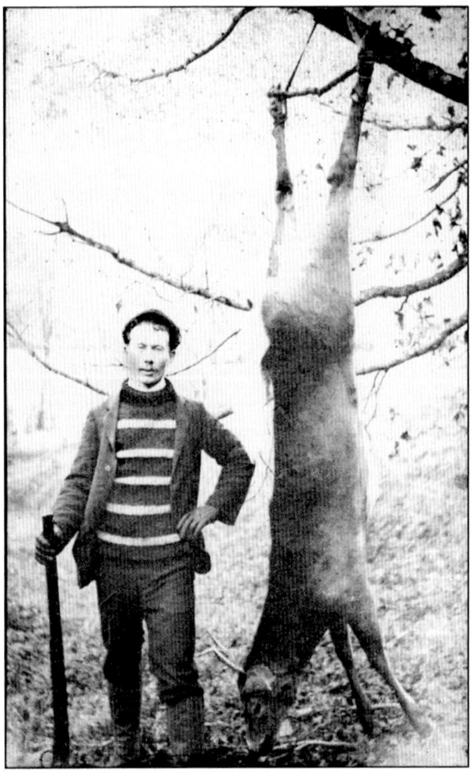

Newbury's heavily wooded hillsides are home to a wide variety of wildlife. The early settlers depended on the plentiful game for food and hides, and trappers found abundant sources of fur. Hunting has remained popular both as a sport and to provide food. Here local hunter Harry Ring poses with his trophy deer taken from property his family owned for many generations along Route 103A. (Steve Hansen.)

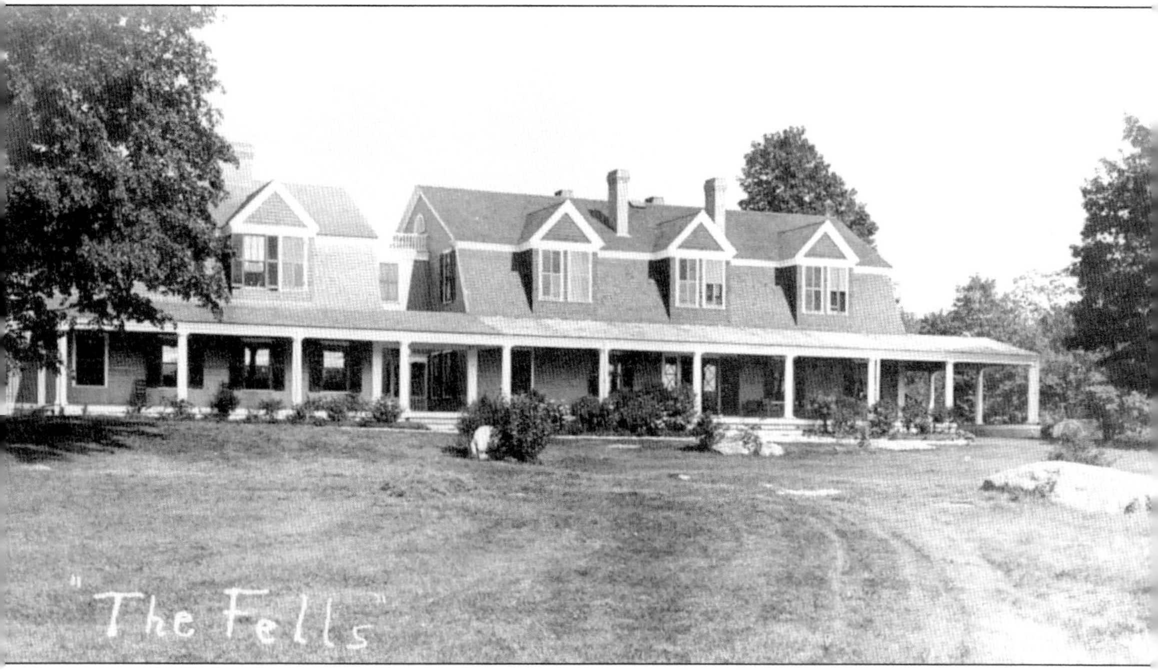

The John Hay estate on the shore of Lake Sunapee was built in the 1890s, and in its early days, the front lawn was home to sheep that grazed the abundant lawns and to crops of potatoes. Known as the Fells, it was the summer home of writer and diplomat John Hay, who served as private secretary to Abraham Lincoln, ambassador to Great Britain, and secretary of state under Pres. William McKinley and Pres. Theodore Roosevelt. Roosevelt visited the Hays at the Fells in 1902 and planted an elm tree on the grounds. Hay's son, Clarence, and his wife, Alice, were responsible for designing and nurturing the beautiful gardens, which include a formal rose garden, alpine garden, Japanese water lily pool, and hidden walled garden. The grounds and surrounding landscape of rhododendrons, azaleas, dogwoods, and heather amid wildflowers and ferns attract visitors from all parts of the country and abroad. They can also enjoy house tours, hiking trails, workshops, and educational programs. (Tracy Messer.)

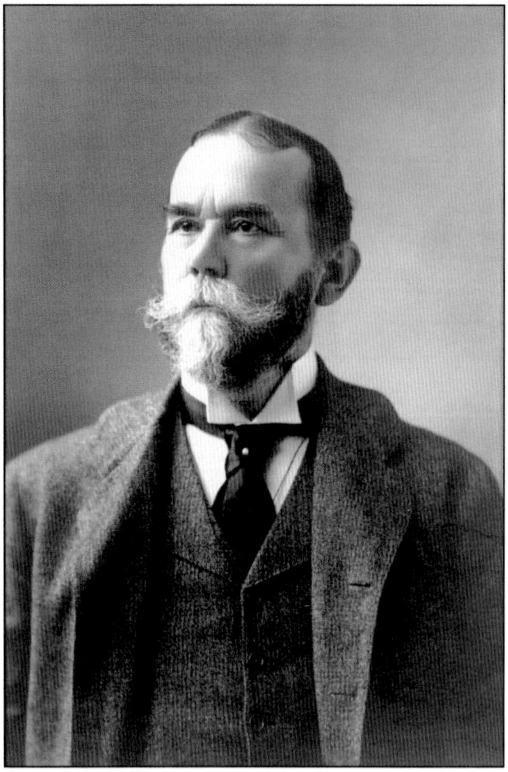

This portrait of John Hay was taken between 1897 and 1905, during the years he spent summers at the Fells. Hay enjoyed quiet time in Newbury with his family and doubtless found opportunities to pursue his personal writing and correspondence with friends such as Henry Adams and William Dean Howells. Hay was a prolific writer and talented poet, publishing *Pike County Ballads* in 1871 and, with friend John Nicolay, a 10-volume biography of Abraham Lincoln in 1890. (Brown University Library.)

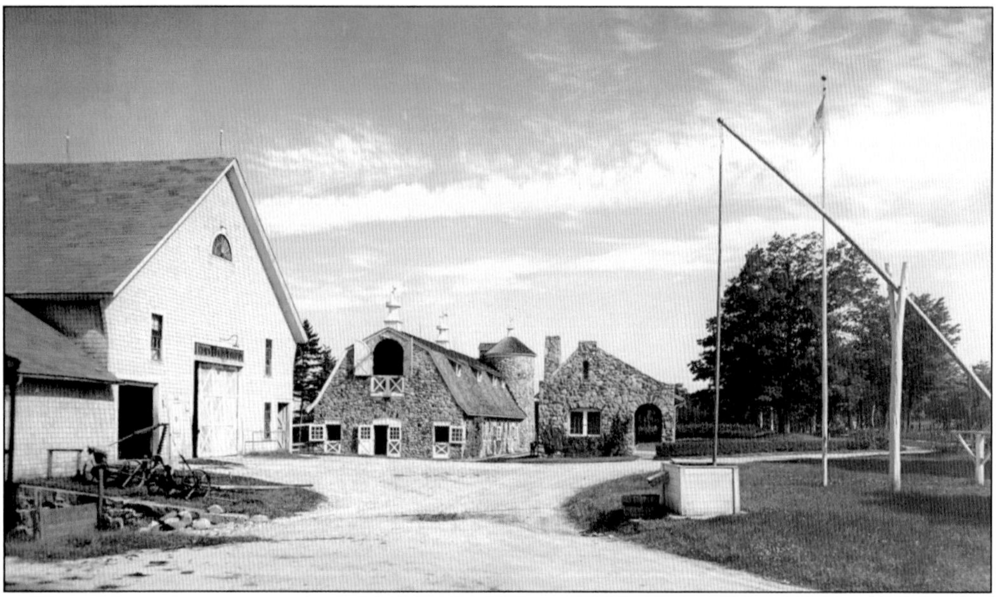

This old stone barn, built around 1912, was originally part of the Hay estate. The property was later named Wellsweep, for the long pole on a fulcrum with attached line. When activated, the bucket on the end of the line dipped into the well to withdraw water. The mechanism is now gone, as is the wooden barn on the left. The stone barn interior was crafted with fir wood for the stalls and the curved stairway leading to the loft. The adjacent stone building was used as an icehouse. (The Fells.)

Six

The Spirit of Blodgett's Landing

George Blodgett was a man of vision, foreseeing a transformation of the family farmland sloping down to Lake Sunapee's shore into a mecca for the tourists pouring into the area after the completion of the Newbury Cut. By 1875, he had established the first campsites at Blodgett's Landing, renting out spaces to Civil War veterans for reunions and to the Masons for their annual meetings.

Close on their heels came the Sunapee Lake Spiritualists, who began holding their annual camp meetings at the landing in 1877. By 1885, many of the tented campsites were sprouting cottages. On the 125 surveyed lots, 32-foot-by-64-foot sites could be rented from Blodgett for a term of 20 years for the sum of $2 per year. Additional accommodations were available at the Forest House, later named Sunapee Anglers' Camp and Blodgett Lodge, catering to visiting fishermen. In the 1890s, the area boasted Messer's country store, a post office, Nelson's livery and boarding stable, George Morrill's barbershop, and J. B. Warren's photographic studio. Blodgett remained active in the growth and diversity of his enterprise, with businesses ranging from real estate to hotels to the ownership of the ill-fated steamboat the *Edmund Burke*, which he renamed the *Wenonah*.

Raising of the spirits not only was offered by the Spiritualists but was available to all visitors in the form of literary and musical entertainments, fairs, and dances. The casino housed ongoing entertainment, including such notables as Will Cressy. He bought the island across from the landing in 1900 and hosted many theater celebrities during the season. Those wishing to commune with nature rather than spirits could enjoy a stroll along the esplanade running along the shore. The air was healthful and bracing, the water pure, and swimming and boating were just a step away.

Blodgett's Landing has preserved a strong sense of community, fostered by the Cottage Owners' Association, which was formed around 1900. In 1917, future congressman Henry L. Bowles led a group that bought the hotel and park and deeded them to the Cottage Owners' Association to preserve them for public use. Over the years, the association has continued to work to protect the interests of the landing's property owners and provides annual events where the community and its history are celebrated.

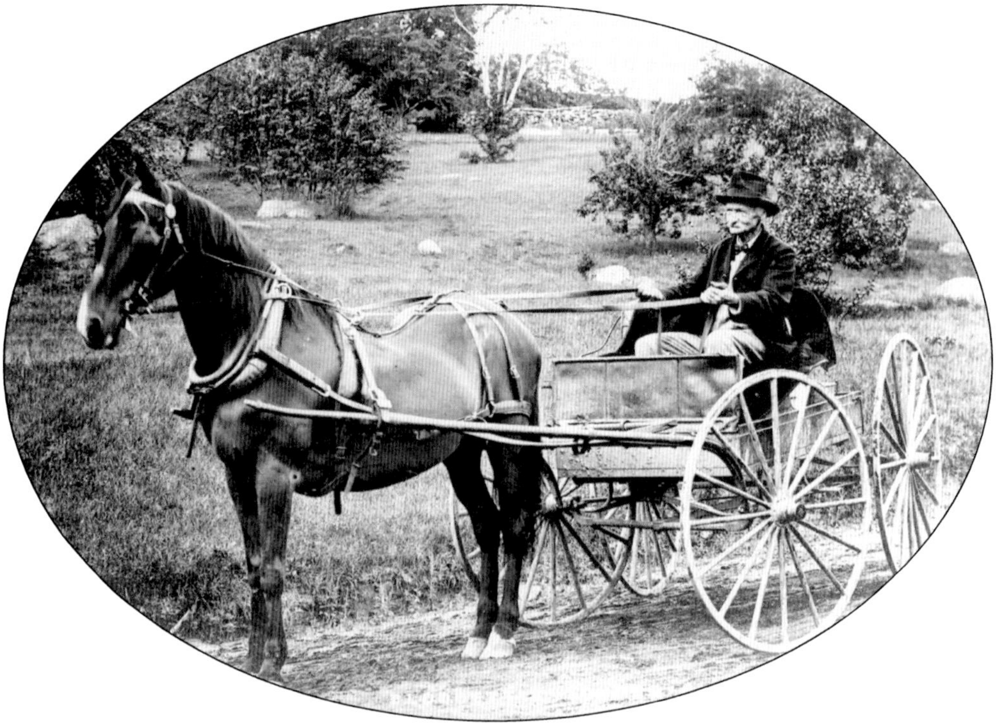

George Blodgett and his horse Billy were a familiar sight as they delivered vegetables and produce around the lake. Billy, of hearty Morgan stock, was foaled in 1864 and had an independent streak that characterized him throughout his reputed 40 years of life. Blodgett and Billy were a daily presence in Blodgett's Landing and throughout Newbury. (Virginia Bates.)

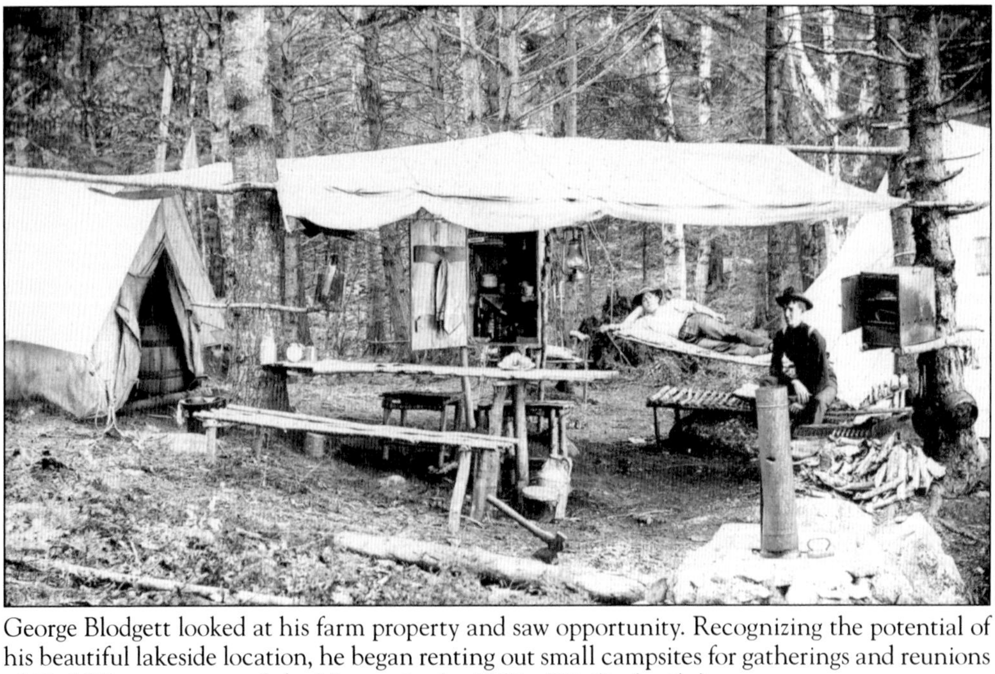

George Blodgett looked at his farm property and saw opportunity. Recognizing the potential of his beautiful lakeside location, he began renting out small campsites for gatherings and reunions of Civil War veterans and the Masons in the 1860s. (Digilio family.)

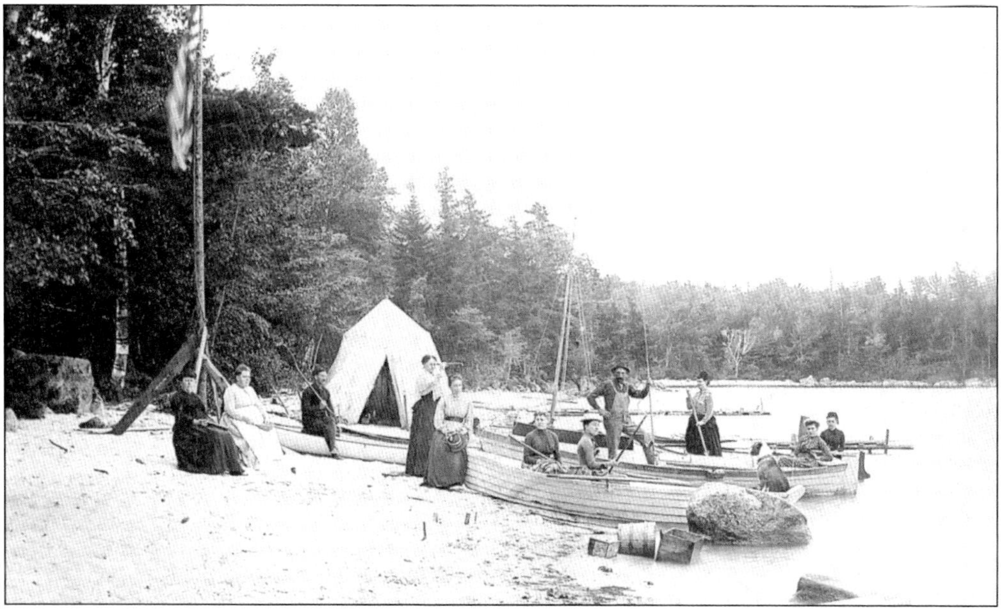

During the 1870s when the railroad and steamboats brought an influx of summer visitors, Blodgett, himself a Spiritualist, invited the Sunapee Lake Spiritualists to convene on his property. They began holding their annual camp meetings there in 1877. Blodgett expanded his number of tent sites and made plans to add a hotel, pavilion, temple, and other amenities to the area. (Digilio family.)

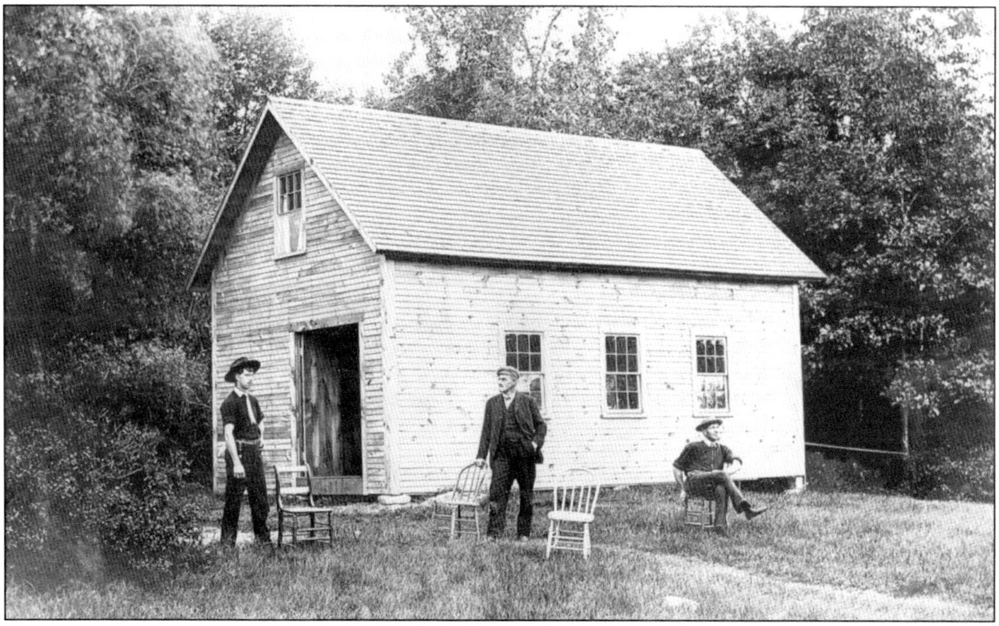

By 1883, Blodgett had surveyed the landing and laid out 125 lots, 32 feet by 64 feet. A flyer at the time noted that 100 lots had been leased and the remaining ones were available for a term of 20 years for the sum of $2 per year. During this decade, tented campsites began to give way to cottages, which were erected on the same small lots and thus created very close neighbors. (William Weiler.)

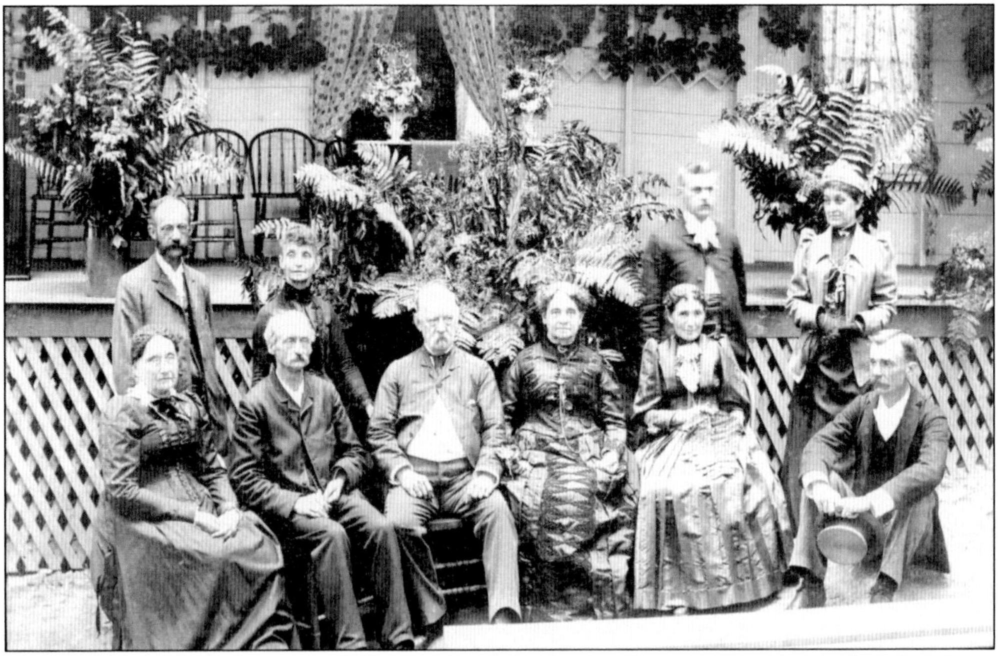

Pictured here are the directors of the Sunapee Lake Spiritualists organization, gathered in front of their Association Hall. George Blodgett (front row, second from left) was an active member of the organization's Grounds and Privileges Committee. (Digilio family.)

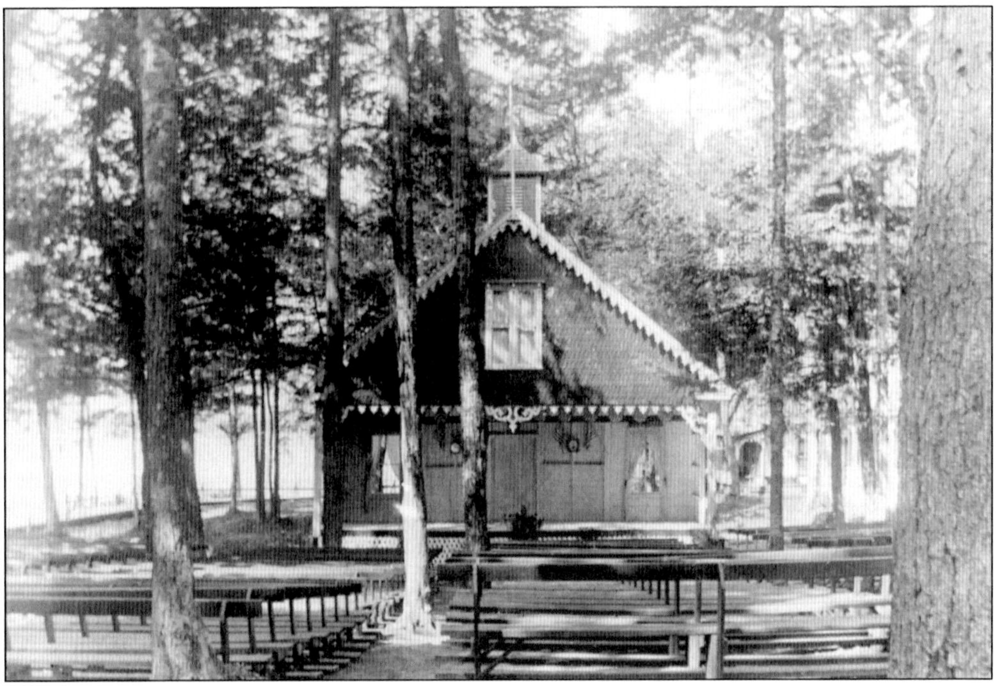

For many years, the Spiritualist meetings were held outdoors in an open-staged structure called Association Hall, with rows of seating provided among the stands of pine. In 1900, George Blodgett leased Harmony Hall, near the casino, for Spiritualist gatherings in inclement weather. (Newbury Historical Society.)

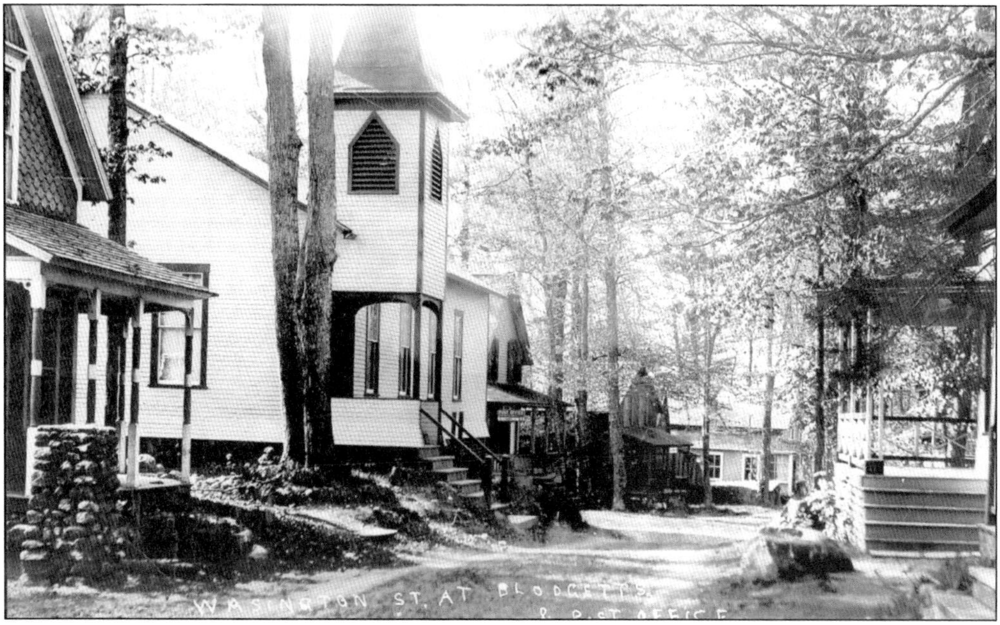

The Spiritualist temple was built at the intersection of Washington and Post Office Streets in 1901. The Spiritualists discontinued their meetings some years later, and the building was taken down. The site then became a small park with a monument to the organization. (Tracy Messer.)

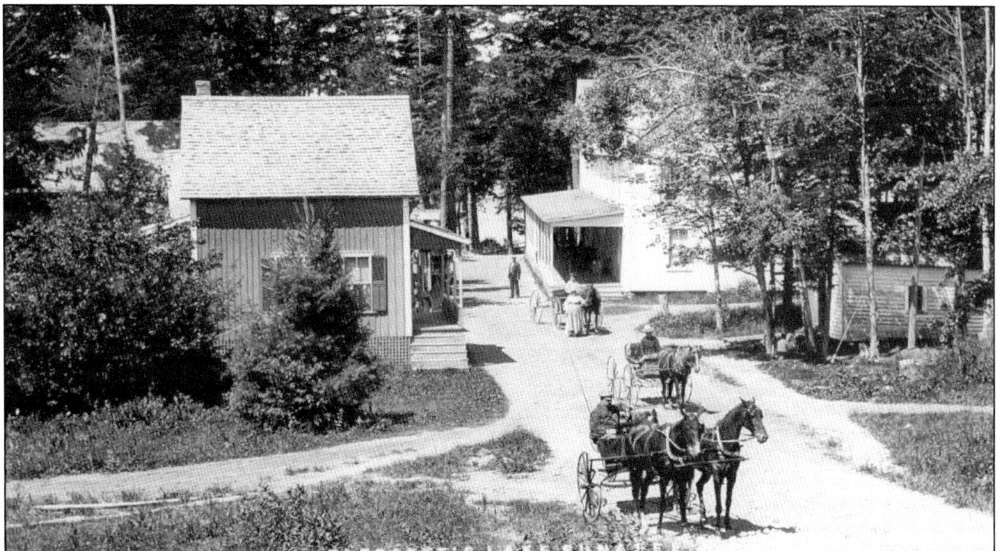

The present-day Blodgett's Landing Road is traveled by horse-and-buggy traffic in this picture that shows the Forest House, with its distinctive porch, on the right and Warren's photographic studio on the left. The present Bowles Road leads off to the left. (Tracy Messer.)

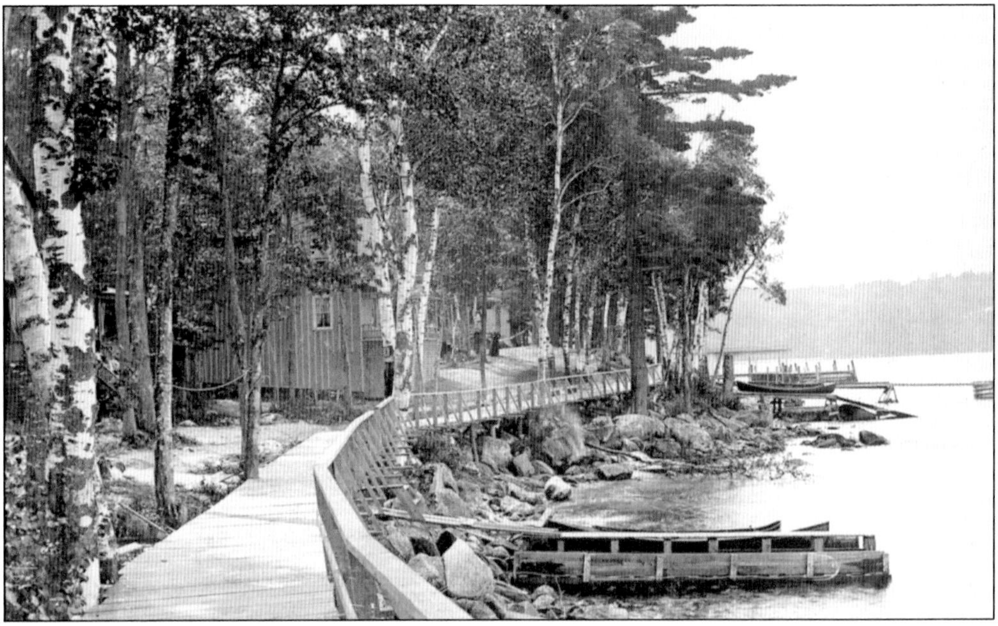

The boardwalk along Front Street (later Lake Avenue) was the promenade for many families and friends. It also served as a safe and convenient way for visitors arriving via steamboat to move from the landing to their cottage or hotel destination. A sturdy and attractive railing ran the length of the walk, preventing accidental dips into the lake. (Digilio family.)

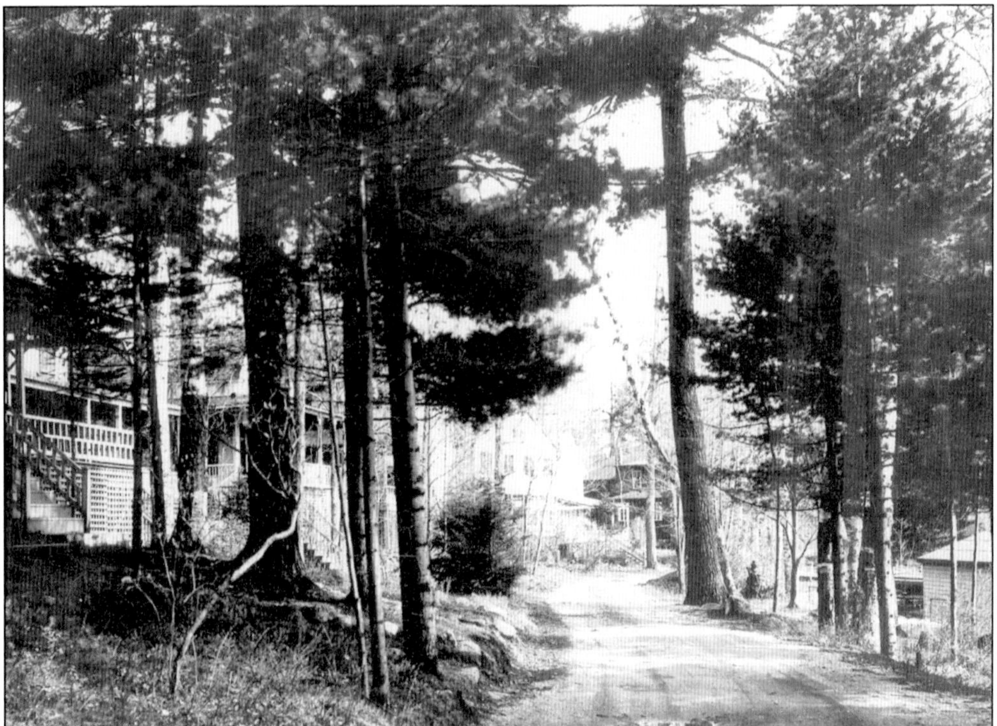

This picture of Lake Avenue, looking south, illustrates the closeness of the cottages and the narrow roadway, lined with towering pines. (Sally Kassman.)

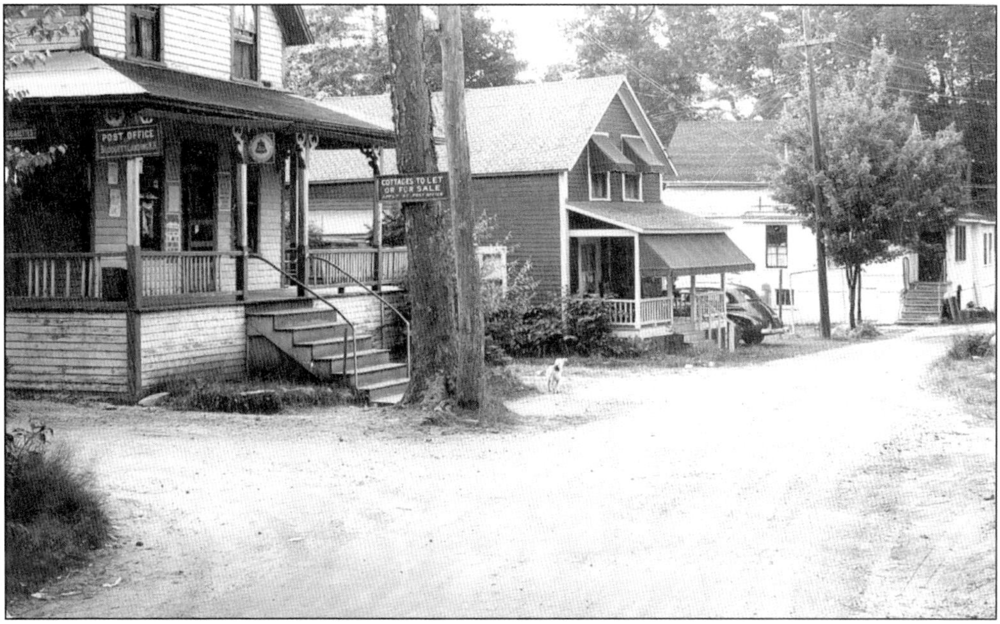

The post office was housed in the building on the left, at the intersection of Post Office and Washington Streets. The roadway to the left leads down to the lake and was the direct route to the busy steamboat landing. (Sally Kassman.)

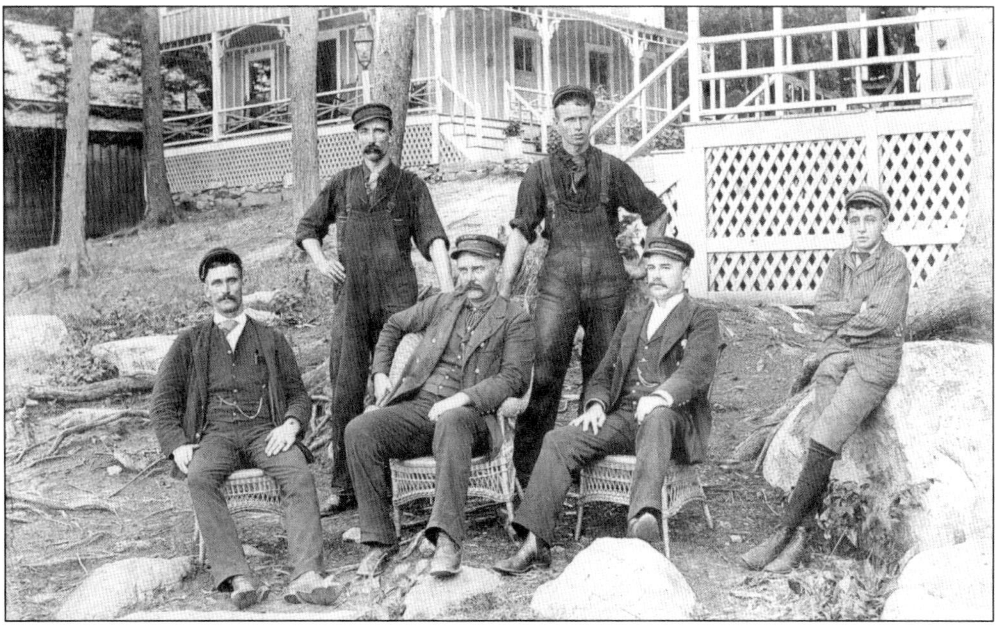

This is the crew of George Blodgett's steamboat the *Edmund Burke* (later *Winonah*). It carried passengers around the lake in competition with the Woodsum brothers' fleet. Blodgett wanted to be sure his summer visitors had priority service. The steamer carried a full crew, shown here with Capt. Wesley Cilley (seated, second from left). Cilley was George Blodgett's nephew. (Digilio family.)

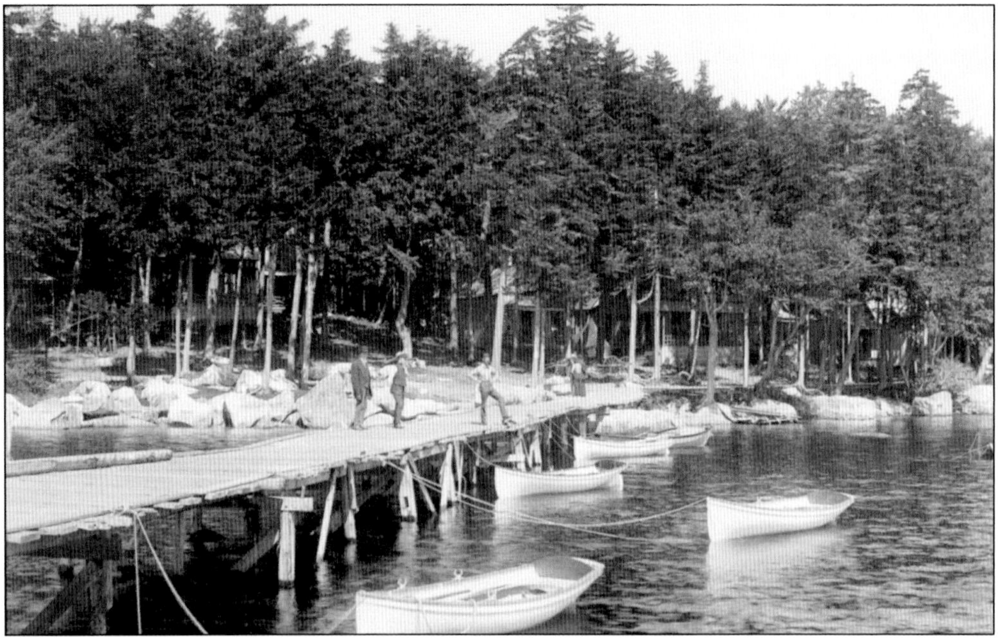

The pier at Blodgett's Landing was a busy spot for fishermen. Salmon, lake trout, and bass were prized catches. Boats could be rented out for sport or for simply enjoying a scenic row along the shore. (Newbury Historical Society.)

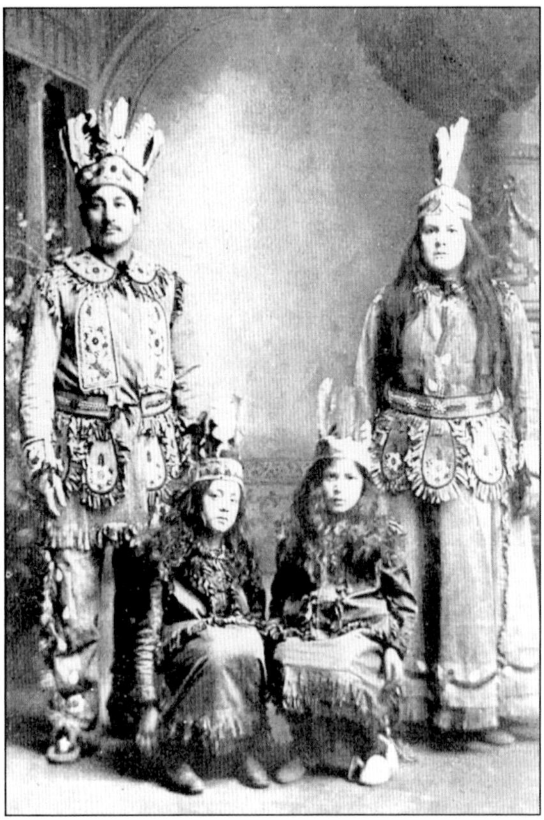

Louis Watso and his wife, Catherine, were Abenaki Indians. They settled at Blodgett's Landing where they sold their fine hand-woven baskets to summer visitors. In 1930, the Lake Sunapee Protective Association hired Watso to visit and inspect 104 cottages around the lake. A few years later, he was acting as a real estate agent for lake cottages, building lots, and farms. Shown here are the Watsos with two of their six children. (William Weiler.)

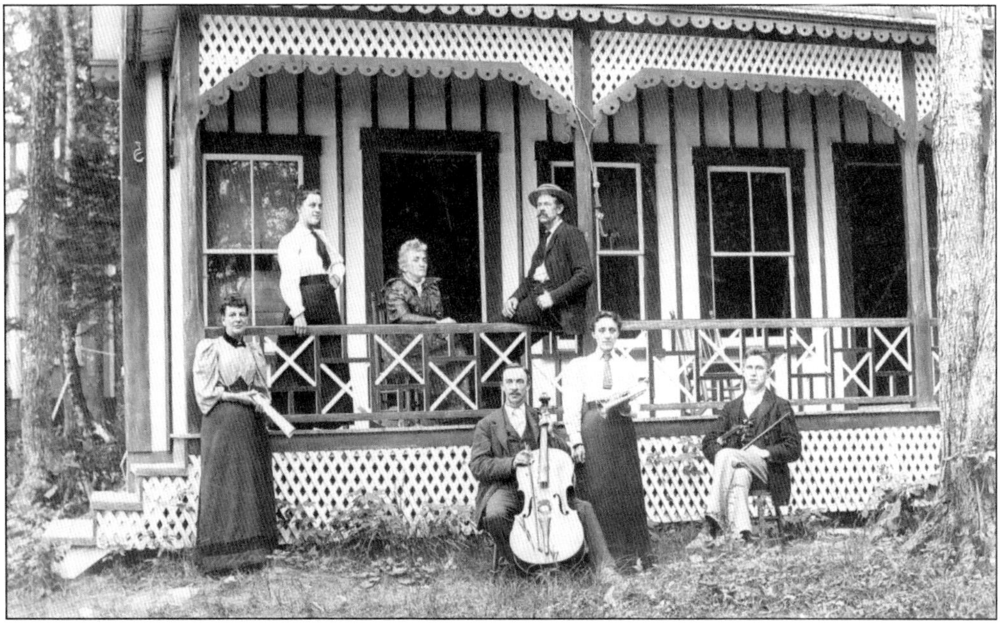

This group is enjoying a musical interlude in front of their elaborately decorated gingerbread cottage. Victorian decor was common to the dwellings at Blodgett's Landing and is seen today in many restored cottages. (Newbury Historical Society.)

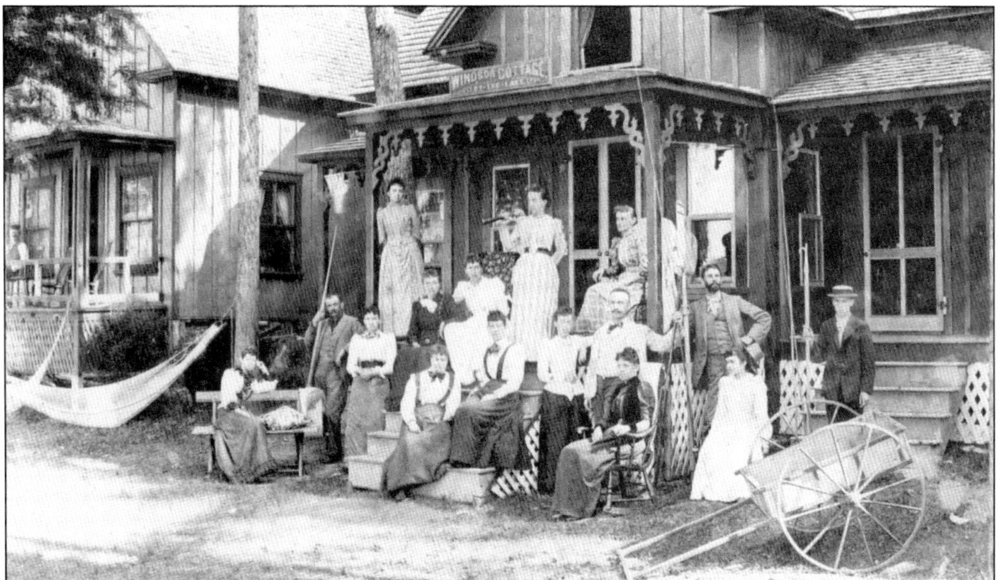

The ladies appear to be at leisure in front of Windsor Cottage, while the men are eager be on their way with their fishing rods. It is easy to see the close proximity in which the buildings exist. (Digilio family.)

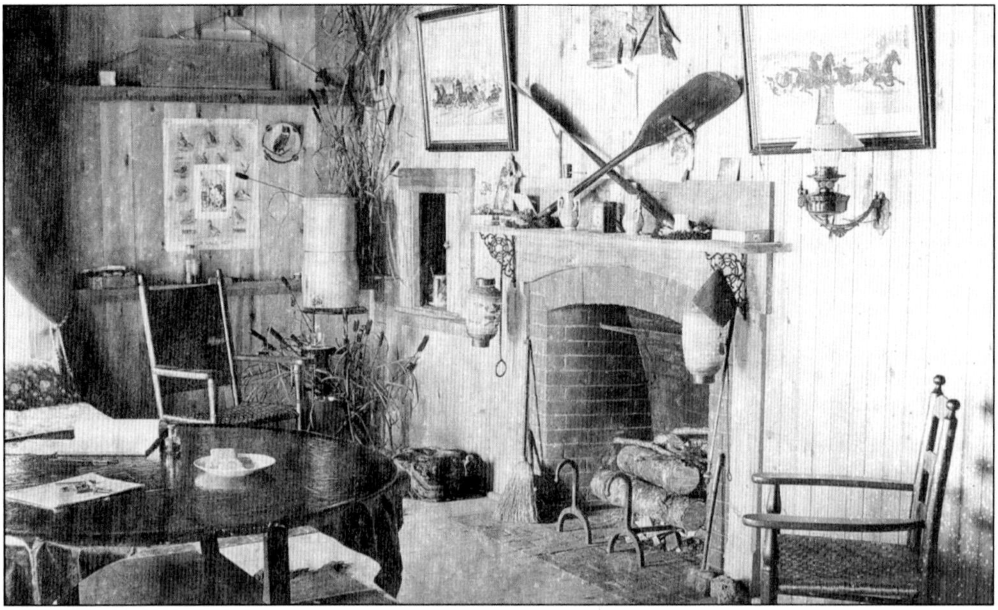

A cottage interior is decorated with an eye to comfort and eclectic furnishings. The collection of wild grasses and cattails were likely gathered along the lakeshore. (Digilio family.)

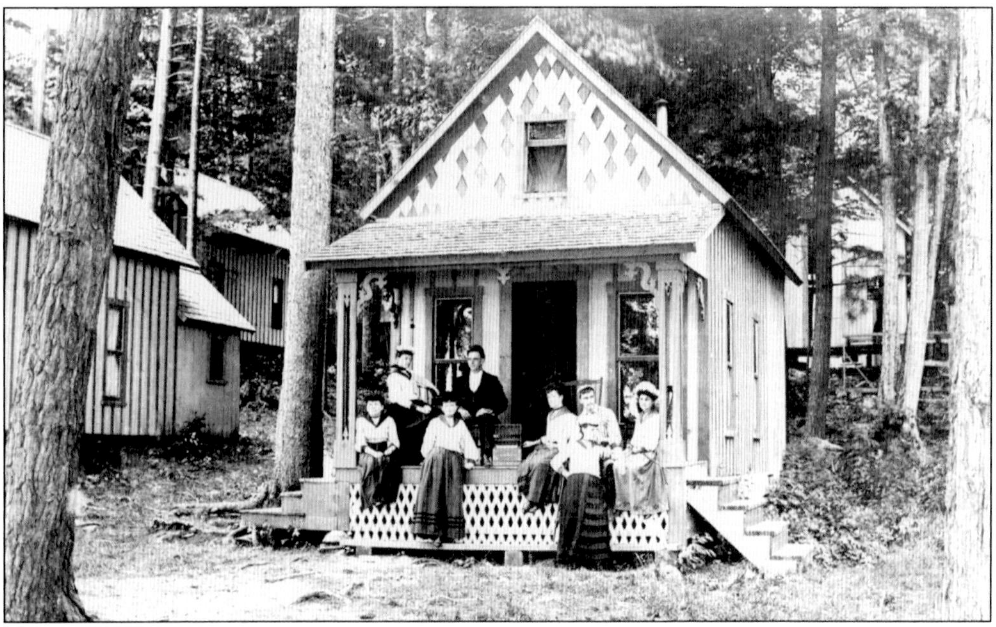

It might look like a dollhouse, but this cottage was vacation headquarters for this group of eight. Many of these small cottages had open sleeping lofts on the second floor. (Newbury Historical Society.)

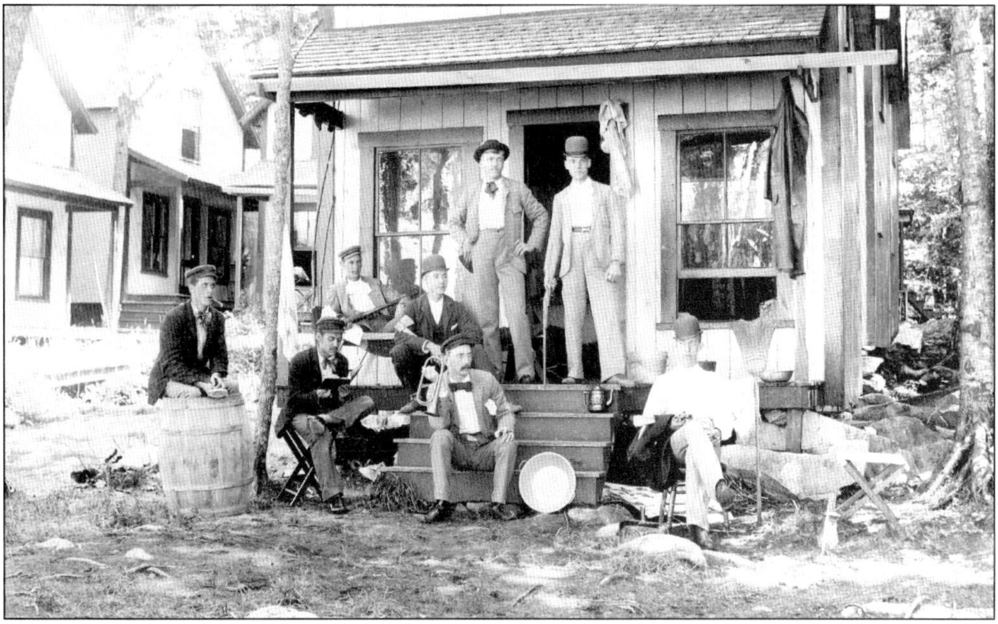

Old Mose Miller owned a group of seven small cottages located in the area of present-day 26 Lake Avenue and extending to the area between Lake Avenue and Washington Street. These young men pose with their props ranging from books to a rifle to a horn. (Digilio family.)

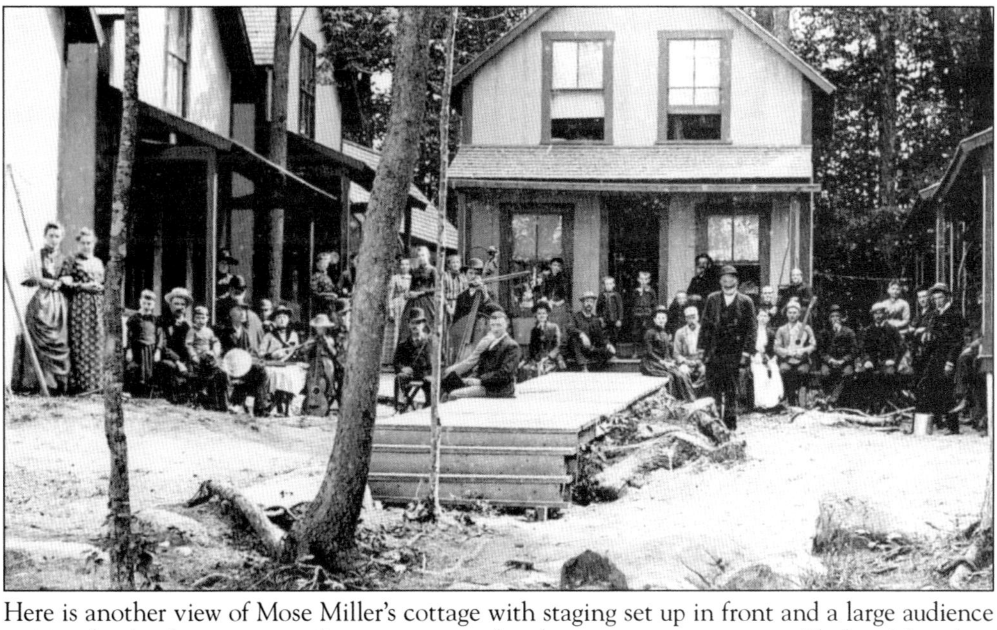

Here is another view of Mose Miller's cottage with staging set up in front and a large audience waiting for the show to go on. Impromptu social gatherings were common at Blodgett's Landing and became more organized as the pavilion and casino provided focal points for entertainment. (Digilio family.)

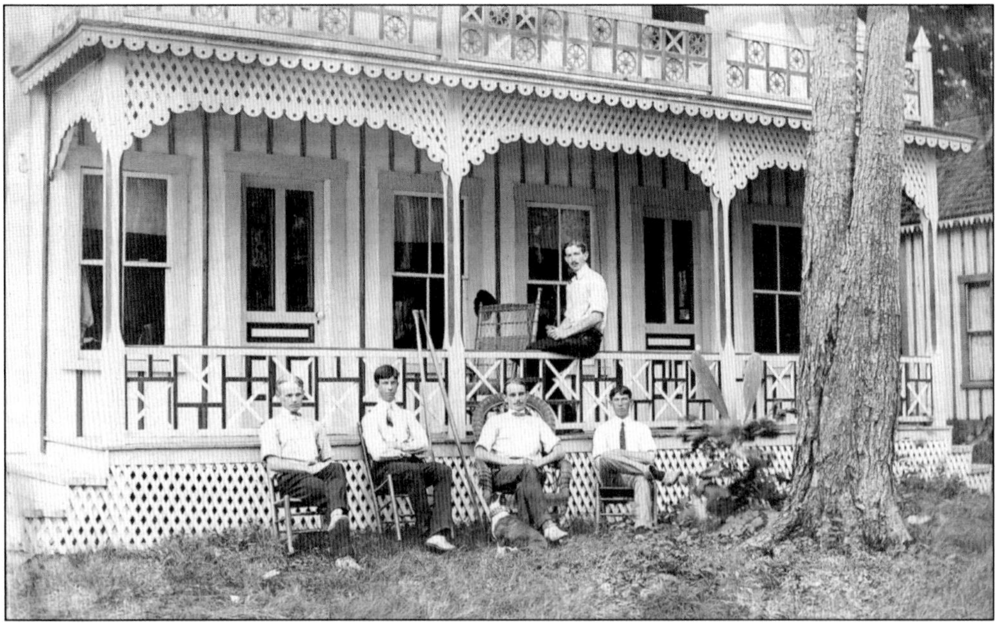

George Blodgett rented out several cottages at the landing. His main cottage was this one at present-day 68 Lake Avenue, next to the outdoor Spiritualist association building. The cottage had distinctive twin peaks and was elaborately decorated in Victorian style, painted white with red and blue trim. (Digilio family.)

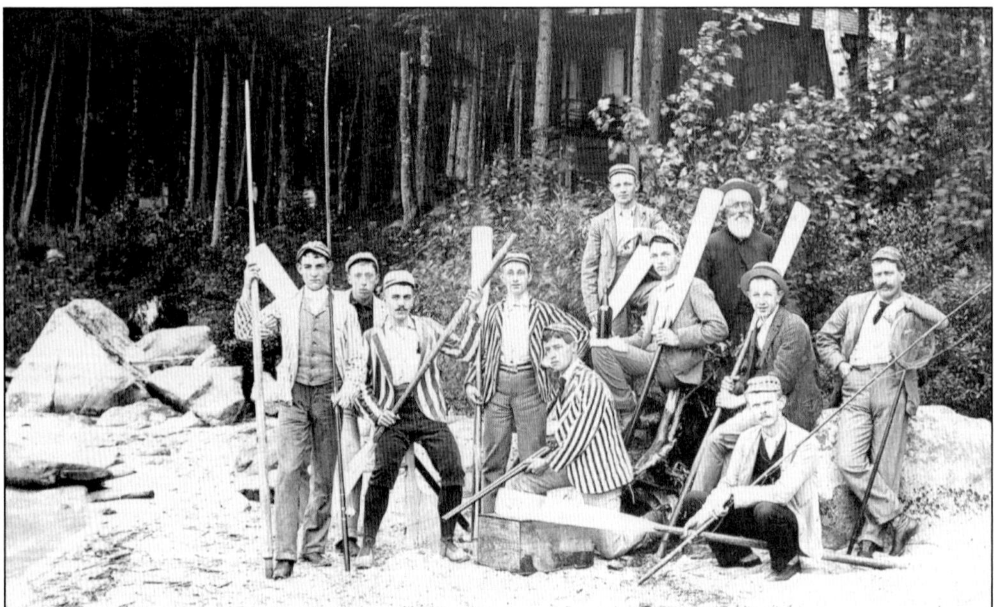

These young men are striking a pose at Kamp Komfort, a private club from Springfield, Massachusetts. The club was established in 1876 at Rowe's Landing (currently 130 Bowles Road). Photographer J. B. Warren took many pictures of the club members in dramatic poses, putting on skits, and clowning for the camera. (Digilio family.)

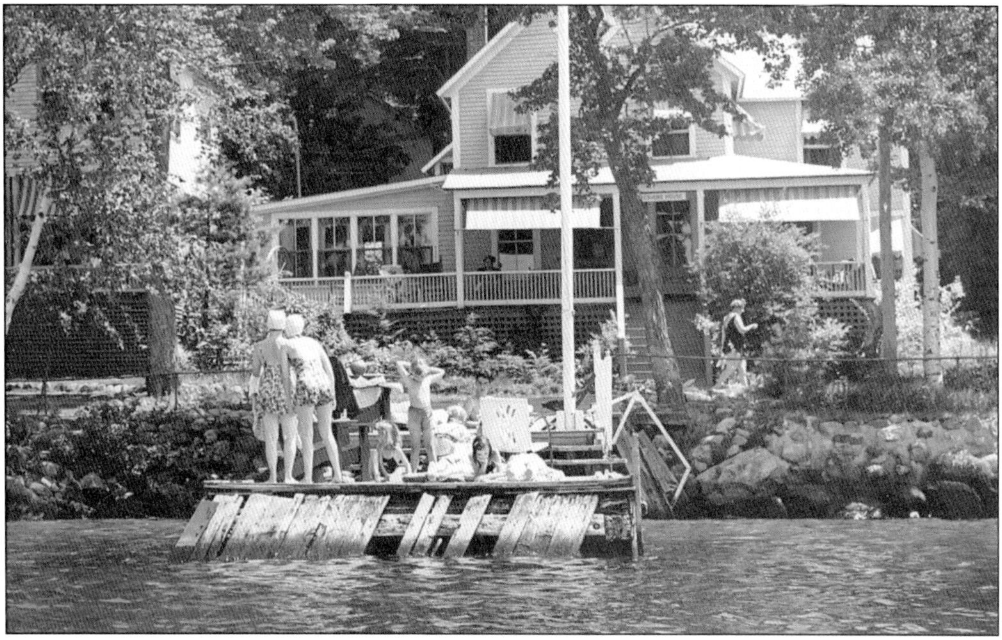

Lakeshore House was one of a small number of boardinghouses welcoming guests during the 1940s at Blodgett's Landing. This one at 18 Lake Avenue provided guests with a wide porch with awnings and a lakefront view, as well as a large dock for swimmers. Many guests returned for successive years. (Digilio family.)

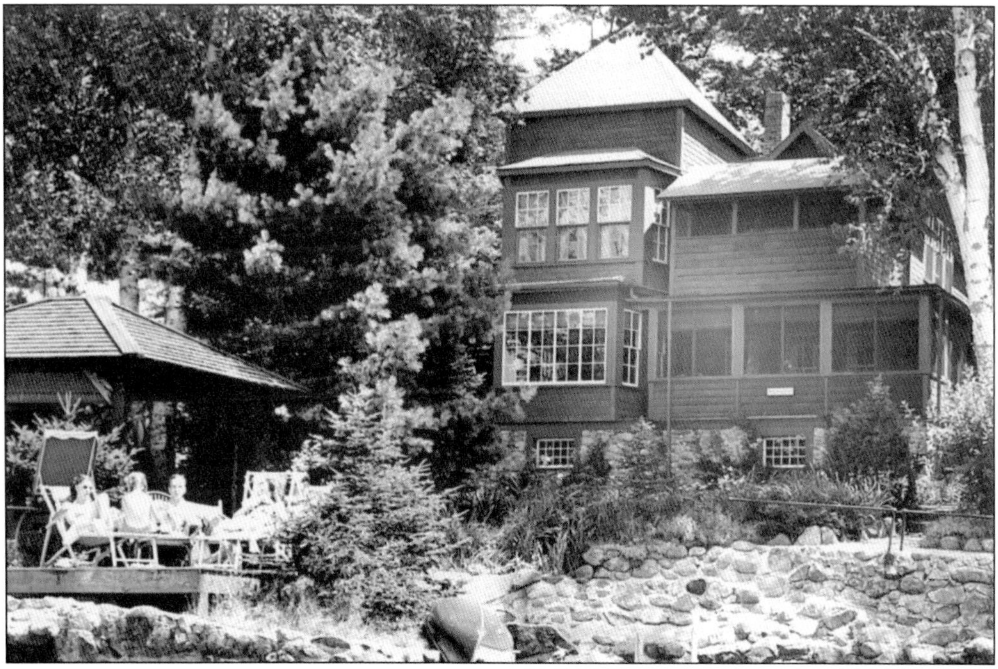

Summer residents at 20 Lake Avenue enjoy the sun and lakeside views from their deck above the water. Their cottage has evolved from humble beginnings to a commodious summerhouse, achieved by adding levels. Building upward has been the only way to enlarge these structures erected on small tent lots. (John Greenwood.)

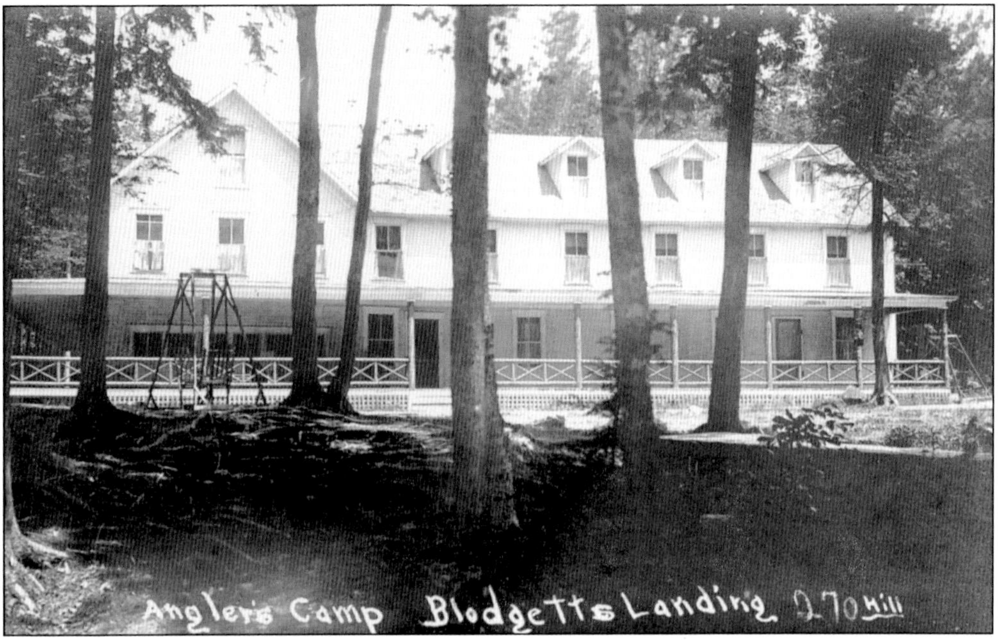

Forest House (later known as Sunapee Anglers' Camp and Blodgett Lodge) was a popular destination for summer visitors. George Blodgett first opened its doors to fishermen and this sport remained an attraction for many gentlemen visitors over the years. Forest House was also summer headquarters for families who enjoyed entertainment and dancing at the casino, shopping for groceries at Frank Messer's store, arranging for group photographs at J. B. Warren's lakeside studio, or simply strolling along the winding Front Street boardwalk that followed the shoreline. Swimming and boating were just a step away, and a bowling alley and pool hall were located by the pavilion. (Above, William Weiler; below, Digilio family.)

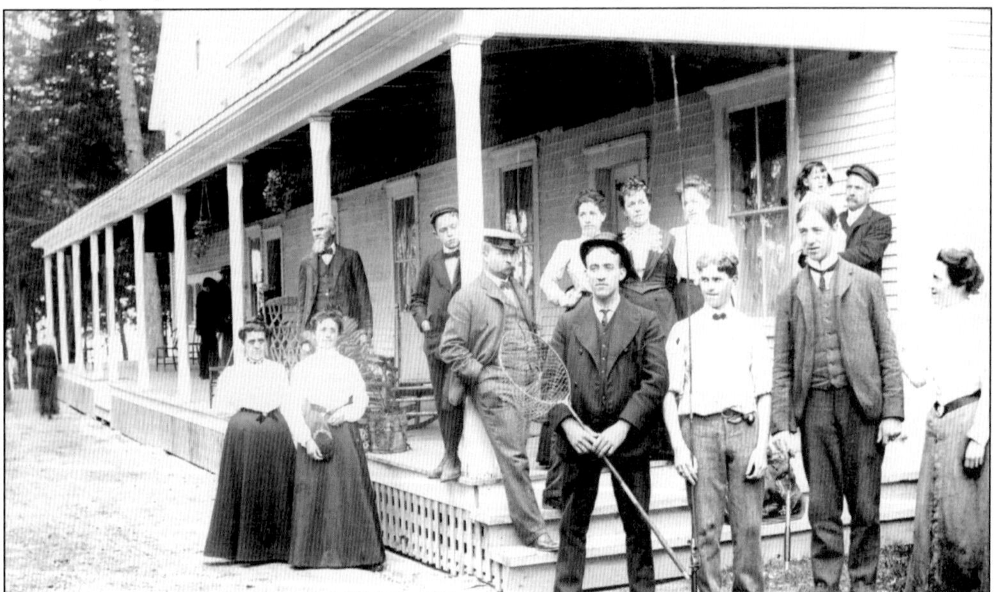

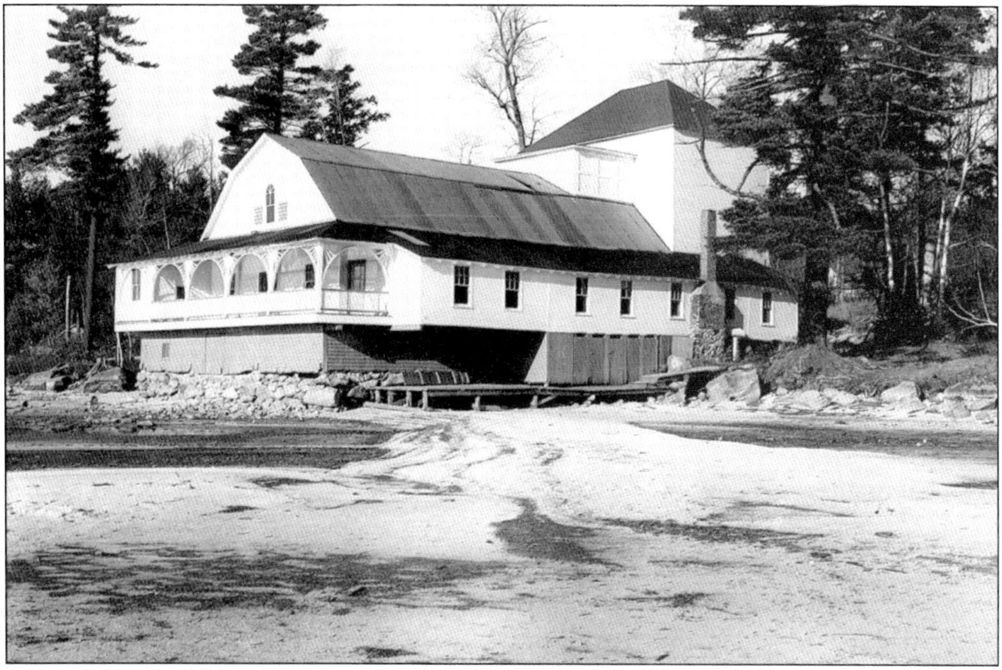

The casino was a highlight of Blodgett's Landing's attractions and a destination for area residents looking for entertainment. Situated across from the hotel, the casino hosted musicals, dances, and plays. During the 1920s, silent movies were a hit and could be enjoyed for the admission price of a nickel. One resident remembers seeing "first-rate theater productions from New York." Noted entertainer Will Cressy was a repeat performer and became a devotee of the area. He and his wife Blanche Dayne bought the island across from the landing in 1900 and hosted many theater celebrities during the season. (Above, Sally Kassman; below, Newbury Historical Society.)

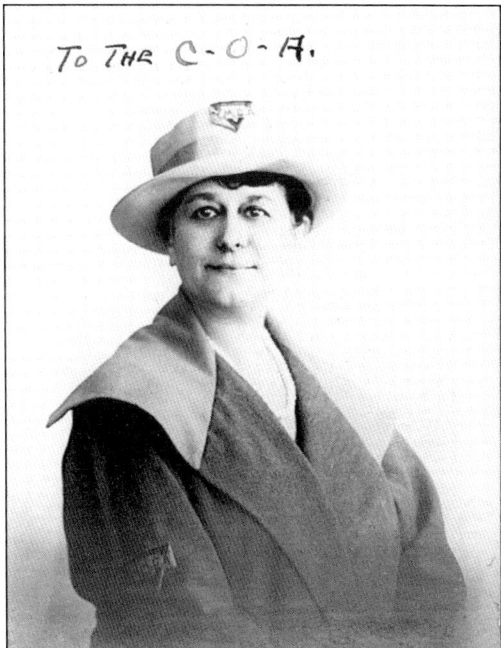

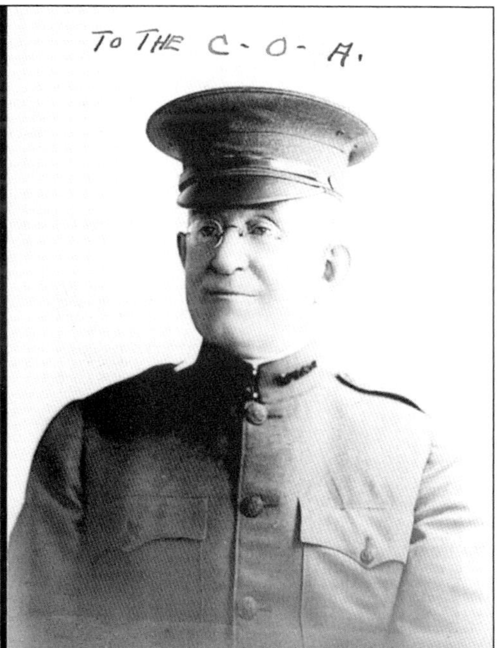

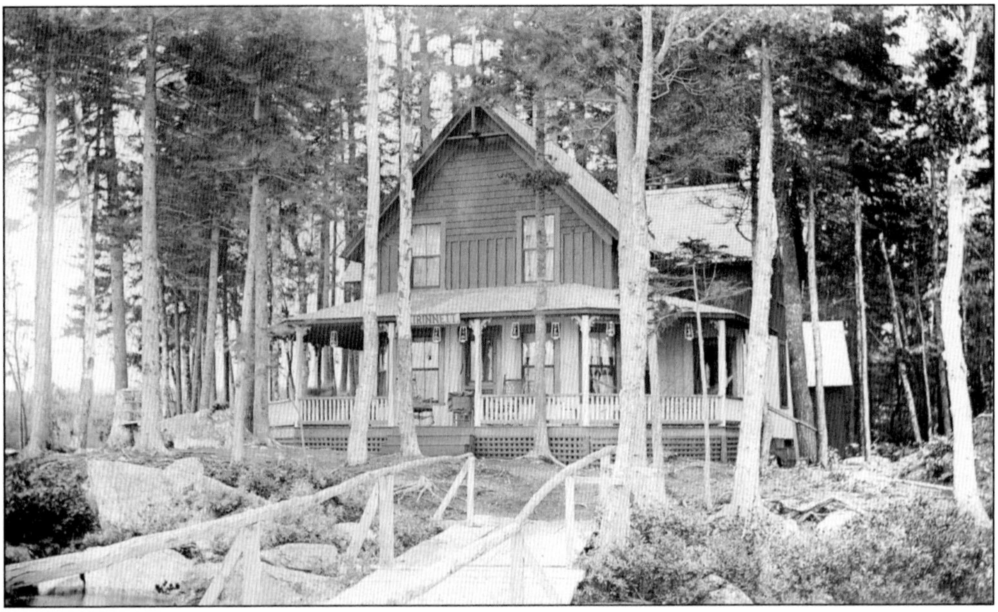

Will Cressy's cottage is seen here in the summer of 1897. The island on which it was built was at one time connected to Bowles Road by a boardwalk. The island is still accessible via Bowles Road, and while the house has had several reincarnations, the site is still known as Cressy Point. (John Hutchinson.)

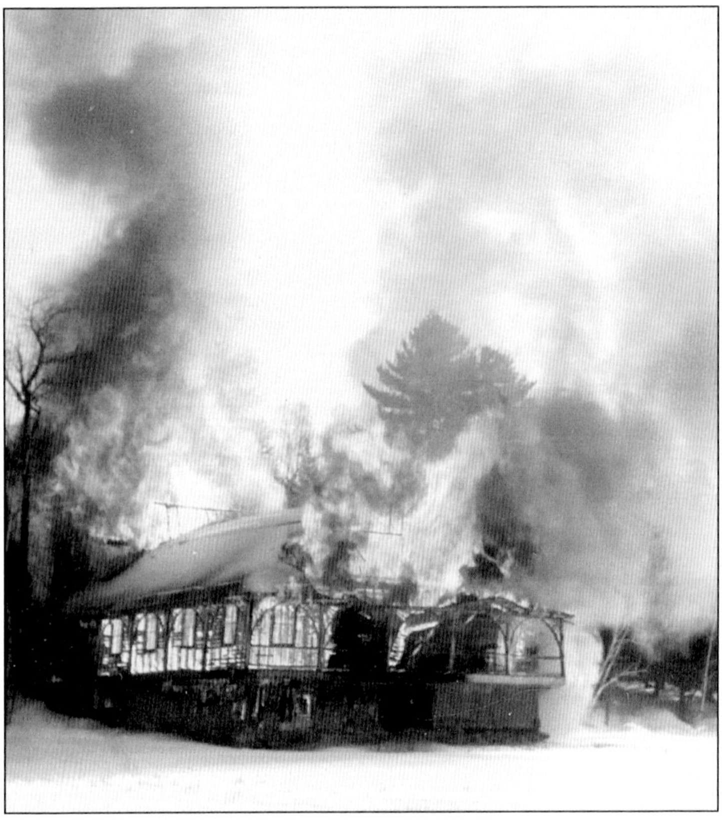

As the automobile replaced the era of rail and steamboat travelers, the number of summer visitors declined and local entertainment spots like Blodgett's casino lost audiences to dance halls and movie houses. Despite efforts of the Cottage Owners' Association to preserve the building, it fell victim to decay and vandalism. It was burned in 1978 by the Newbury Fire Department, which used the occasion as a training exercise. (Newbury Historical Society.)

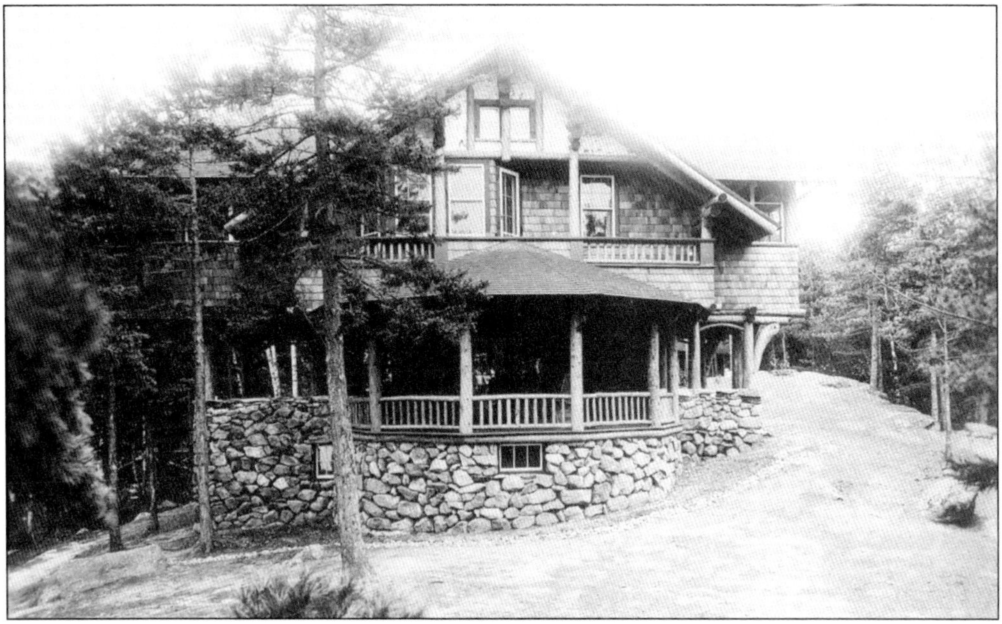

Around 1910, Henry Bowles, future congressman, purchased more than 300 acres of land running south on Lake Sunapee's shore and east to Chalk Pond. He and his wife Edna moved into their house in 1912. He was a highly successful self-made man, was generous with his time and money, and led a group at Blodgett's Landing that bought the hotel and park and deeded them to the Cottage Owners' Association for future public use. (Digilio family.)

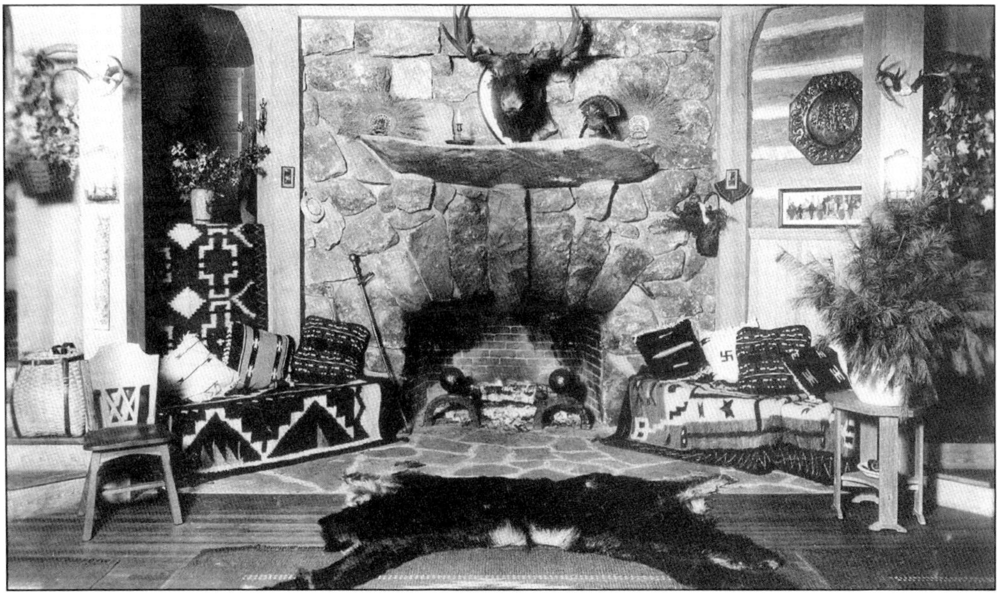

The Bowles "cottage" was built in the rustic Adirondack style on a grand scale with all the conveniences of the day. Granite for the huge double fireplaces built by the Digilio brothers came from the site. The kitchen had a restaurant-capacity stove; the dining room featured a canopied ceiling of inlaid wood and a double fireplace shared with the living room. The great room, seen here, had a beamed ceiling, long built-in window seats, and numerous hunting trophies. (Digilio family.)

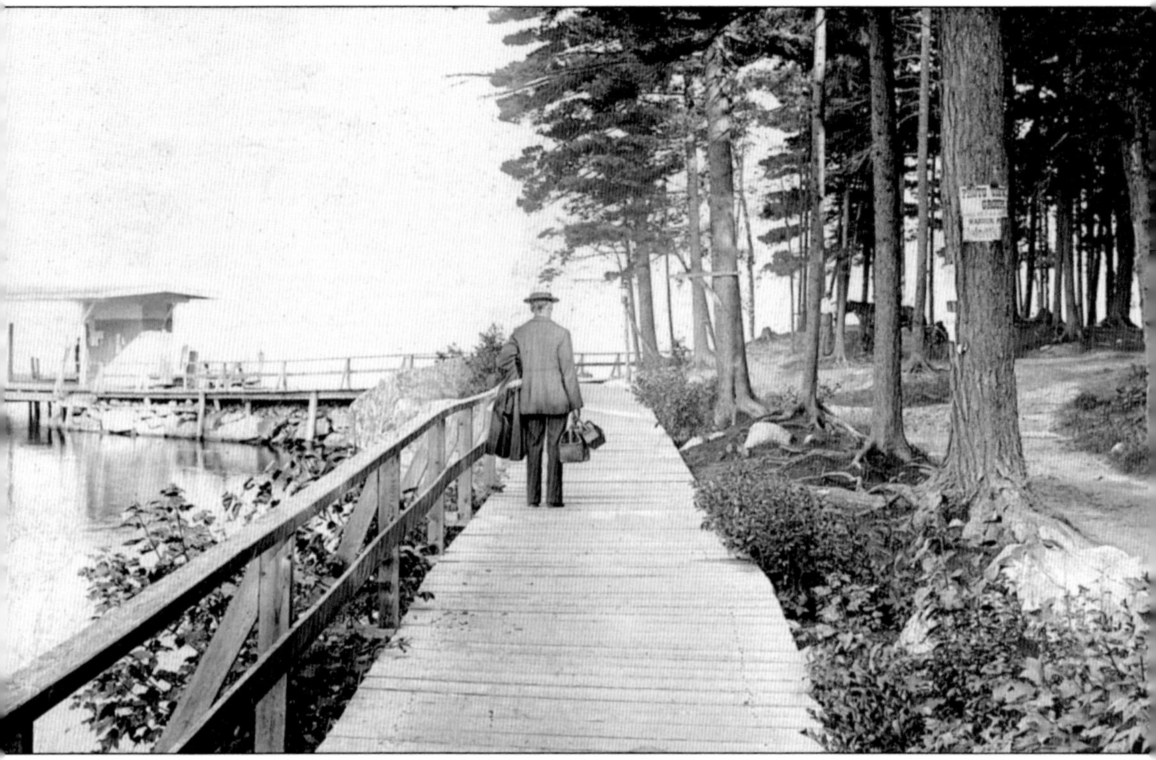

At day's end or summer's end, it is not easy to leave a place of such beauty and tranquility. Here a departing traveler is frozen in time on the boardwalk, waiting for the steamer and a whole era to quietly slip away. (Digilio family.)

Seven

On the Road

The automobile signaled the end of an era for the railroads, steamboats, and ultimately Lake Sunapee's grand hotels. The railroads were in decline by the 1890s, and the branch line serving Newbury discontinued passenger service in the 1950s. In 1964, the track between Bradford and Newbury was taken up. Steamboat operations on Lake Sunapee ceased even sooner—the last in operation was the *Kearsarge*, ending service in 1933.

The end of one era opened the way for the next. The automobile carried a new type of tourist to the area and spurred new business ventures. Visitors were still drawn by Newbury's undisturbed beauty, but the pace of life became a little faster. People were on the go and did not have the entire summer to enjoy the amenities of the grand hotels. They preferred campsites and cottages, along with the means to fill their appetites and those of their cars. Newbury responded.

The venerable Cilley Tavern took on a new life. By 1926, Charles Dicey had put it to use as a garage. After World War II, the LaPorte family added two open garage bays to the former first floor. Texaco gas was dispensed, and Richard LaPorte operated a Sonoco gas station across the intersection. Cottages sprang up adjacent to the tavern on the Frost Top road and Olive J. Lear dispensed ice cream at her Why Not store. At the harbor, the Lake Sunapee Trading Post and a marina opened their doors.

Cottages and cabins met the demand for accommodations—comfortable, rustic, and situated to take full advantage of the natural attractions. Davis Cabins and Wild Goose Lodges, built on the site of the old Lake Sunapee steamboat landing, offered lodging by the night, the week, or the season. These two side-by-side sites began operations during the 1930s and had dining facilities, a gift store, and a pavilion where dancing and indoor roller-skating were popular. Even today, Davis Cabins continues to draw a faithful clientele.

New and improved roads carried tourists to the lake and mountain where they could stretch their legs with a hike over mountain trails, a refreshing swim, or a run on the ski slopes. With automobiles, this could be done in a day and could be repeated at will. Many visitors extended their stays into permanent residency, swelling Newbury's population.

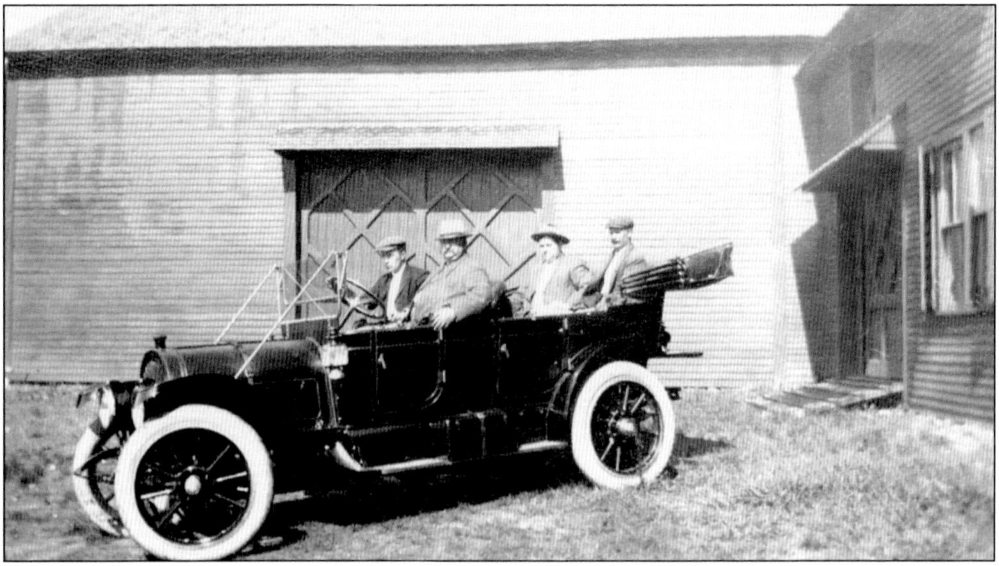

When the automobile made its early appearances in Newbury, few realized the profound impact it would have on this peaceful rural town. For Mark Shultis (second from left) and his companions, it was a vehicle for pleasure and for moving his produce more quickly to local markets. (Sally Harris.)

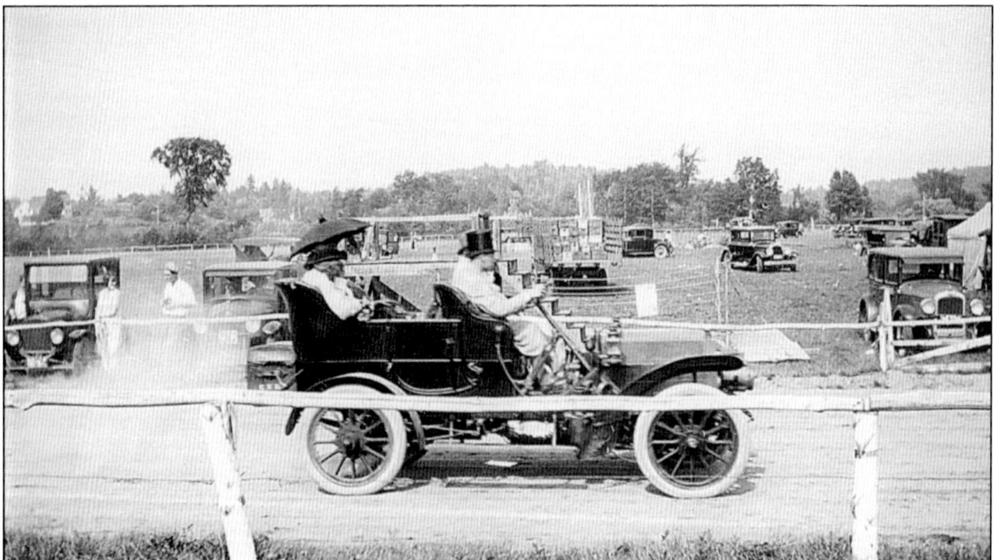

Attendance during the 1920s at the Bradford-Newbury annual fair swelled as people arrived by car from far afield. The event also provided an opportunity for attendees to look over the latest automotive features and motoring finery. (Bradford Historical Society.)

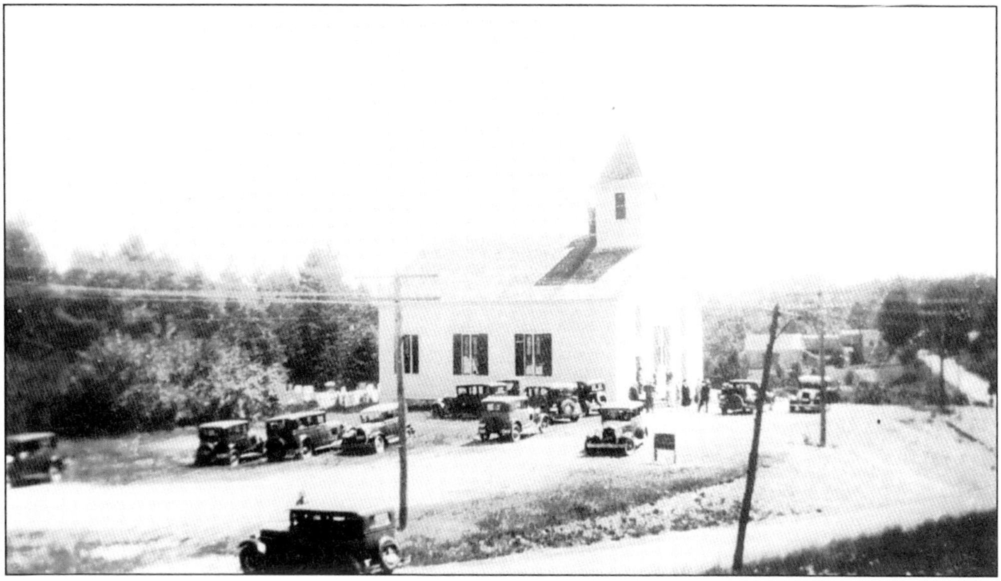

Parking was a casual affair in the early days of the automobile. Here at the South Newbury Union Church, many used the empty field between the church and the schoolhouse (later the Friendship House). Early roads were often not wide enough to allow for parking along their sides. (Elizabeth Folsom.)

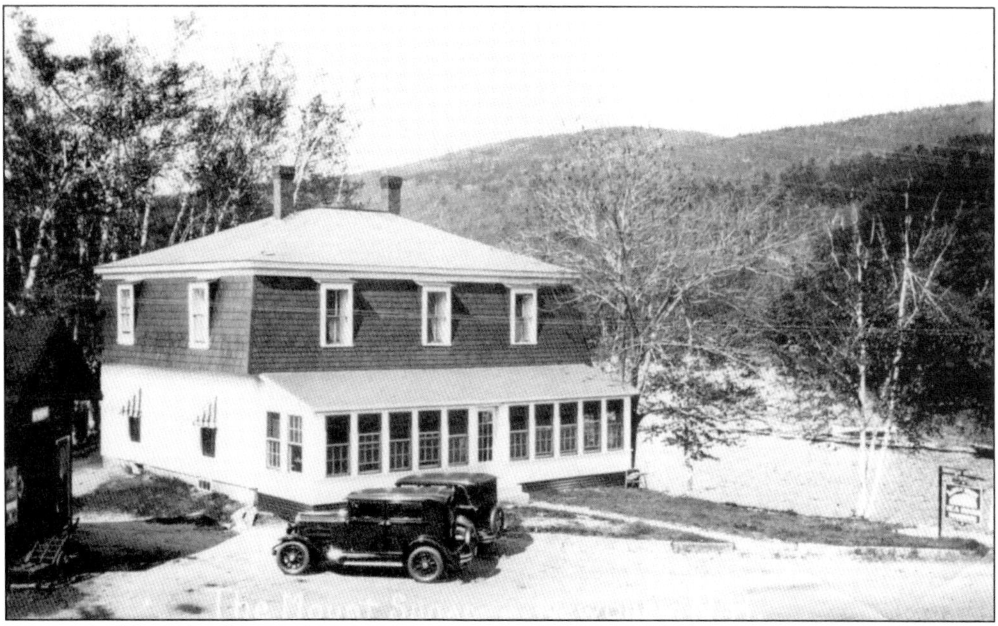

Guest- and boardinghouses became increasingly popular for visitors on the move. With the demise of the steamboats and the decline of the grand hotels, motorists cruised the area to seek out accommodations along the lake. In Newbury harbor, the Durgin House, adjacent to the train station, enjoyed a brisk business. Statesman John Hay stayed here while work was being done on his summer home, the Fells. (John Hutchinson.)

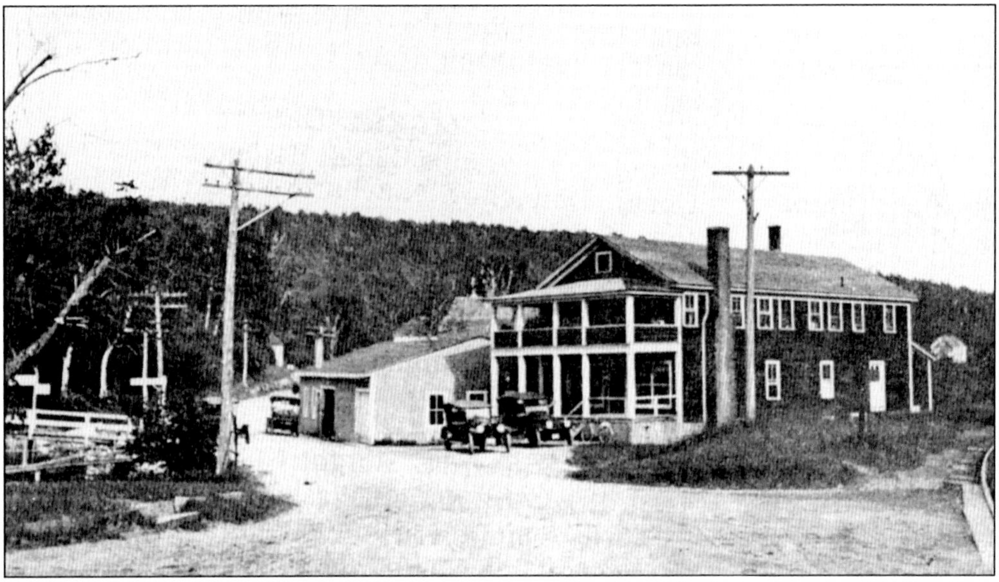

Businesses catering to passing tourists sprang up along the lake. The Lake Sunapee Trading Post at Newbury harbor featured gas pumps, snacks, and refreshments, including a soda fountain. The building underwent renovations over the years to attract tourists and serve residents with the latest amenities. The photograph above was taken in the 1920s. The photograph below reflects 30 years of changes: removal of the porches, enlarged display windows, modern gas pumps, and a fresh coat of paint. (Above, Town of Newbury; below, William Weiler.)

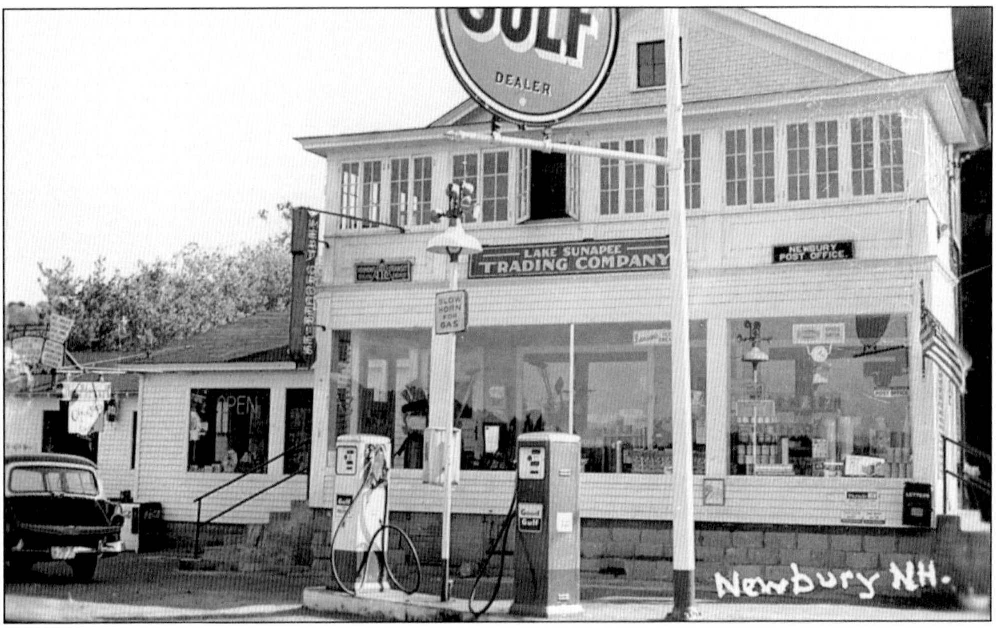

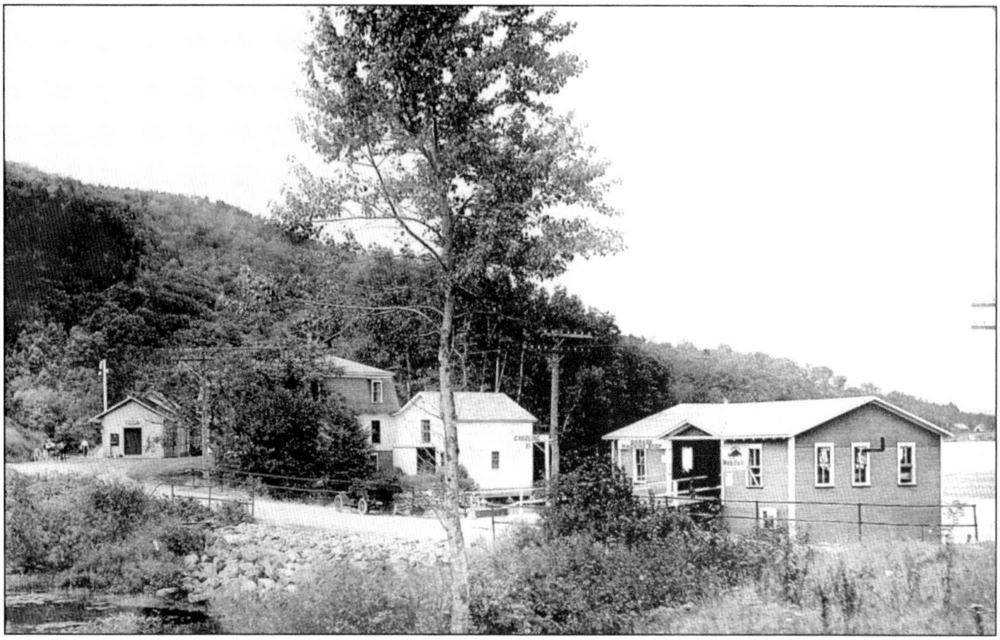

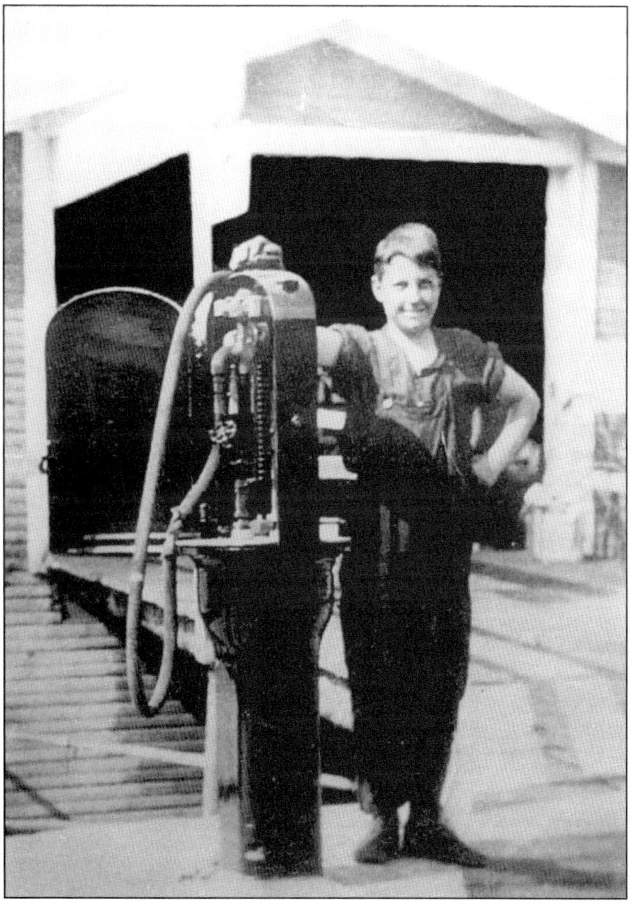

A dual enterprise was located at Newbury harbor on the site of the present town dock. This repair shop, catering to automobile traffic on the land entrance and to motorboat traffic at the lake entrance, offered mechanical repairs to motors of just about any sort. Young Earl Rowe, manning an early gas pump on the land side of the shop, looks happy to "fill 'er up." (Above, John Hutchinson; right, Newbury Public Library.)

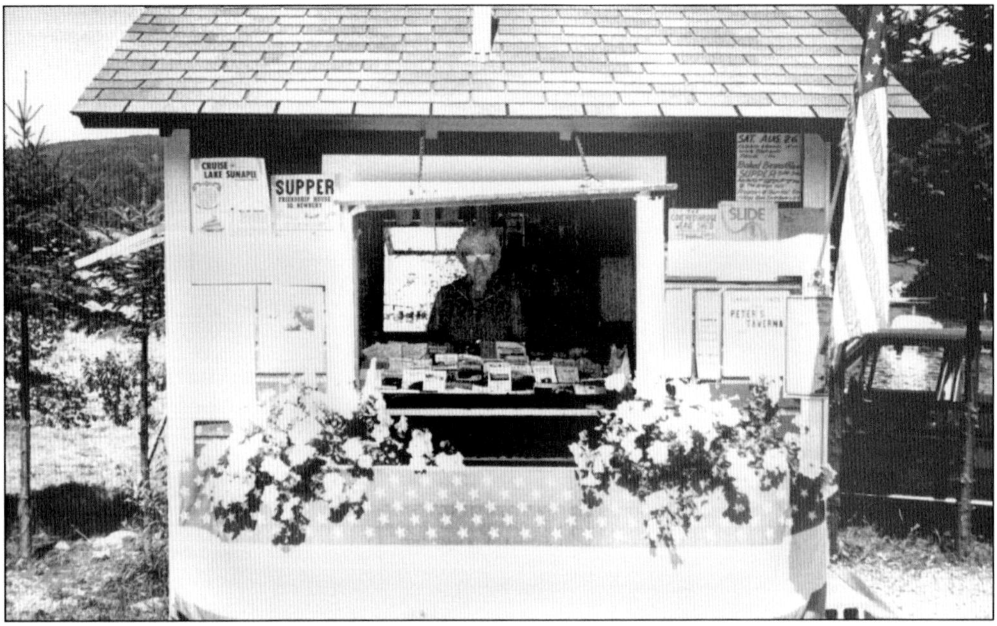

Newbury's information booth is all decked out to greet Independence Day motorists, answer their questions, and provide helpful information. In addition to a friendly welcome, visitors could find out about local happenings, hiking trails, and dining and lodging recommendations. Many took the opportunity to stretch their legs and admire the lake and mountain views. (Wayne and Judy LaPorte.)

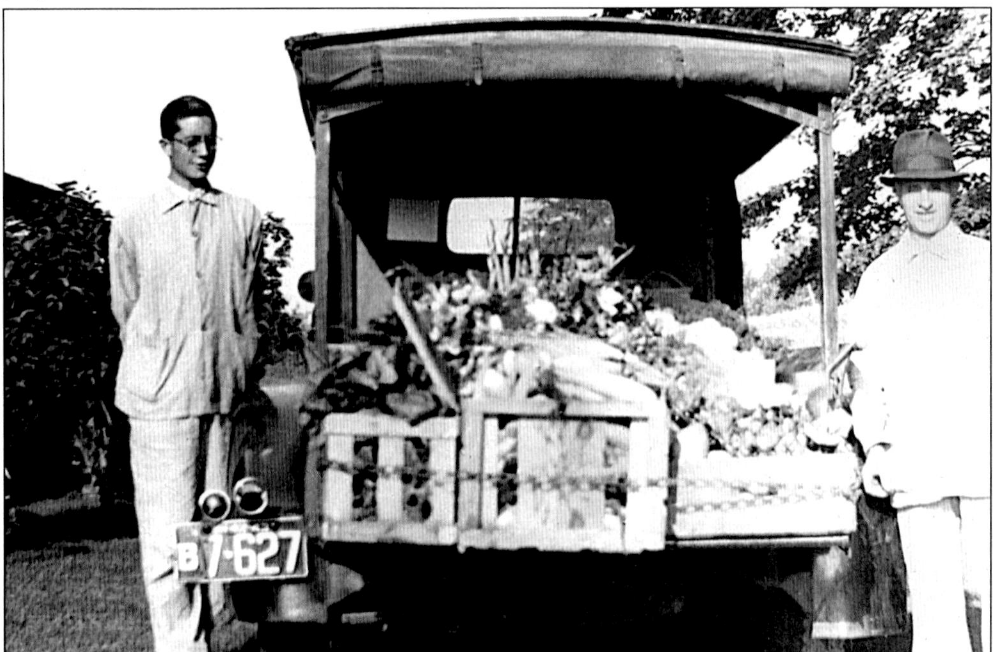

Local farmers were able to bring fresher produce more quickly to their customers with the help of motorized vehicles. Here Carl and Dominic Digilio get ready to make the rounds with their abundant produce around 1940. (Digilio family.)

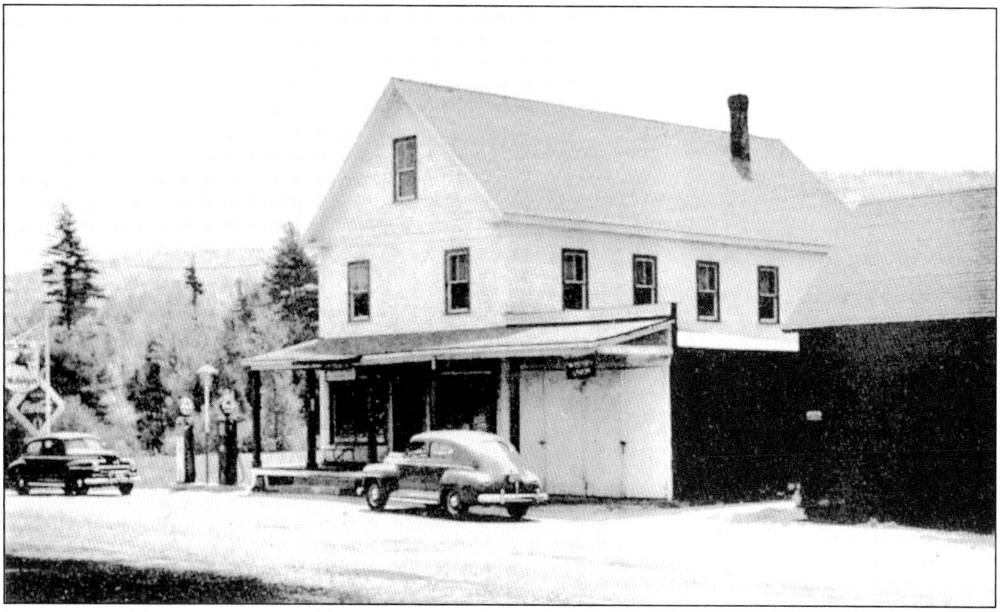

The Mount Sunapee store, still operating today, is located at the base of the mountain at the present-day traffic circle. For passersby, it offered gasoline and refreshments, and for residents, it had the added attraction of housing the local post office. (John Hutchinson.)

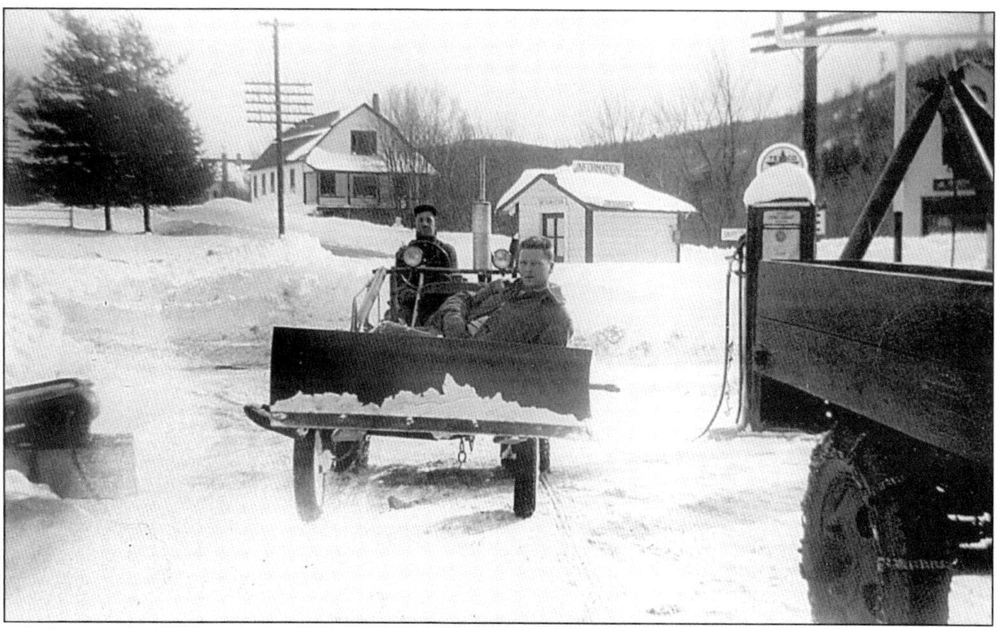

By the 1940s, the highway crew's work had changed drastically. Motorized equipment offered tremendous advantages for road maintenance and for removing snow. Gone were the snow rollers—roads had to be cleared to allow for the passage of vehicles. Pictured here are Wayne LaPorte and Paul Berglund working at the intersection of Routes 103 and 103A in 1949. (Wayne and Judy LaPorte.)

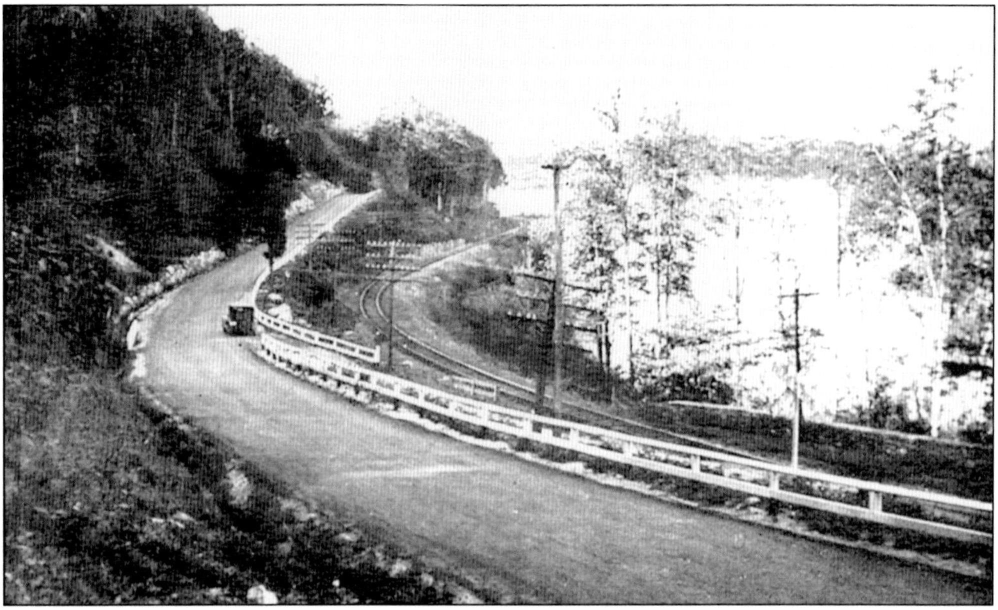

Seen here in 1935, Route 103, heading north toward Newport, parallels the railroad tracks and offers wide views of Lake Sunapee. While the town worked to upgrade local roads, the state devoted efforts to improving routes to accommodate the growing number of travelers from afar. (Tracy Messer.)

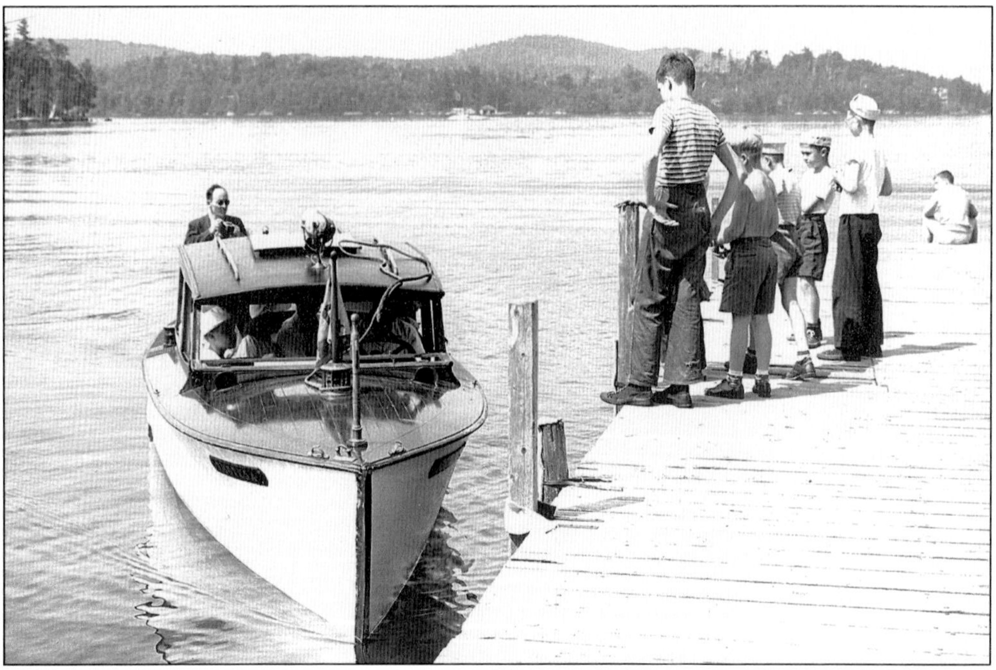

A group eagerly awaits the arrival of the mail boat *Fortuna* as it makes a stop at Blodgett's Landing. Mail to summer residents was supplied by boat since the days of the great steamers, which picked up packets from the Newbury depot and delivered them with passengers around the lake. The motor craft that replaced the steamboats were able to make the rounds faster and more frequently. (John Greenwood.)

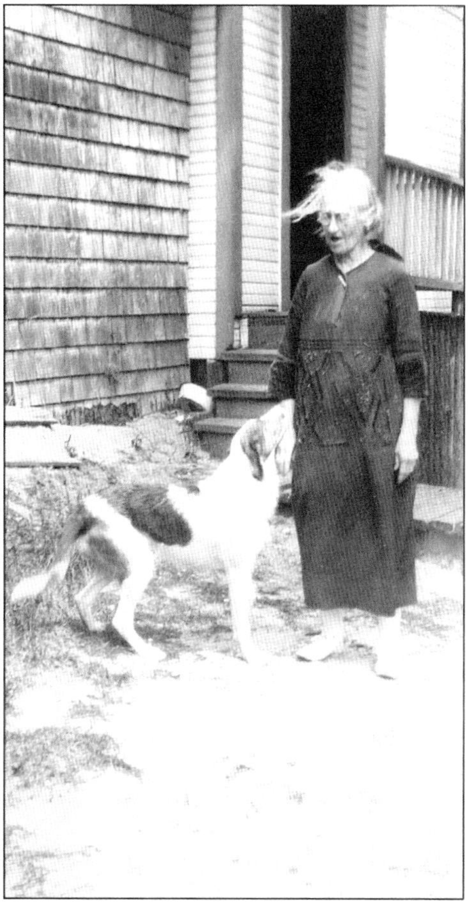

Davis Cabins, located on the site of the old Lake Station steamboat landing, has been welcoming guests for nearly 80 years and continues to do so today. This family business began when Mindwell Davis (right) opened a small store and rented out rooms at her lakeside home. Her son, Everett (next page), former stationmaster at Lake Station, began building cabins (below) on an adjoining hillside in 1933. He expanded the operation in 1941, after buying abutting railroad property, and added rustic cabins until 1956, reaching a total of 16, 10 of which had housekeeping amenities. (Davis Cabins.)

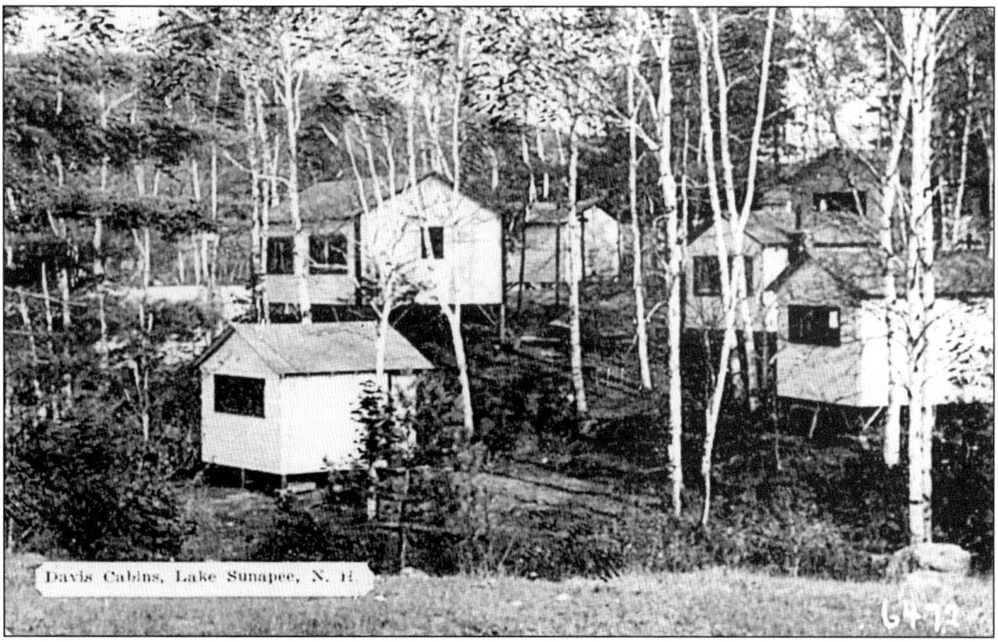

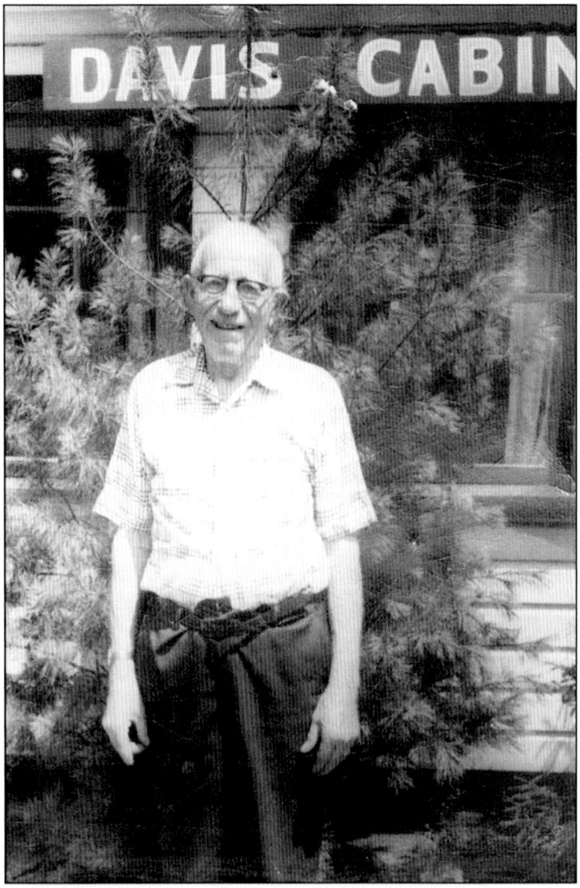

The Davis Cabins complex included a main house with dining room and deck, a laundry, a workshop, and a boathouse with boats for rent and an open porch for taking in the view on the second floor. In the early days, railroad tracks leading into the lake held a cradle and cable that was attached to the workshop and was used to pull steamboats up onto land for winter storage. The *Kearsarge* spent several winters here, as did the MV *Mt. Sunapee* (shown here around 1950). Everett Davis's daughter Florence had a gift shop in the present-day office and library. Another daughter, Muriel Guild, was a longtime manager who welcomed returning families year after year. (Davis Cabins.)

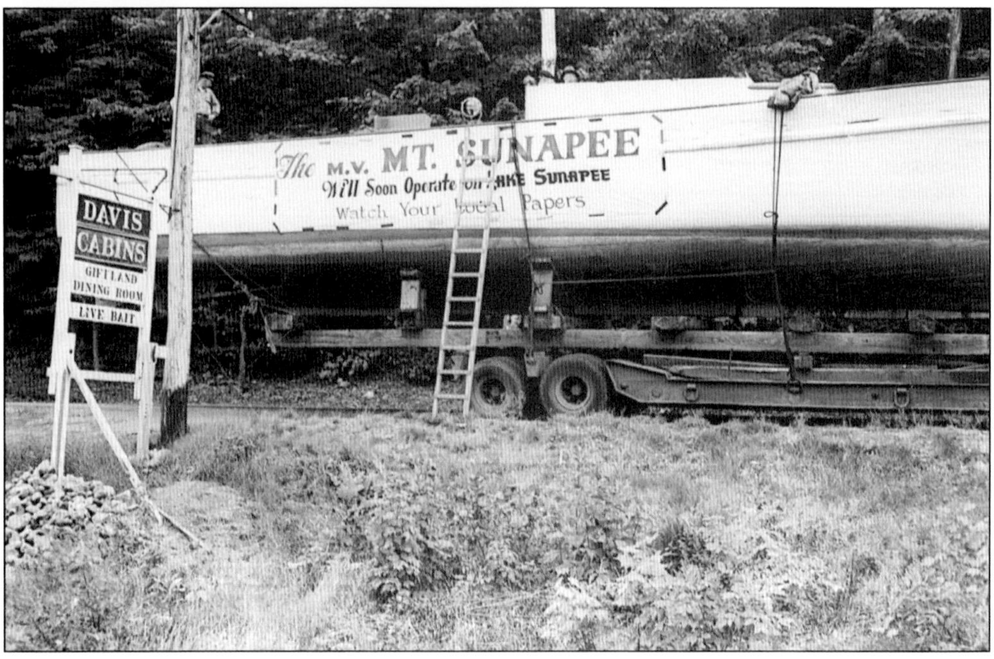

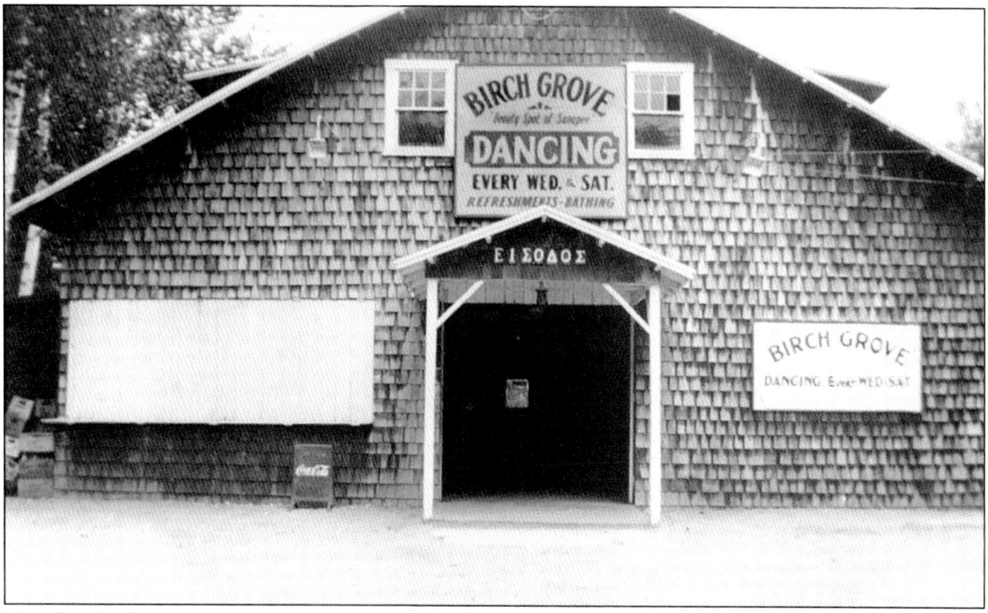

The Birch Grove, adjacent to the Davis Cabins, was a popular destination in the 1930s and early 1940s. The dance hall hosted outstanding bands from as far away as Boston and was also used for roller-skating. A long open porch on the lake side offered cooling breezes. In the mid-1940s, William Slater Jr., a son-in-law of Everett Davis, purchased the pavilion and had it carefully demolished, using the timber to help construct Wild Goose, which had 10 cabins and a recreation hall with lunch counter. A cottage formerly used by visiting bands was moved to the entrance area shared with Davis Cabins and became headquarters for the owners. Subsequent owners made changes, adding a motel and updating and winterizing cabins. Today the cabins are gone, and the land is owned by the State of New Hampshire. (Above, Katheryn Holmes; below, William Weiler.)

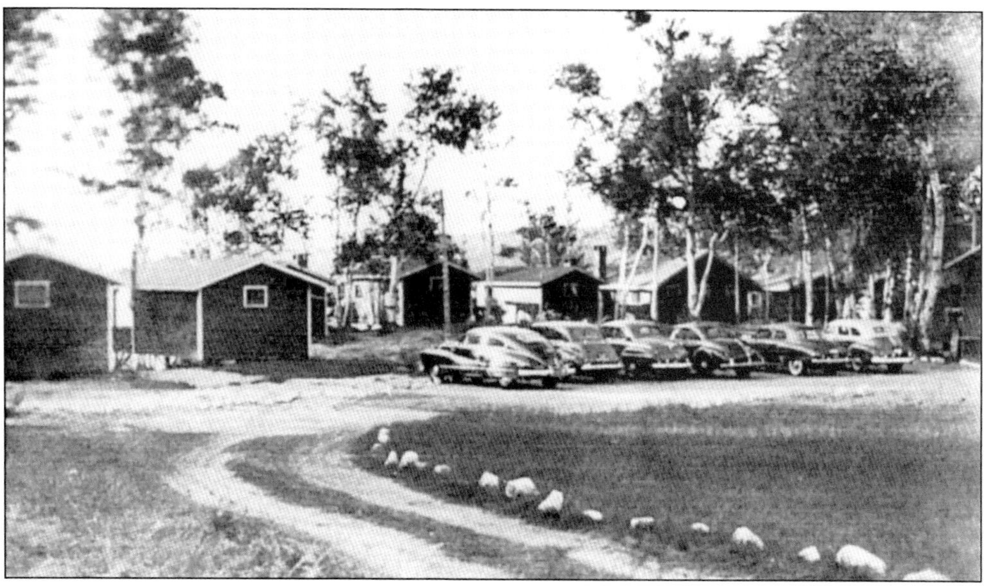

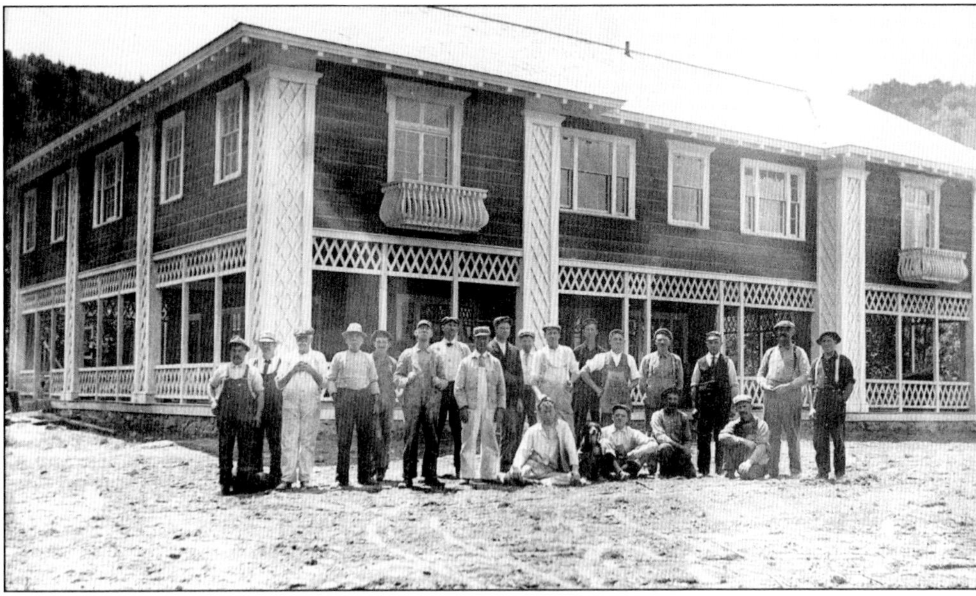

Lakewood Manor was the private estate of Col. Frederick G. King, a manufacturer from Boston. It boasted elaborate walkways, gardens, lake views, and a protected boathouse that stands today. On King's death, the Earl Abbe family bought the property and opened a hotel, which enjoyed popularity until World War II, when tourism took a backseat to the war effort. The Abbe family sold to William Glynn, who reopened the establishment as Lakewood Manor Lodge and Cabins in the early 1950s. He advertised motorboat trips, fishing, parties, square dancing, and magic shows. He also turned several outbuildings into motel-type units. After 1960, the property underwent additional ownerships until the 1970s, when the estate was torn down to make way for individual lots. Shown here is the estate at the time of construction, about 1910, and the beautifully detailed common room. (Above, Newbury Historical Society; below, William Weiler.)

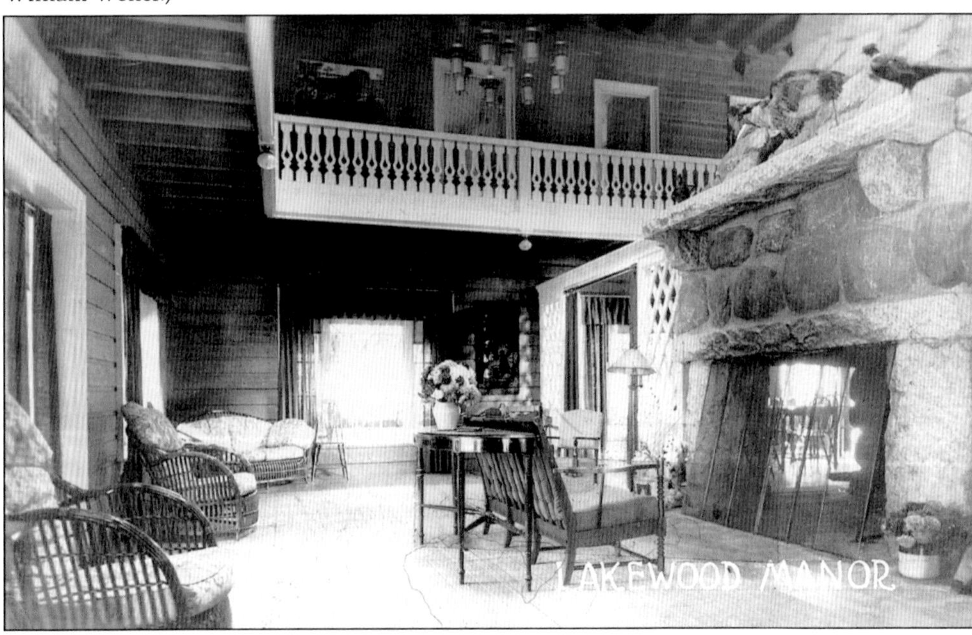

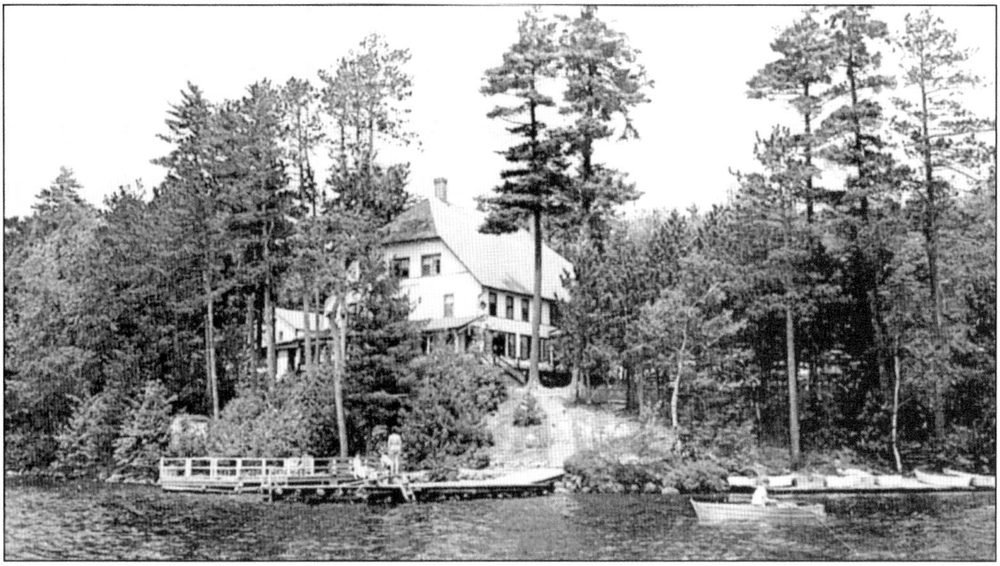

Pine Cliff Inn on the easterly side of Lake Sunapee had its heyday as a summer retreat during the steamship era, and it served tourists under the name Maxner's Hotel until the end of World War II. Pine Cliff Inn was formerly the home of Armenia White, benefactress to the Woodsum brothers, who named their flagship in her honor. Early summer residents at the Pine Cliff colony were from prominent Concord families, closely allied by birth and social standing. A group of residents is seen waiting for the daily mail boat delivery. (Above, William Weiler; below, Newbury Historical Society.)

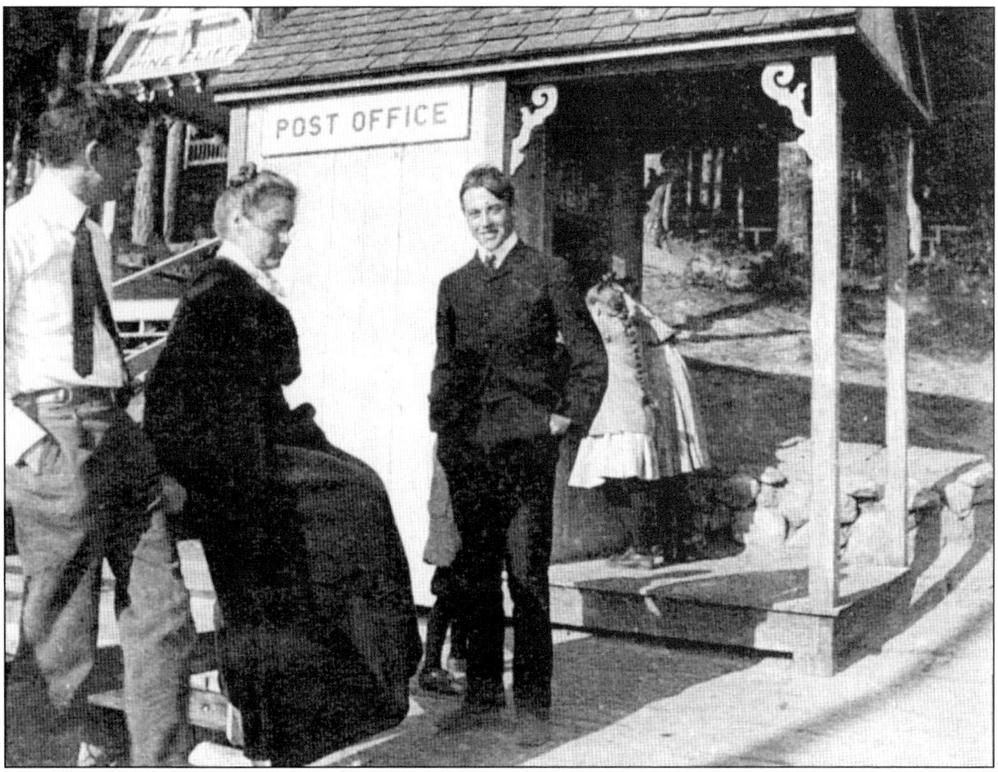

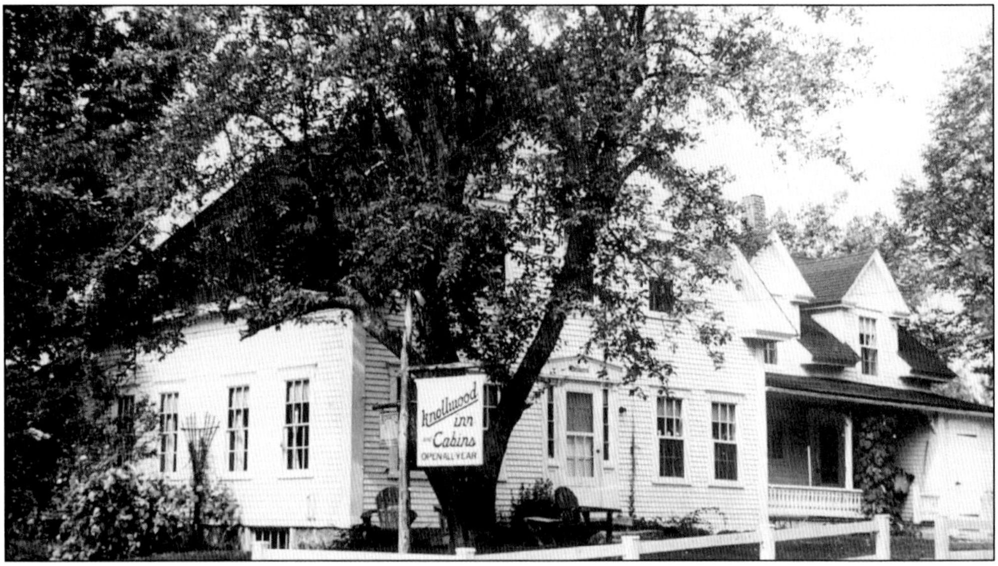

The Knollwood Inn on Route 103A boasted 350 feet of lakefront and 100 acres of fields and woods. Built on land that belonged to Moses Ring and his descendants, it passed through several hands during the 1940s and 1950s. Frank and Janet Yager purchased it in 1965 and continued the tourist business started by the Butterfields, operating the inn and adjoining cabins and cottages. The inn was demolished in the 1990s to make way for the Bly Hill Landing development. (Maureen Rosen.)

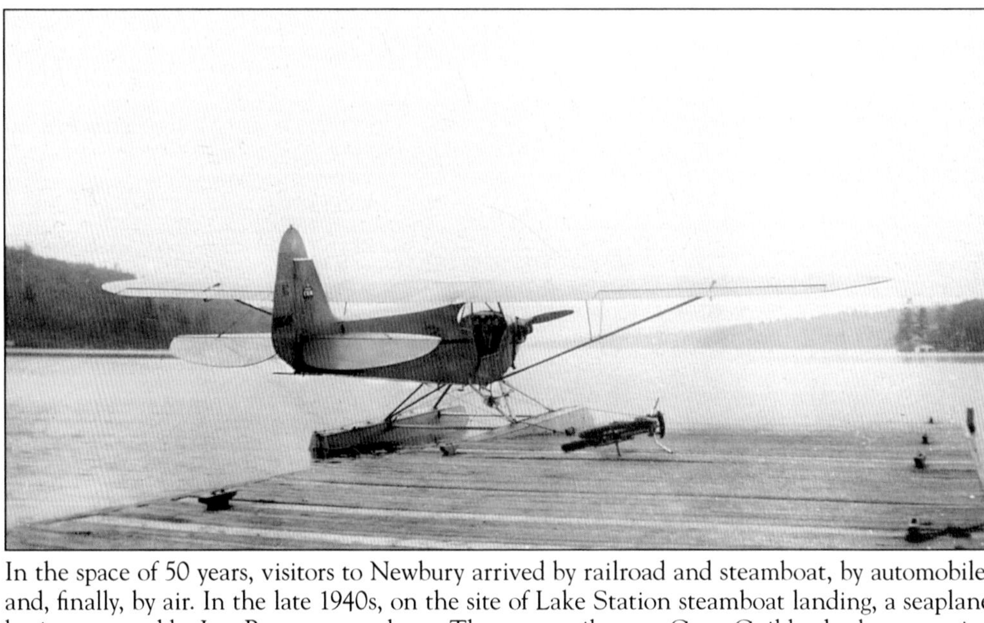

In the space of 50 years, visitors to Newbury arrived by railroad and steamboat, by automobile, and, finally, by air. In the late 1940s, on the site of Lake Station steamboat landing, a seaplane business owned by Lee Bowman was born. The young pilot was Gene Guild, who later married Muriel Davis of Davis Cabins. Guild ran a charter service from that location for several years. (Wayne and Judy LaPorte.)

Eight

SERVING NEWBURY'S CITIZENS

Ever since Zephaniah Clark posted notice of the first town meeting to be held at the home of Charles Emerson on January 18, 1779, resident involvement in town government has been at the heart of Newbury's growth and development. At that first meeting, residents were charged with selecting a moderator, town clerk, selectmen, constable, surveyor of highways, and other town officers "that shall be thought proper." Many early settlers served the town in multiple capacities. Some found an affinity for the political scene: Zephaniah Clark served as a state representative in 1786, as did Rev. Timothy Morse, who moved from town selectman and moderator to representative in the legislature from 1816 to 1822.

Although fire was a constant menace to the early residents, they had to rely on family and neighbors to fight blazes. Over the years, there were many devastating property losses. The Newbury Volunteer Fire Department was organized in 1927. Charles Dicey was appointed as the first fire chief, although it was not until 1928 that the town acquired a fire truck. In 1928, Thomas Leach Jr. donated land for construction of a firehouse. Early fire chiefs included Charles Brockway, Shirley Powers, Moses Bly, and George Croteau. A small auxiliary firehouse was built at Blodgett's Landing around 1945.

Law and order were also concerns of the Fishersfield settlers. Reeves were appointed to round up errant hogs, while constables and sheriffs addressed lawlessness among the population. Town-appointed constables upheld the law in Newbury through the 1930s. In 1940, Ralph Shaw was named police chief, followed by Reginald LaPorte, Richard LaPorte, and William Pomeroy. In 1958, Arthur Jones was appointed police chief, and held that position until 1980.

In the face of rapid growth, townspeople agreed that Newbury should retain its rural character. Protection of its natural resources—lake, mountain, and forests—was also a concern. A planning board was formed in 1969, led by Alice Lynn. By 1970, zoning and building regulations were in place. Richard Wright chaired the first conservation commission established in 1969 to monitor land use and environmental quality. Arthur Larson was named historical society chairman, devoted to safeguarding Newbury's past. All of these organizations, vital to preserving the town's assets, continue to draw their memberships from dedicated Newbury volunteers.

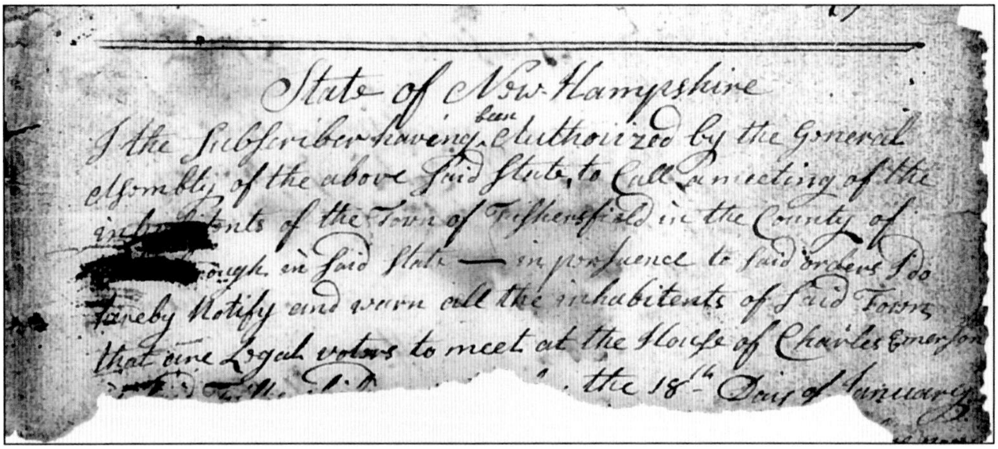

State of New Hampshire
I the Subscriber having been Authorized by the General Assembly of the above said State to Call a meeting of the inhabitents of the Town of Fishersfield in the County of [illegible]rough in said State — in persuance to said orders I do hereby Notify and warn all the inhabitents of said Town that are Legal voters to meet at the House of Charles Emerson [illegible] the 18th Day of January

Zephaniah Clark announced the first town meeting to Fishersfield residents via posted notice, perhaps at the Cilley Tavern, on December 31, 1778. The meeting was called for January 18, 1779, at the home of Charles Emerson, and its purpose was to elect town officers. Minutes of that meeting reveal that Clark was voted moderator and selectman, Jonas Hastings town clerk and selectman, and John Lain selectman. Also elected at that meeting were a constable, highway surveyors, and "all other necessary Town Officers that shall be thought proper." (Town of Newbury.)

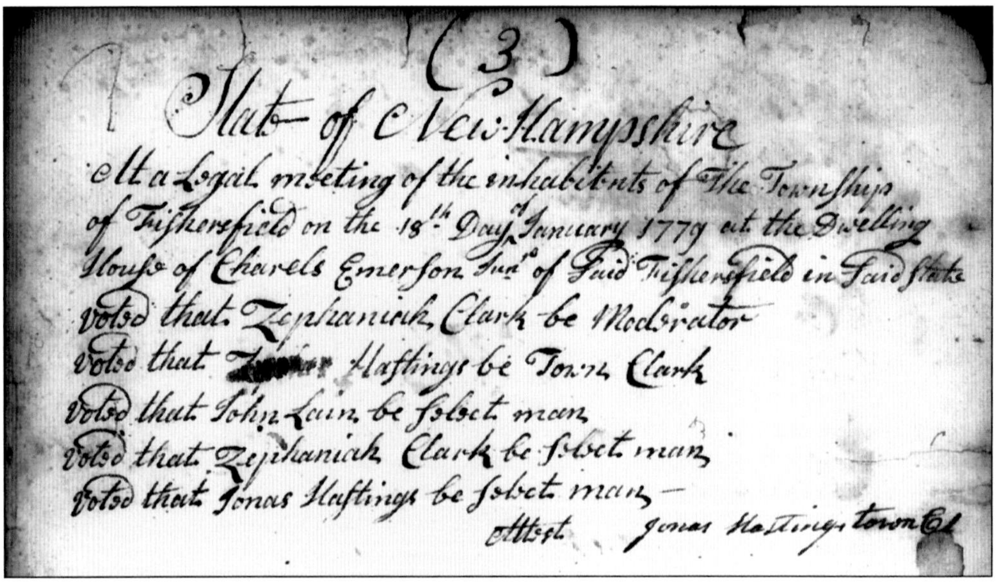

(3)
State of New Hampshire
At a Legal meeting of the inhabitents of the Township of Fishersfield on the 18th Day of January 1779 at the Dwelling House of Charels Emerson Jun. of said Fishersfield in said State
Voted that Zephaniah Clark be Moderator
Voted that [illegible] Hastings be Town Clark
Voted that John Lain be Select man
Voted that Zephaniah Clark be Select man
Voted that Jonas Hastings be Select man —
Attest Jonas Hastings town Cl

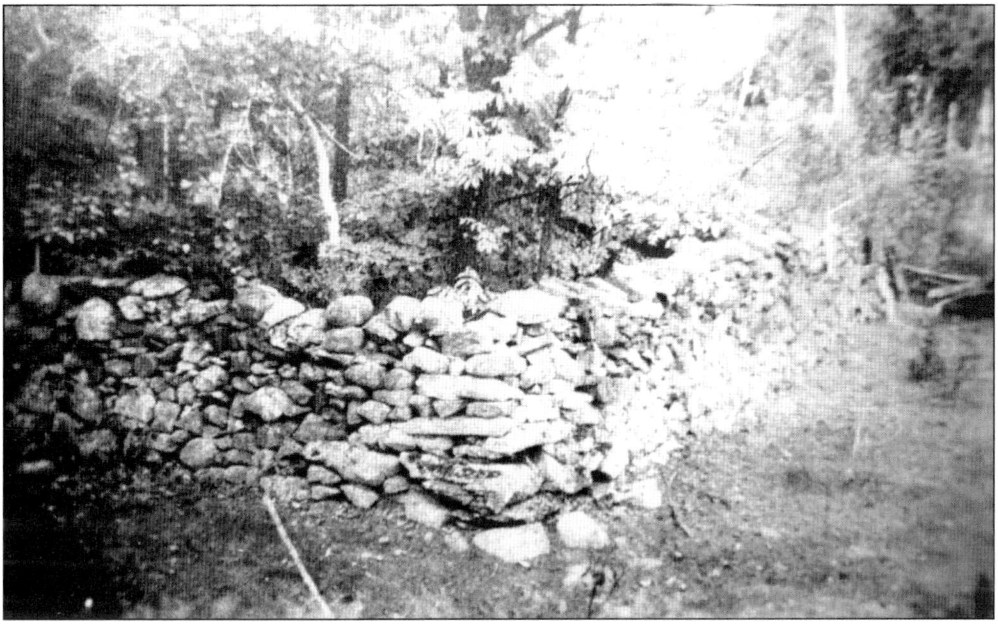

In 1792, an article discussed at town meeting addressed the acceptance and fencing of land provided by Capt. John Burns designated for a pound and burying ground on Bly Hill. William Cross, who lived adjacent to the old meetinghouse, made a bid to the town in 1798 to build the enclosure for corralling wayward animals. The remains of the pound can be seen today, adjacent to the Bly Hill cemetery. (Newbury Public Library.)

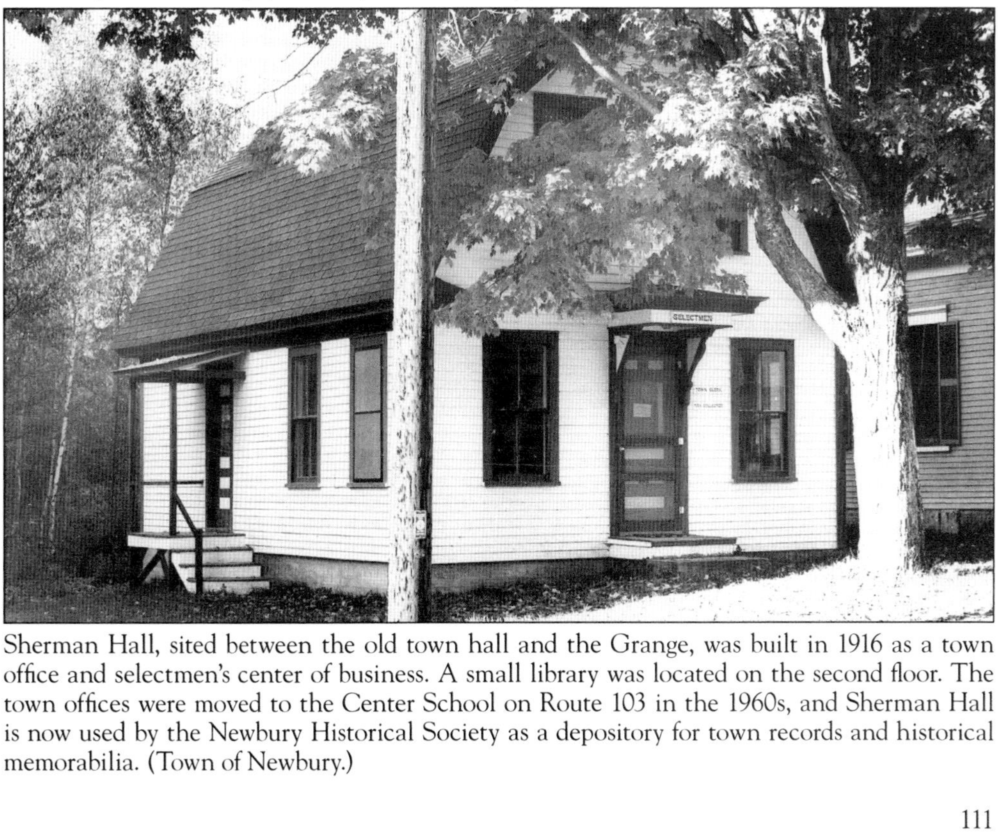

Sherman Hall, sited between the old town hall and the Grange, was built in 1916 as a town office and selectmen's center of business. A small library was located on the second floor. The town offices were moved to the Center School on Route 103 in the 1960s, and Sherman Hall is now used by the Newbury Historical Society as a depository for town records and historical memorabilia. (Town of Newbury.)

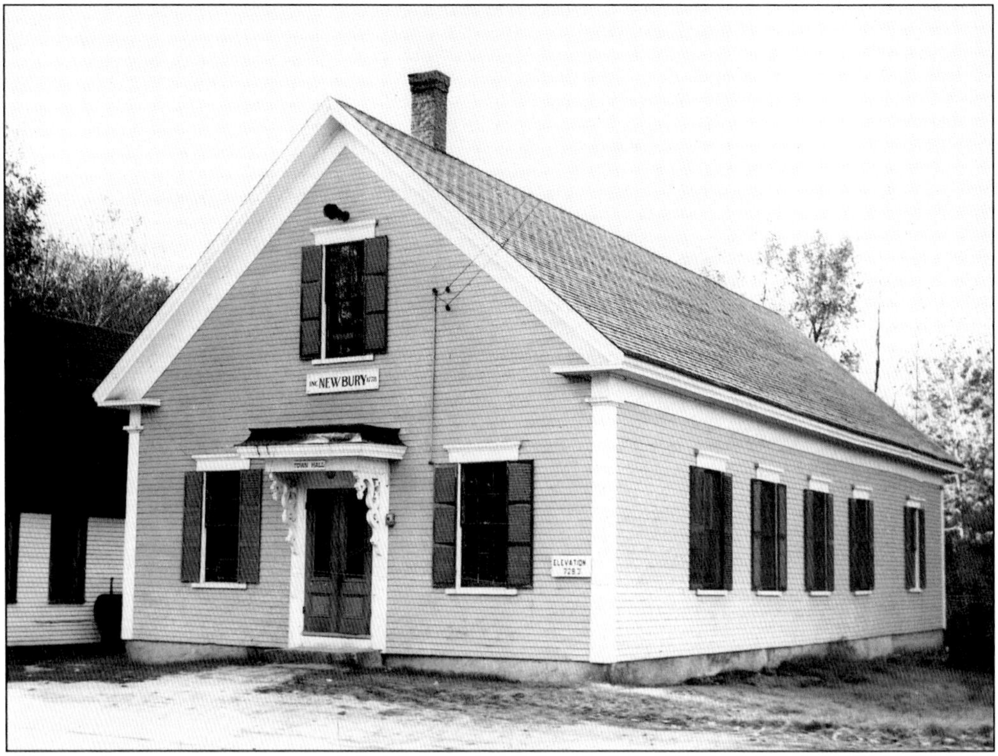

The town hall in South Newbury was built in 1876. It was the center of town activity for many years, hosting the selectmen's meetings and the annual town meeting. The settees, or benches, in this building were made by the Fowler brothers in 1877 and purchased for $150. They are still in use today in several town buildings. (Newbury Historical Society.)

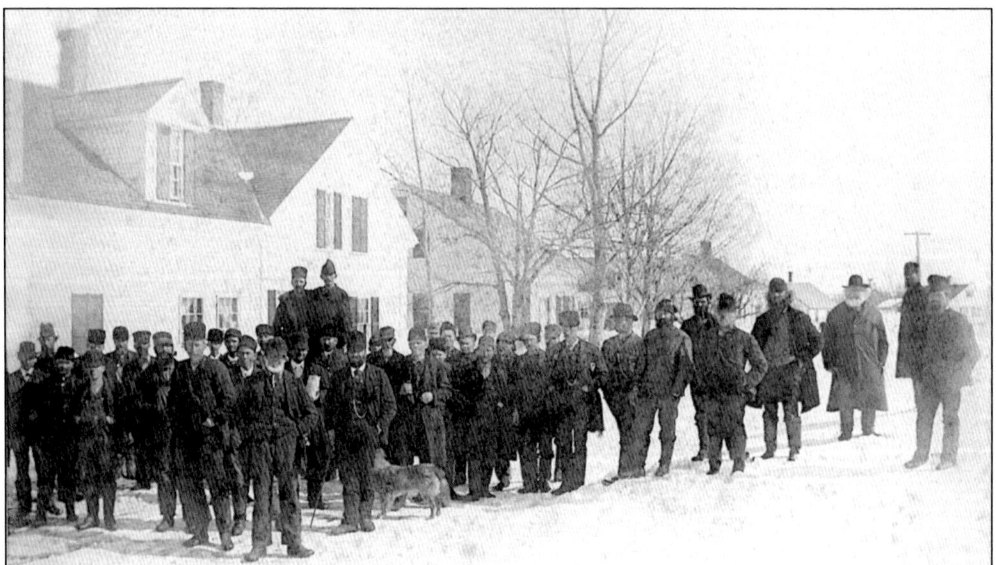

This group of men in South Newbury village has gathered on a snowy March day to attend the annual town meeting. Women were excluded from the privilege of voting on town affairs. (Newbury Historical Society.)

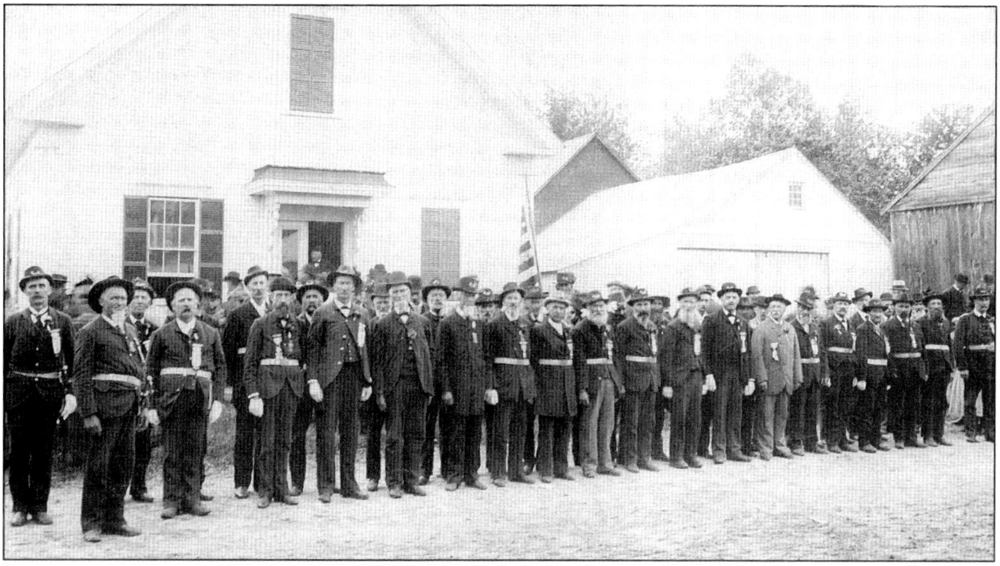

Veterans of the Civil War are gathered for a reunion in front of the South Newbury Town Hall in the late 1880s. Such militia gatherings were common after the war and included parades and exercises as well as socializing. (Steve Hansen.)

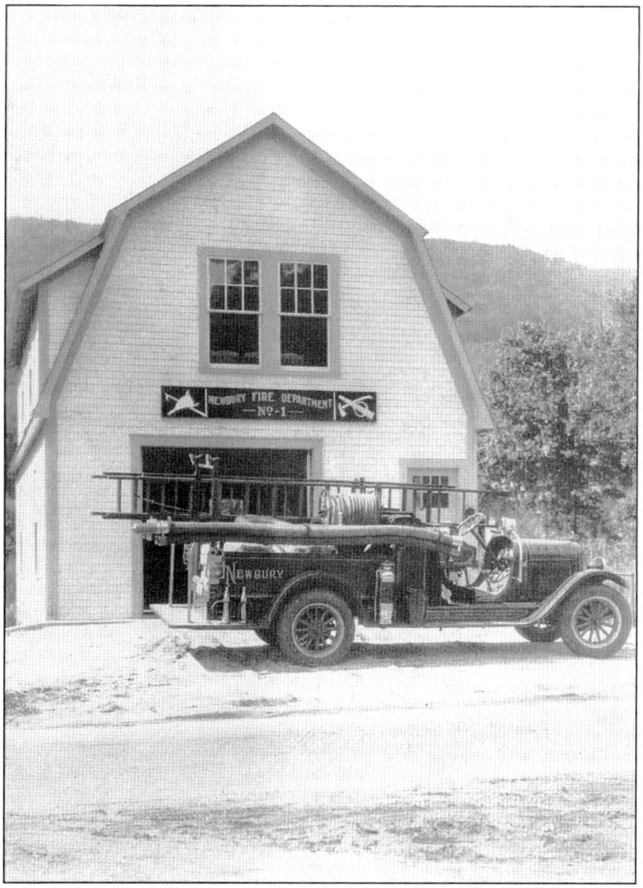

The Newbury Volunteer Fire Department was organized in 1927 with 66 members. The first fire station was built in 1928 at Newbury center, across from the Cilley Tavern (then known as Dicey's Garage). The first fire truck was purchased that year and stored at Dicey's Garage until the station was completed. (Elizabeth Folsom.)

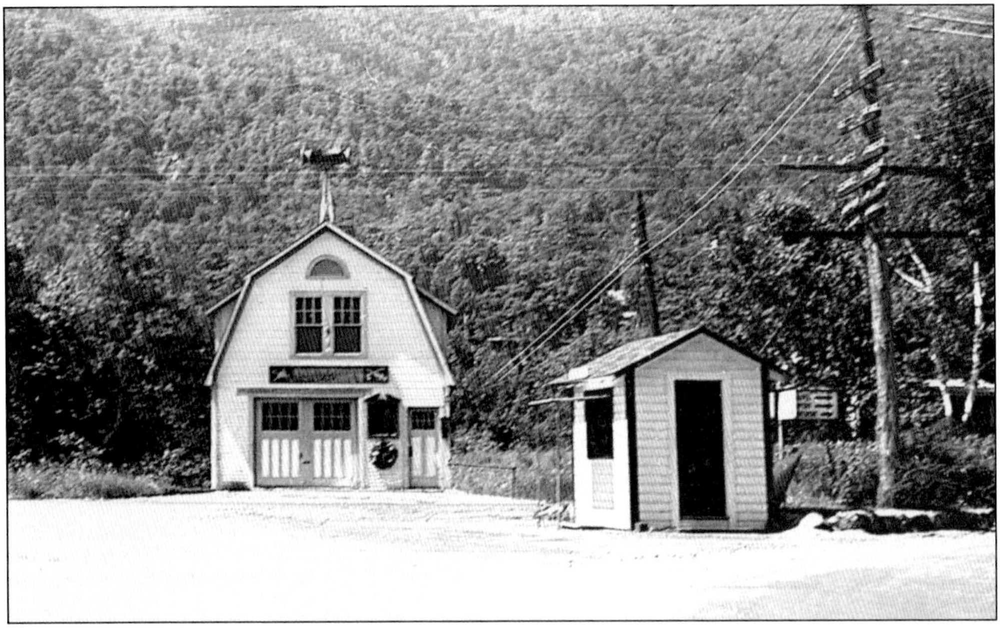

The fire station was enlarged in the 1940s to accommodate new equipment, including a 600-gallon tank truck and portable pumps and accessory equipment. A siren was added to the firehouse, replacing the old alarm system of ringing the meetinghouse bell for emergencies. The building burned in 1984 and was rebuilt and enlarged in 1985 to house both the fire and police departments. (Newbury Historical Society.)

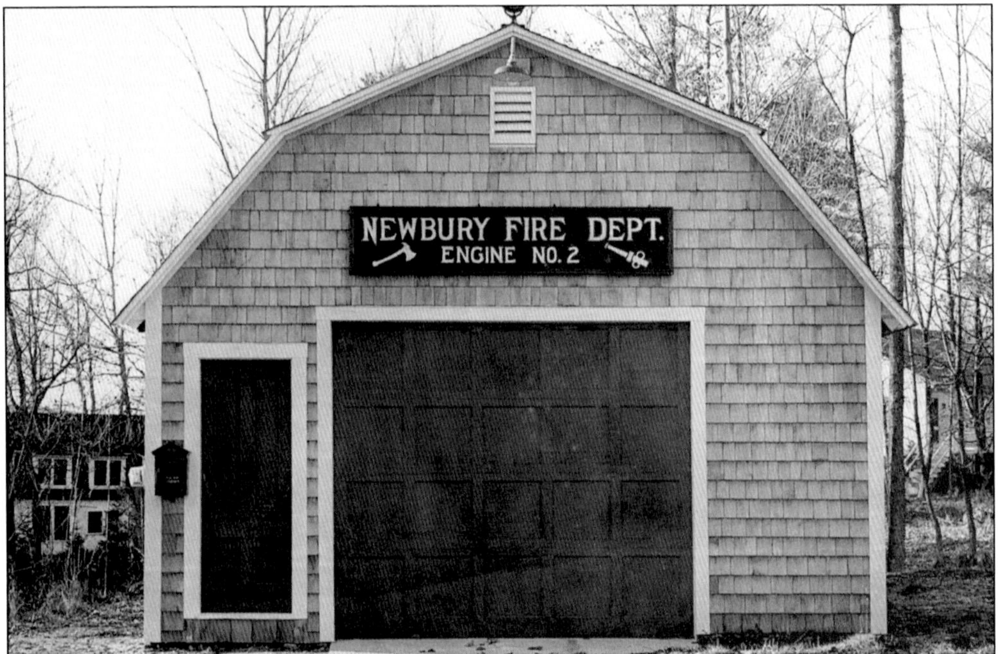

An auxiliary firehouse was built at Blodgett's Landing in the mid-1940s as a precaution against the ever-present threat of fire in that densely populated settlement. An engine continues to be stored there. (Sally Kassman.)

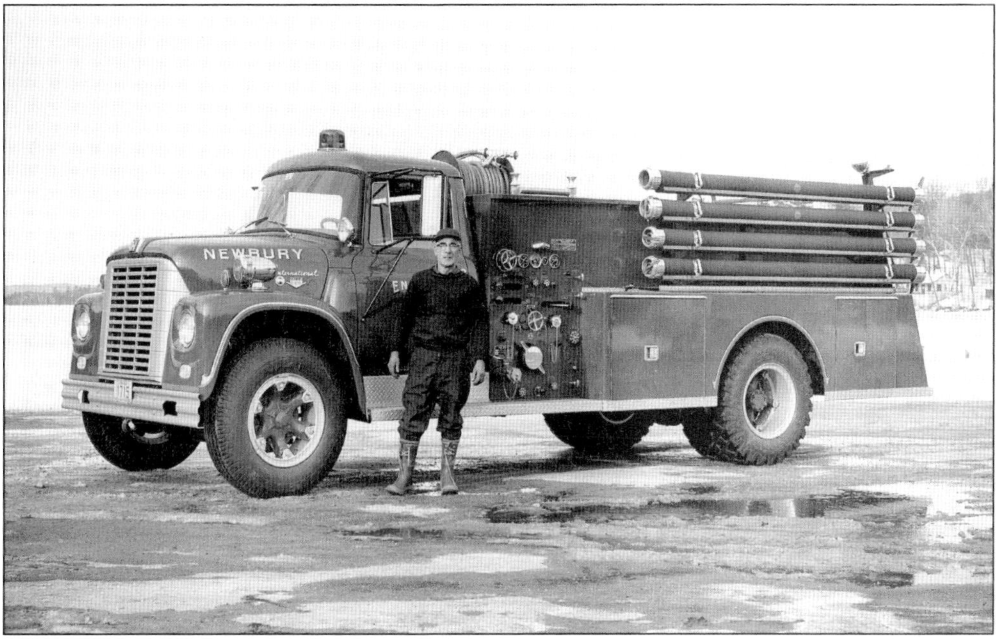

Fire Chief George Croteau stands beside the Maxim fire truck on its delivery day in 1964. Croteau was fire chief during the time of the great 1947 fire on Mount Sunapee, which raged across the mountain from October 19 until October 30. More than 500 men from 15 communities and the National Guard fought the wind-driven blaze that burned eight miles along the Sunapee ridge to within two miles of Goshen village. (Newbury Historical Society.)

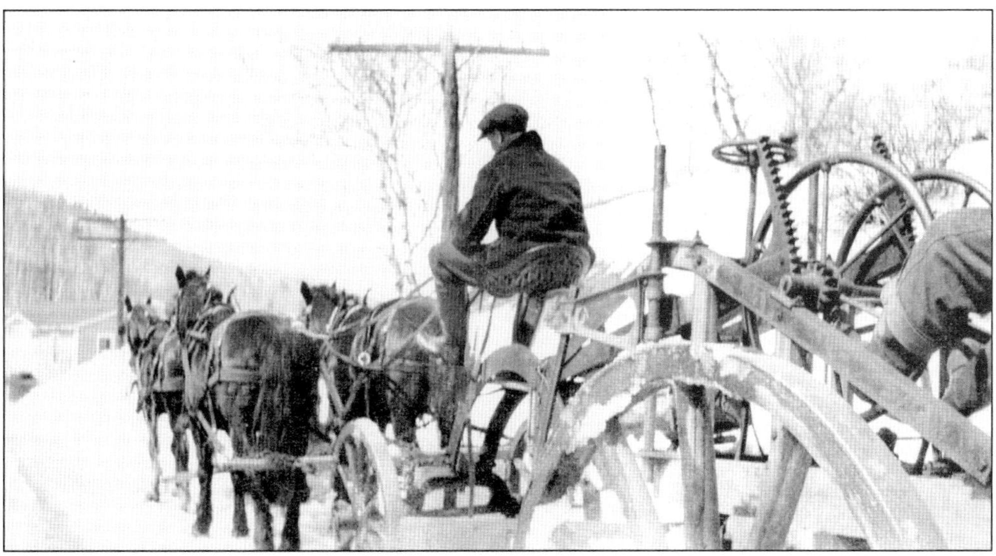

The highway department's manpower and equipment have expanded over the years to provide service to the ever-growing miles of road requiring maintenance. Home owners on Newbury's hillsides and remote farmlands need safe access, and this can be a challenge in winter weather. Here an early road machine heads out on a snowy day. (Elizabeth Folsom.)

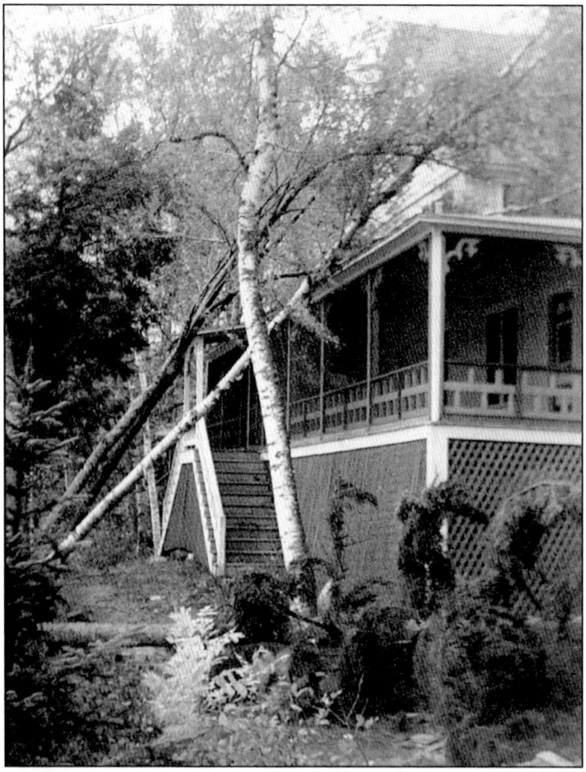

The infamous Hurricane of 1938 left a long-lasting mark on Newbury. Much of the mature timber on Mount Sunapee was blown down, leaving a floor of dead timber to serve as fodder for the great fire of 1947. Naturalist John Hay, grandson of the statesman, lamented, "All those cathedral pines . . . pluming by the lake shore for a hundred years or more went down like so many matchsticks." Along Lake Sunapee, flimsy summerhouses were badly damaged or blown off their foundations, while shoreline trees where uprooted and water turbulence shattered docks. These two pictures were taken along the Bay Point area on Lake Sunapee. (Katheryn Holmes.)

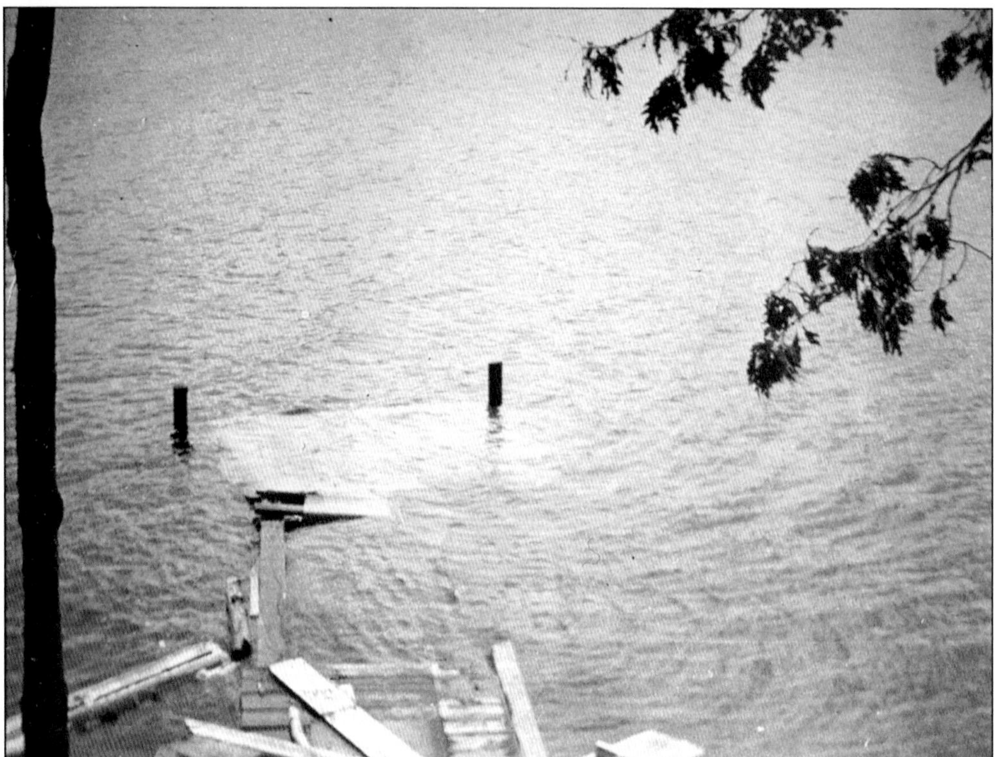

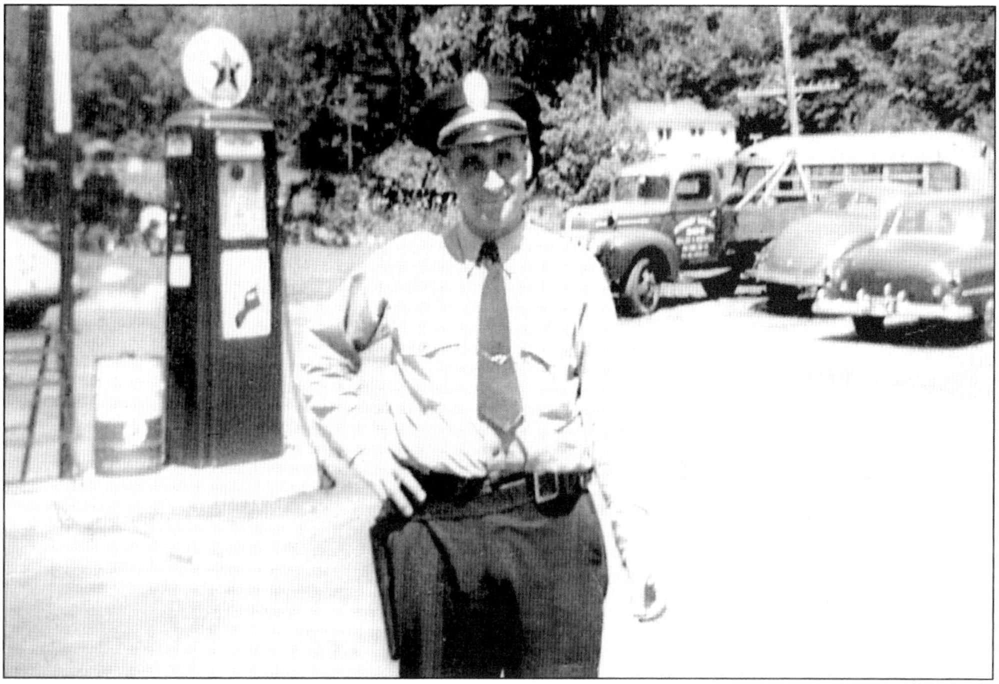

Newbury's police chief Reginald LaPorte served the town from 1946 to 1956. His son Richard followed in his footsteps. During the 1920s and 1930s, Edwin Stearns was town constable. (Wayne and Judy LaPorte.)

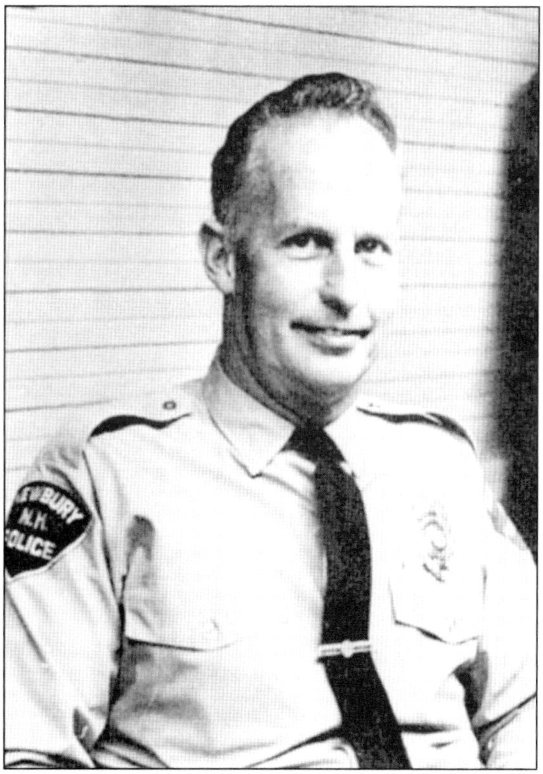

Longtime police chief Arthur Jones kept the peace in Newbury from 1960 until his retirement in 1980. During his tenure, the town grew in population, and he and his part-time officers were increasingly busy with law enforcement. (Town of Newbury.)

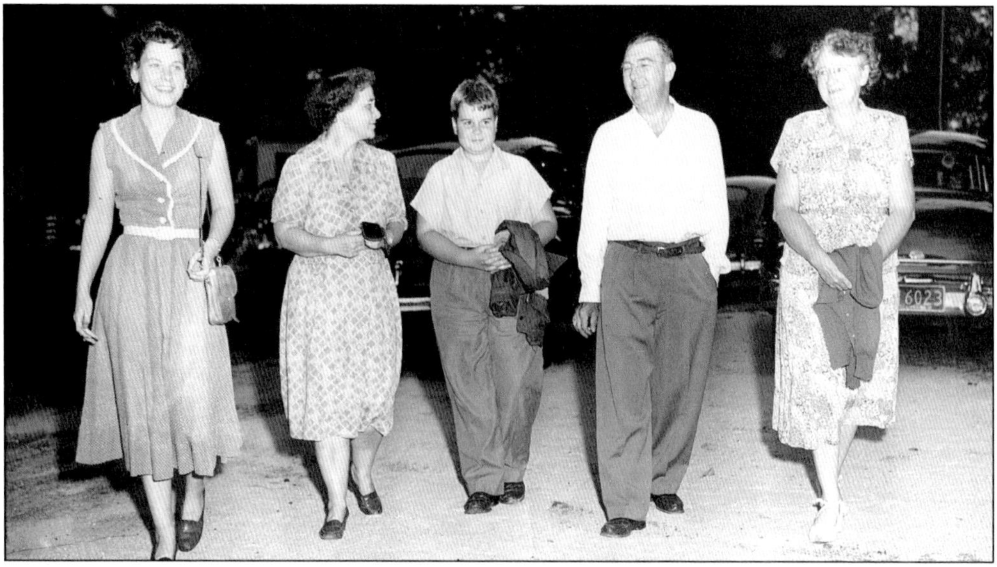

Summer informational meetings are held as a courtesy to the summer residents who are not able to attend the traditional March town meeting. These residents make up a large proportion of Newbury's tax revenue, and this is their opportunity to ask about and give their opinions on town issues. In 1952, 91 people filled the South Newbury Town Hall to discuss a variety of topics. Above, friends and family arrive ready for a lively meeting. Below, property owner C. L. Sheldon of Watertown, Massachusetts, asks a question of moderator Randolph Milligan regarding town roads. (Boston Globe, Charles Carey/Landov.)

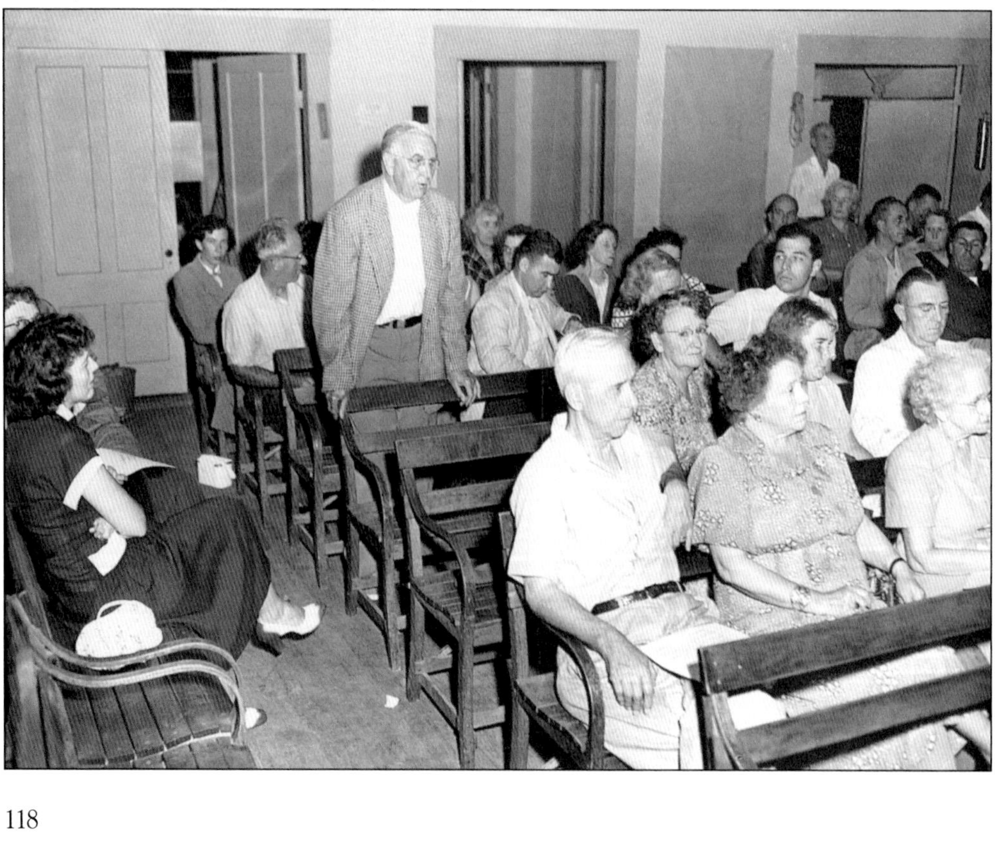

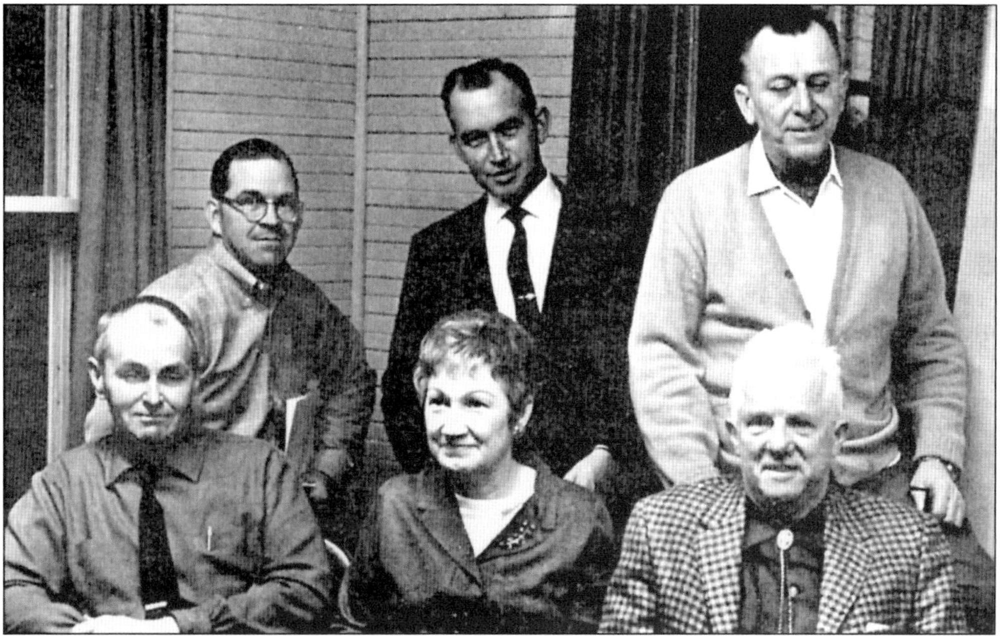

The Newbury Planning Board was formed in 1969 to develop guidelines for directing the town's rapid growth and development and to preserve its rural character. Seen here are, from left to right, (first row) Harold Folsom, Alice Lynn, and Arthur Larson; (second row) Herbert Smith, Roy C. Parsons, and Paul Diekmann. Ernest Sherman is not pictured. (Town of Newbury.)

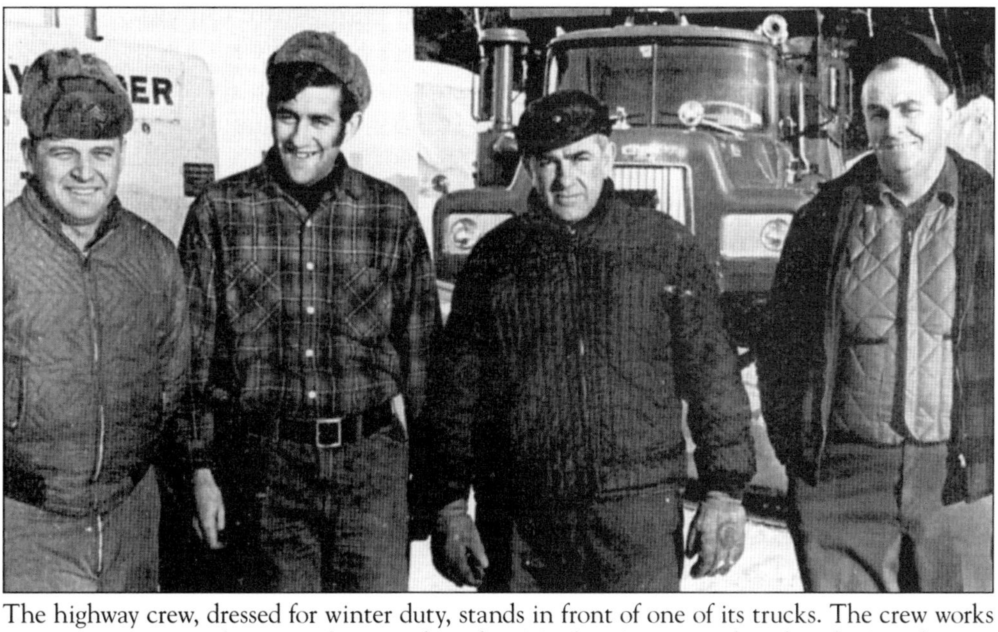

The highway crew, dressed for winter duty, stands in front of one of its trucks. The crew works overtime in winter, clearing, salting, and sanding Newbury's many miles of roads. Seen here in 1969 are, from left to right, Norman Smith, Howard Eaton, Walter Leach, and Harold Folsom. (Town of Newbury.)

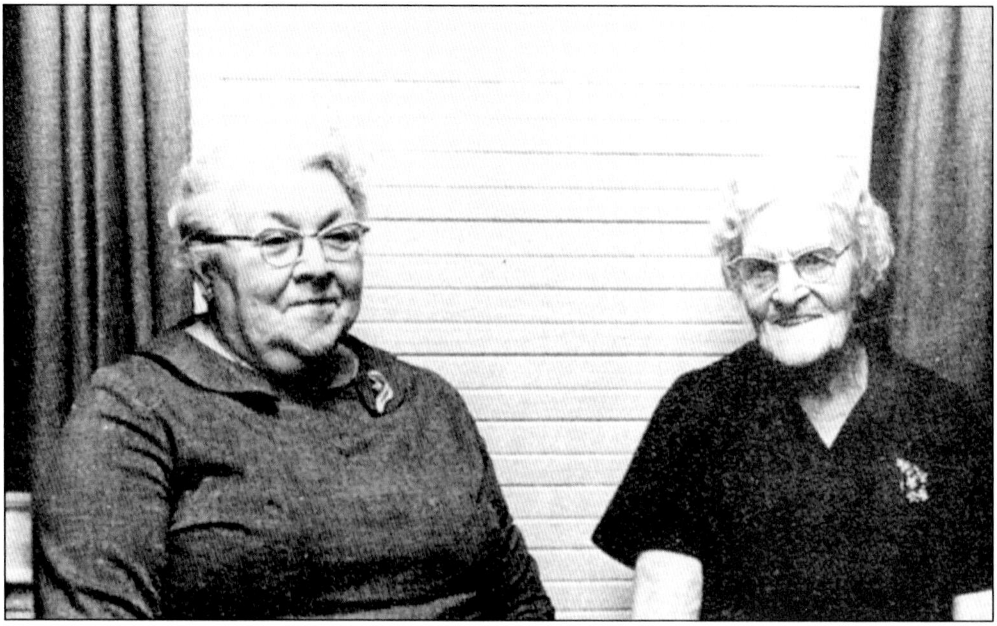

Newbury's information booth attendants serve the public on behalf of the town, offering information and advice to hundreds of travelers from across the country and overseas. Common questions pertain to area activities, places to dine, hiking trails, lodgings, boat rentals, and beach areas. Bertha Rich (left) and Mabel Pomeroy provided information in the 1960s. (Town of Newbury.)

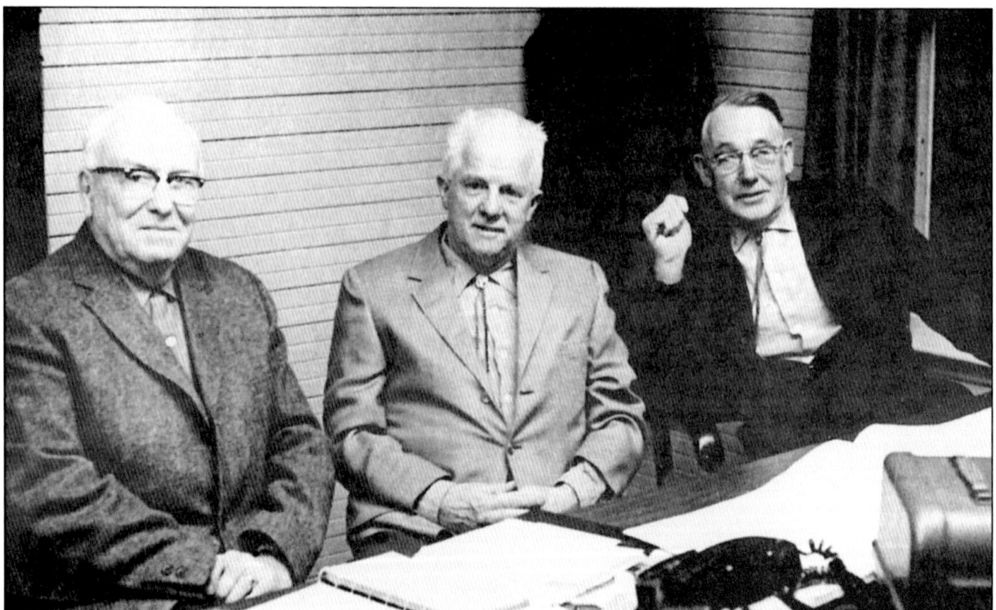

The Newbury Board of Selectmen has been in charge of town government since the first board was elected in 1779. Acting in the best interests of the residents, it rules on issues impacting the town, oversees the town budget, and provides guidance to town departments and organizations. Seen here in 1969 are, from left to right, Kenneth Sherman, Arthur Larson, and Merle Rich. (Town of Newbury.)

Nine

THE 1978 BICENTENNIAL

Just two years after the national bicentennial celebration, Newbury threw a grand party on July 28, 29, and 30 to commemorate 200 years of rich heritage. The event, with a theme of Newbury Past and Present, was chaired by Martha Blake.

Festivities began on Friday with a church supper at the Friendship House in South Newbury. This was followed by a pageant in the South Newbury Town Hall, billed as offering "special features." Those highlights included a cast of townspeople impersonating important historical figures from Newbury's past: John Fisher, Gov. John Wentworth, many of the original pioneer families, statesman John Hay, and Pres. Theodore Roosevelt.

Saturday's events included exhibits of historical memorabilia in the library and Center School, a parade of children in period costumes, games, snacks, and a sold-out chicken barbecue hosted by the firemen. The Hopkinton-Weare Community Band provided music. During the day, the bicentennial quilt worked by 24 local ladies was on display in advance of a raffle to be held in the fall. The quilt depicted scenes from Newbury's notable landmarks and town organizations. The raffle winner donated the quilt to the town, and it hangs in a place of honor in the town offices today.

Another highlight of the weekend was the presentation of the Newbury Bicentennial Cane by the selectmen to Moses Bly, the oldest town resident and descendant of one of Newbury's founding families.

Sunday services at the Center Meeting House were conducted by Dr. J. Duane Squires, who recounted the highlights of Newbury's past 200 years.

Souvenir items were sold to help defray costs of repairs to the Center Meeting House. These included 1892 town maps, postcards, pennants, and Ernest Sherman's *History of Newbury*, Part I. A commemorative coin was also struck for the occasion. The coin, cast in silver, bronze, and pewter, depicted the town seal on one side and the meetinghouse on the reverse.

The bicentennial celebration brought together many descendants of the town's first settlers as well as 13 of the original members of the Sunapee Lake Grange. Some families had representatives from four generations in attendance. The celebration honored those who paved the way, remembering their struggles and determination to establish a strong community and forge ties that would last over the centuries.

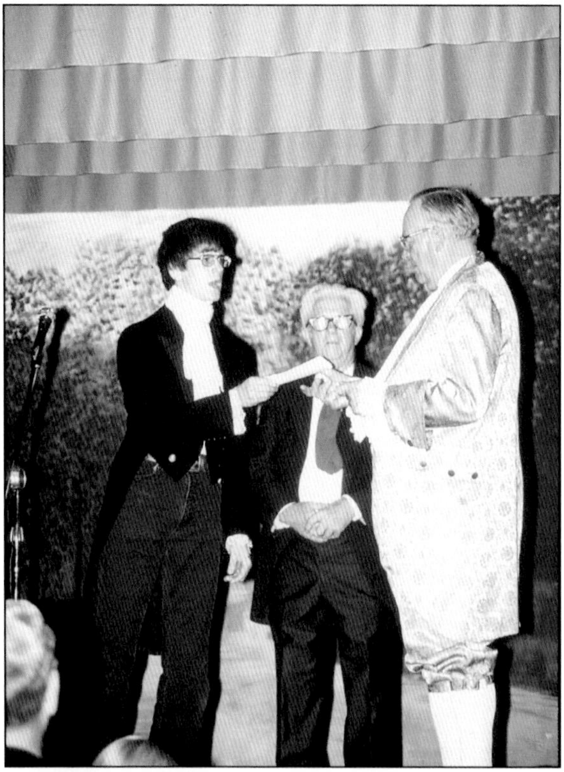

Newbury began its bicentennial celebration on Friday, July 28, 1978, with a supper at the Friendship House in South Newbury, followed by a pageant in the town hall featuring townspeople in costume portraying historical figures from Newbury's past. Shown here, Tracy Messer (left), playing Gov. John Wentworth, presents the town charter to John Fisher, acted by Ernest Sherman. The man in the center is Arthur Larson, playing Mark H. Wentworth. (Kay Sanborn and Marion DeRoche.)

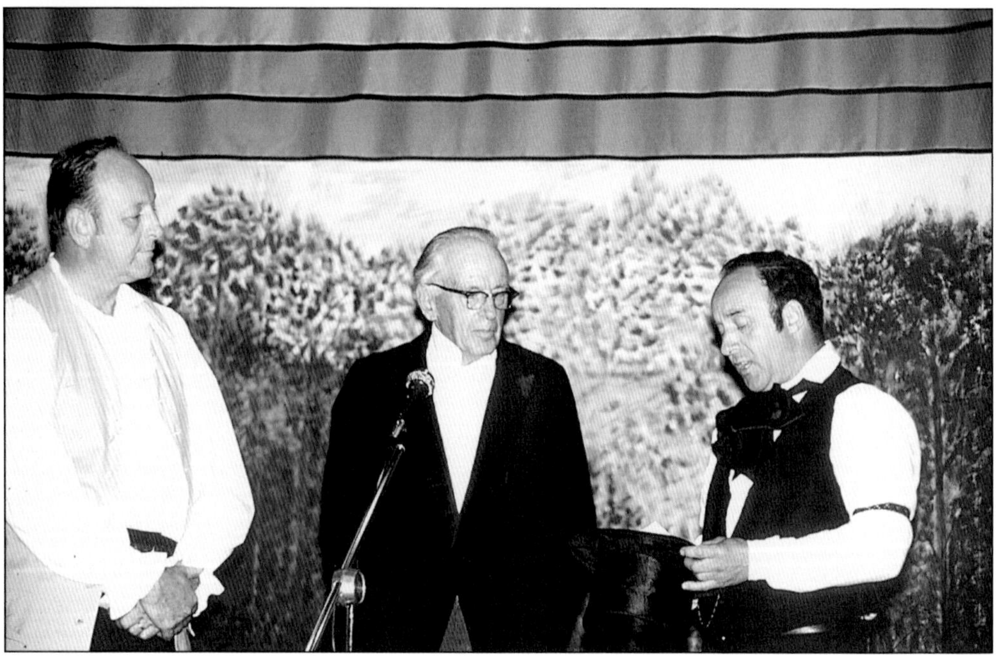

At the 1796 town meeting, selectmen discuss a petition to grant a southern portion of the town known as the Bradford Plains to the town of Bradford. Pictured here are, from left to right, Luther Sweet as Timothy Morse, Milford Newell as Paul Towle, and Wayne LaPorte as Joseph Webster. (Kay Sanborn and Marion DeRoche.)

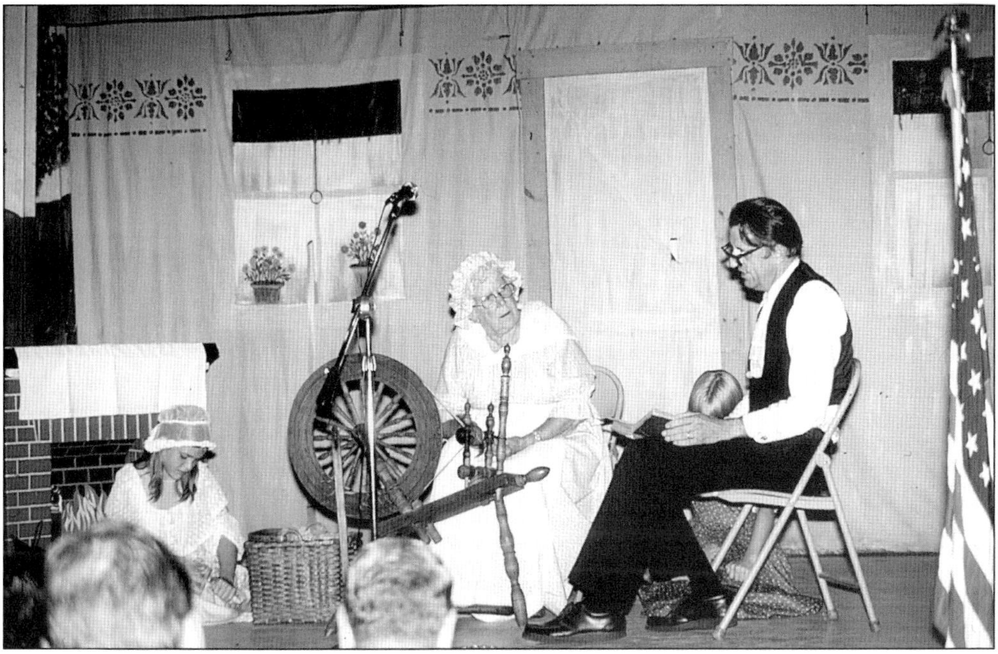

Dea. William Gunnison (right), played by Harold Newell, discusses some fine points of theology with his wife, Hannah (played by Jeannette Sherman), as she spins wool in a depiction of a quiet evening at home in Colonial Fishersfield. The child sitting by her mother was played by Karen Sherman. (Wayne and Judy LaPorte.)

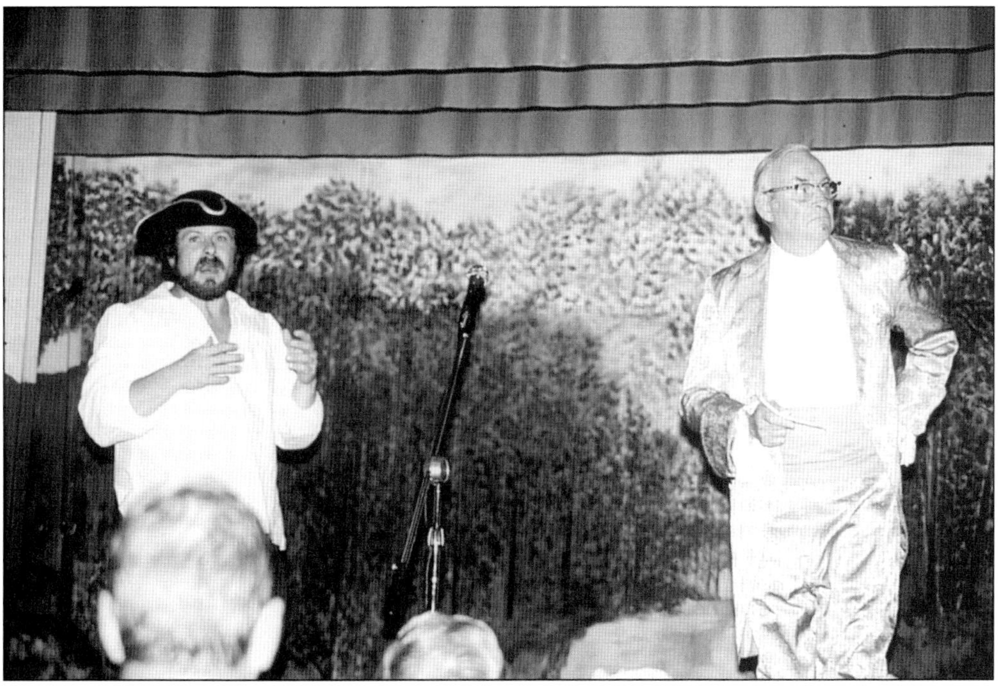

Zephaniah Clark, Fishersfield's first settler, strikes a deal with John Fisher in which he will survey the town in exchange for clear title to his house and lot. Tom Biuso (left) and Ernest Sherman portray the two gentlemen. (Kay Sanborn and Marion DeRoche.)

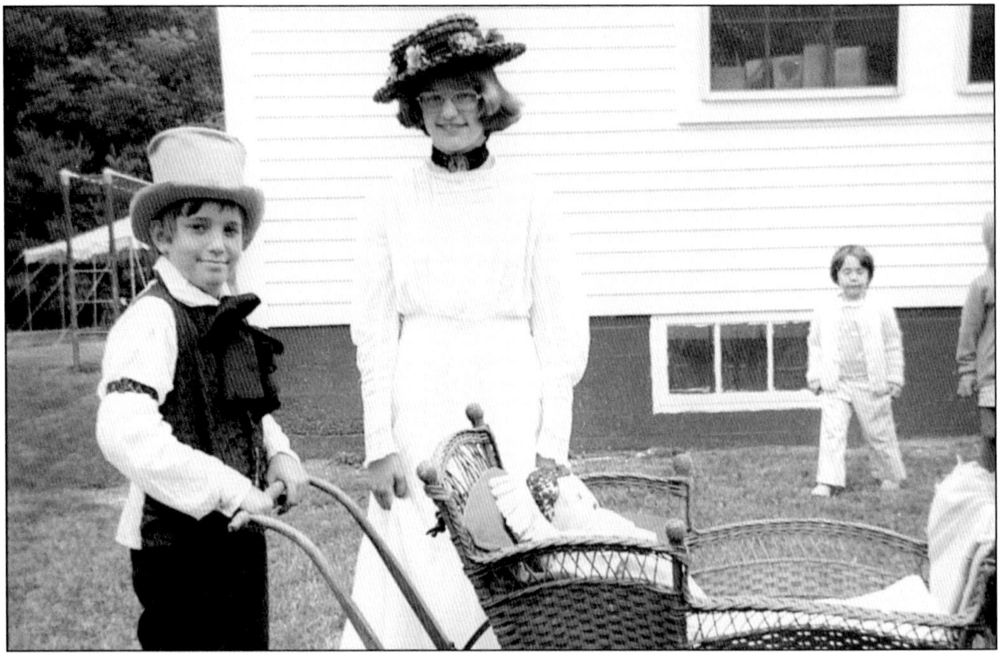

Children enjoyed the parade, contests, and games on Saturday. Here Wayne Jr. and Teriko LaPorte don their great-great-grandparents' clothing and get ready to push their great-great-grandfather's baby carriage in the parade. They won an award for "most in keeping with the bicentennial theme." (Wayne and Judy LaPorte.)

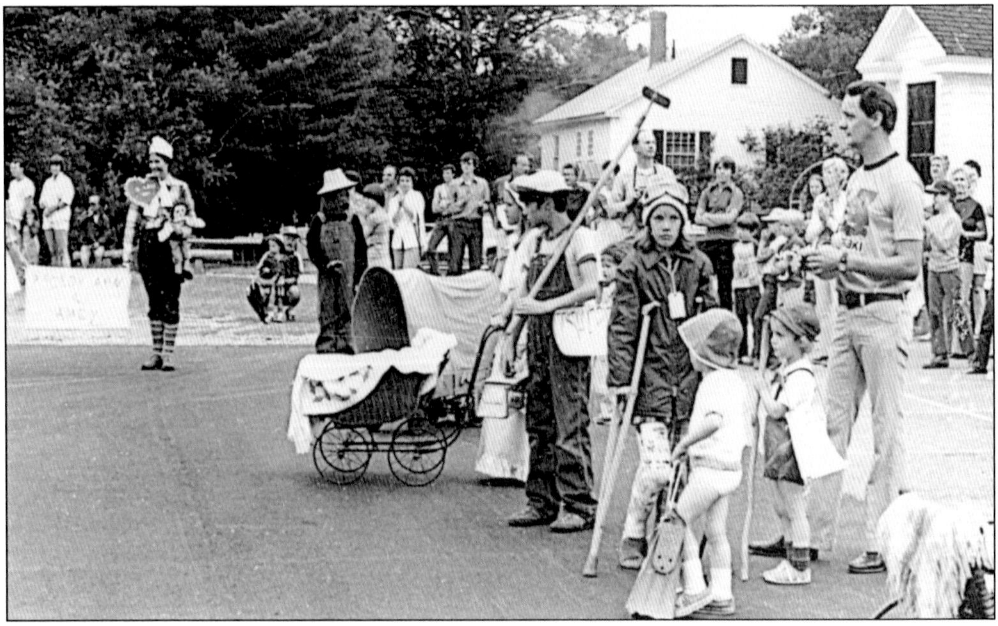

Let the games begin! This group is ready for action. The boy with the hoe is Tim Gove and directly behind him, to the left, is Karen Sherman. The covered wagon belongs to the Stoddard children (not identified). Standing on the right, without costume, is Bill Gove (Tim's father) with his daughter Karla (on crutches) and his twins, James and Evonne. (Kay Sanborn and Marion DeRoche.)

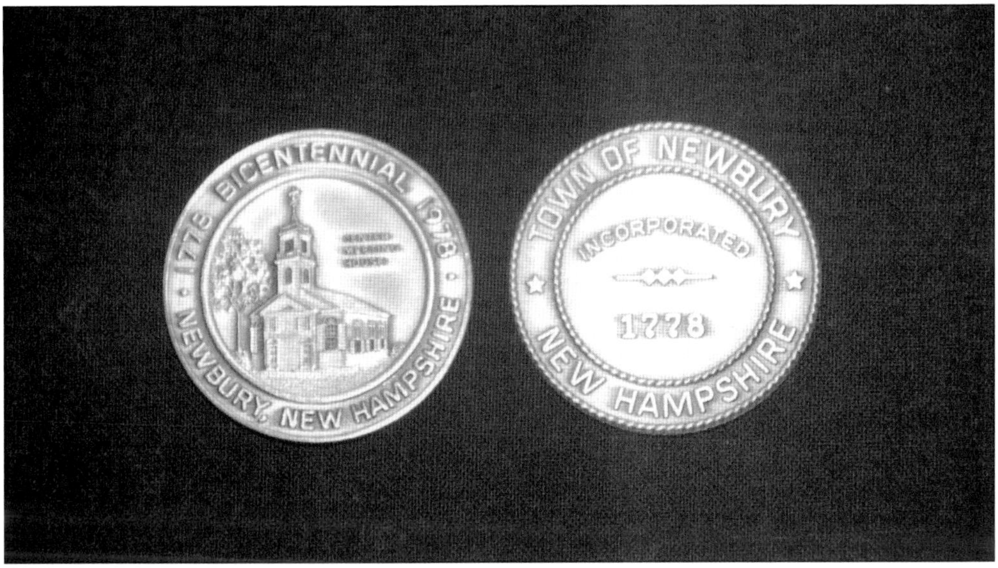

Among the souvenirs of the bicentennial celebration was a commemorative coin depicting the Center Meeting House on one side and the town seal on the reverse. The coins were available in silver, bronze, and pewter and were sold in numbered sets of three for $30 or individually for $4 or $5. (Donna Long.)

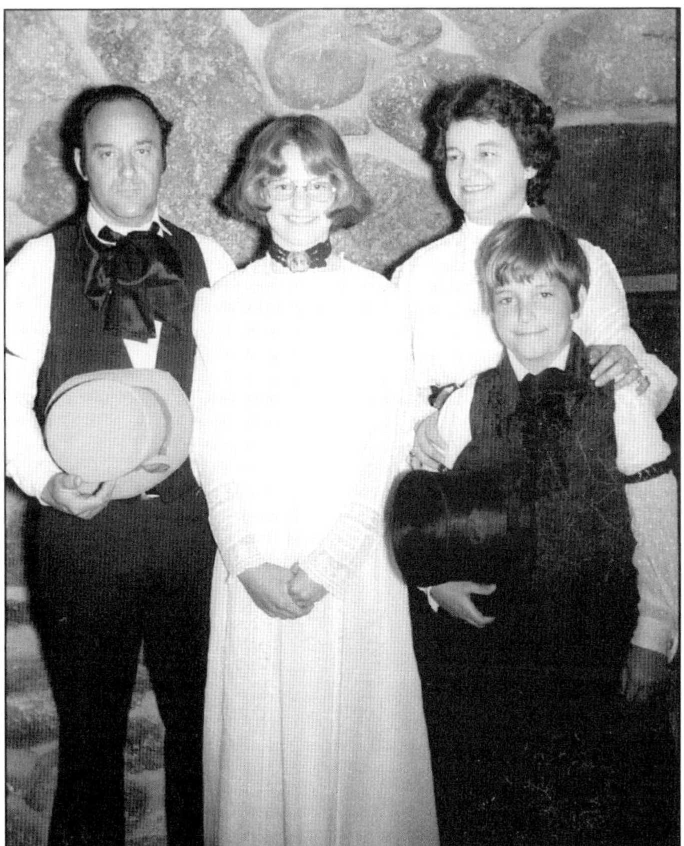

The LaPorte family takes time out during the festivities to pose for a picture in period costume. From left to right are Wayne, Teriko, Judy, and Wayne Jr. (Wayne and Judy LaPorte.)

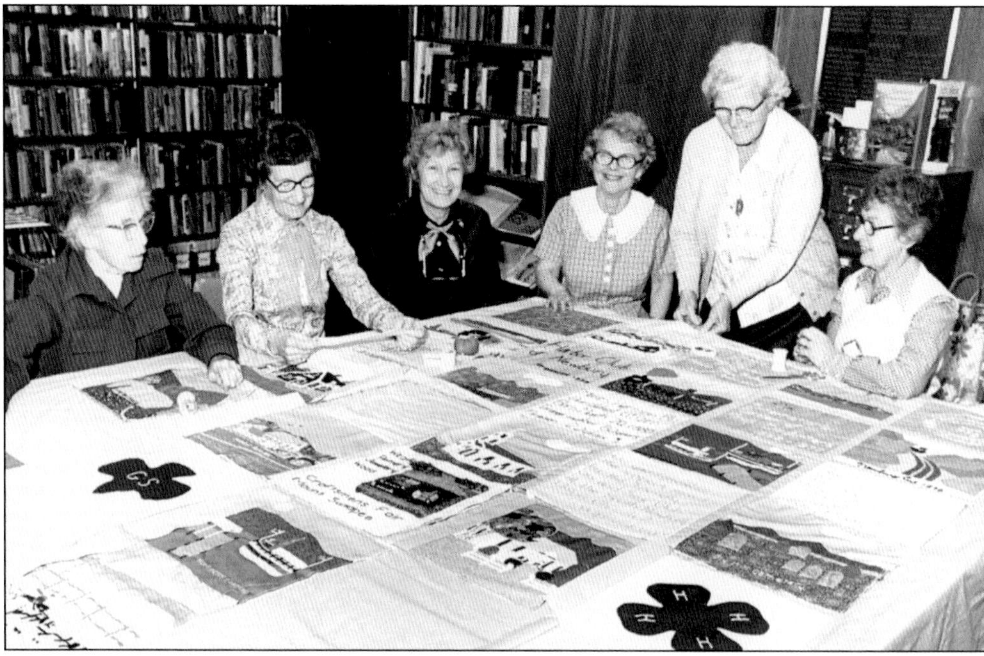

Newbury ladies assemble to work on the bicentennial quilt, which was a raffle prize at the celebration. Pictured here are, from left to right, Marie Lubinger, Ruth Croteau, Alice Lynn, Dorothy Perkins, Martha Blake, and Janet Yager. The quilt depicted various town associations and landmarks unique to Newbury's history. (Kay Sanborn and Marion DeRoche.)

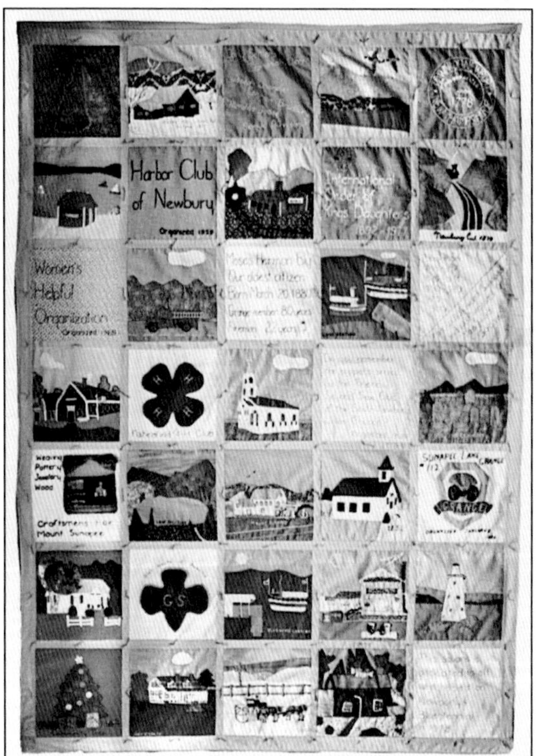

The winner of the bicentennial quilt raffle was Helen Weisskirchen, who graciously donated this historical treasure to the town. It hangs in a place of honor today in Newbury's community meeting room, which was added to the town offices as part of a major renovation in 2005. (Kay Sanborn and Marion DeRoche.)

Newbury selectmen made a special trip to the home of Moses Bly during the celebration to present him with an honorary cane, which traditionally goes to Newbury's oldest citizen. Bly was 98 years old, living independently and enjoying good health. He died in 1980 at age 100. Pictured are, from left to right, George Beal, Moses Bly, James Wright, and Frank Veazie. (Kay Sanborn and Marion DeRoche.)

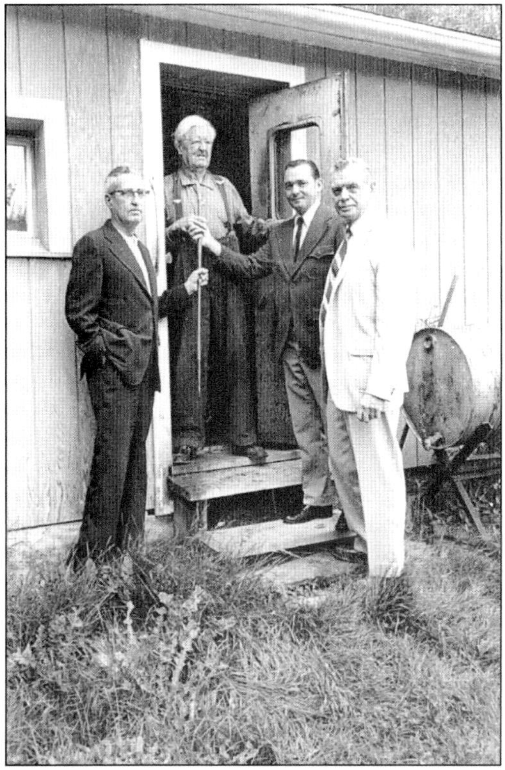

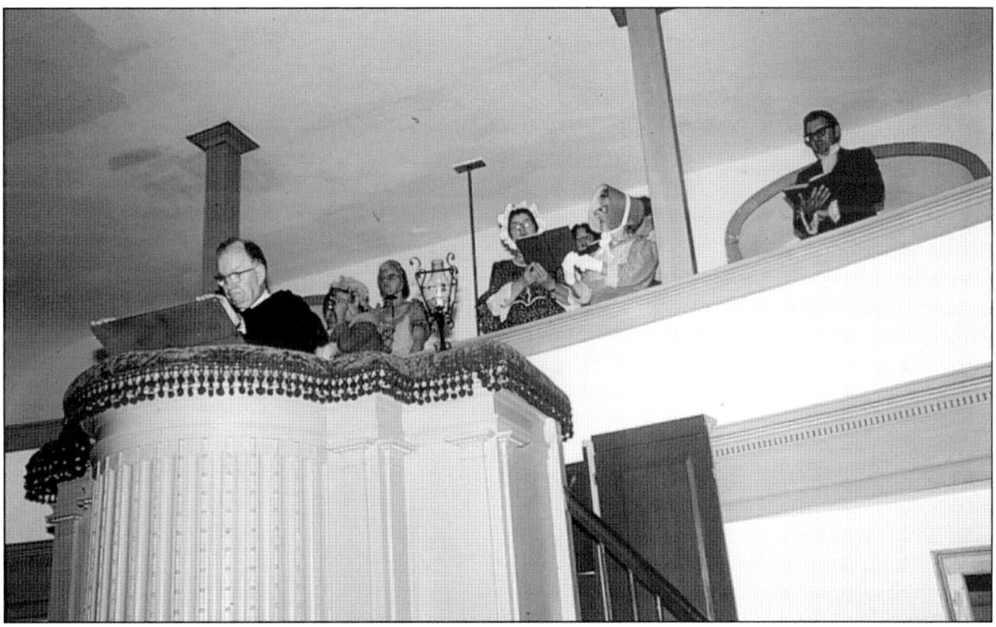

Dr. J. Duane Squires of New London conducted the Sunday service at the Center Meeting House. He recounted the highlights of Newbury's history from its earliest days to the present and returned time and again to the scripture text from Job 8:8–10: "Inquire, I pray you, of bygone ages and consider what the fathers have found; for we are but of yesterday." (Kay Sanborn and Marion DeRoche.)

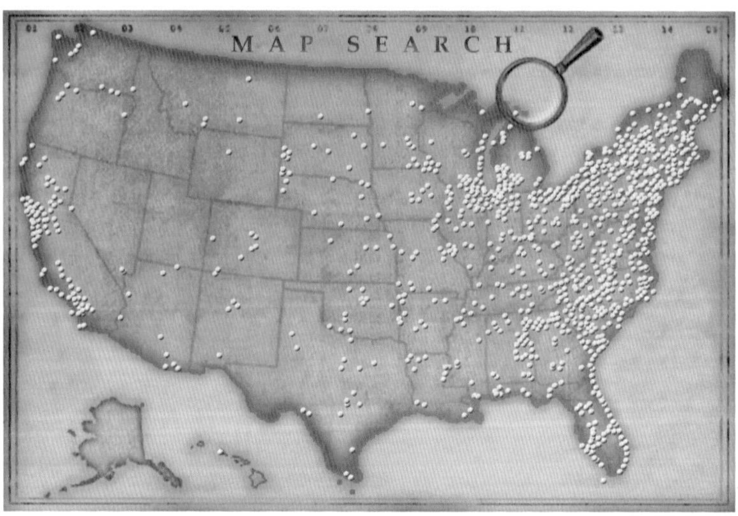

MAP SEARCH